Medieval Celebrations

Medieval Celebrations

SECOND EDITION

Your Guide to
Planning and Hosting
Spectacular Feasts,
Parties, Weddings,
and Renaissance Fairs

Daniel Diehl

Mark P. Donnelly

STACKPOLE
BOOKS

Copyright ©2001, 2011 by Daniel Diehl and Mark P. Donnelly

First edition published 2001. Second edition 2011

Published by
STACKPOLE BOOKS
5067 Ritter Road
Mechanicsburg, PA 17055
www.stackpolebooks.com

Printed in China

10 9 8 7 6 5 4 3 2 1

Cover design by Tessa J. Sweigert

Cover photo credits: Main photo and center bottom, Eugene Siren; bottom left, Valerie Rowe/ Fantaysia Limited; bottom right, Scarborough Renaissance Festival, Waxahachie, Texas.

Page iii photo courtesy Cathy Rich

All photos by the authors unless noted

Library of Congress Cataloging-in-Publication Data

Diehl, Daniel.
    Medieval celebrations : your guide to planning and hosting spectacular feasts, parties, weddings, and renaissance fairs / Daniel Diehl, Mark P. Donnelly. — 2nd ed.
       p.   cm.
    Includes bibliographical references and index.
    ISBN-13: 978-0-8117-0761-9 (pbk.)
    ISBN-10: 0-8117-0761-X (pbk.)
    1. Festivals. 2. Medievalism. 3. Manners and customs. I. Donnelly, Mark, 1967– II. Title.
GT3932.D44 2011
394.26—dc22

                                     2010043609

Contents

Preface to the Second Edition

Since the beginning of recorded history people have been fascinated with the idea of recreating events from the past. The Greeks and Romans reenacted earlier military victories and made the struggles of their ancient gods and goddesses come to life on the stage. Medieval European monarchs also reenacted Greek and Roman battles, both real and legendary, and in the nineteenth century, medieval tournaments were recreated by the nobles and gentry of England and Europe. The enjoyment of much of this historical recreation was, however, limited to the privileged classes. By the twentieth century the stories of kings, knights, and courtly love became common themes in popular entertainment, but seeing history on stage and screen was very different from actually being there in person. It was not until the 1960s that a few people in the US, UK, and Europe became brave enough to risk being mocked by their neighbors and began recreating medieval life on a regular basis. It was a bold step backward.

Obviously these fanciful, popular recreations were a far cry from the bleak realities of medieval life. The Middle Ages were a time fraught with political turmoil, brutal and incessant warring, random violence, unsanitary living conditions, plague, and famine. Despite these shortcomings, there are few images more appealing than a magnificently armored knight riding out in the name of his lady, his king, and the church to do battle against the forces of evil. Who among us does not long to change places with one of those glorious warriors or fair maidens from the past?

Since their introduction in the 1960s, the popularity of these splendidly archaic recreated medieval feasts, tournaments, and Renaissance fairs has increased tremendously. Medieval military reenactments are staged in nearly every culture old enough to have a recorded medieval history, and medieval weddings are among the most popular themed weddings in all of Western culture. If the United States has added its own unique contribution to the celebration of all things medieval it is the concept of the medieval or Renaissance fair. According to online listings, there are now no less than 127 medieval and Renaissance fairs scattered across the forty-eight contiguous states.

It is no wonder that the Renaissance fair is so popular; the romance of escaping, at least for a day, from the stress-filled, work-a-day modern world can be very attractive and a lot of fun. Beyond question, a medieval theme can help make any special occasion even more memorable. A wedding with people dressed in fairy-tale clothes or a Christmas party with minstrels and a table groaning under the weight of strange and rich-smelling food will always be remembered as something spectacular, daring, and magical.

But wanting to hold a medieval event and having access to all of the relevant information are two distinctly different things. Naturally, you can hire a company to plan your event for you, but unless you have a whopping budget and are convinced the party planners know their history, you have no way of knowing what you may wind up with or how much it may cost. By far the most economical—not to mention enjoyable—way to host a medieval celebration is to plan and execute it yourself. So, to those of you who feel the attraction of diving headlong into the past but really don't know where to begin, this all-color, greatly expanded edition of *Medieval Celebrations* is dedicated specifically to you.

We wish the very best of luck to all of you.

Daniel Diehl & Mark P. Donnelly

Acknowledgments

First we would like to thank everyone who bought the first edition of *Medieval Celebrations*; your enthusiasm helped make this updated and expanded version possible. Next, thanks to our editor, Kyle Weaver, for suggesting this updated volume. The time we spent in revisions and updates was very much like visiting an old friend who turned out to be even more fun than we had remembered, and we hope our readers, both old and new, are as enthusiastic about this new version as we are. Naturally, we re-extend our thanks to everyone who made contributions to the original edition of this book and again acknowledge their generosity. Specific to this new edition, we first owe a tremendous tip of the hat to Barton Branstetter and Cara McCandless for allowing us access to their stunning castle home; thanks guys. Thanks also go to Bob Rich for granting us permission to reproduce his wall paintings from the Branstetter home and for overseeing our photo session. We would also like to thank Valerie Rowe of UK event planners Fantaysia Ltd, and the Scarborough Renaissance Festival of Waxahachie, Texas, for allowing us to use some of their copyrighted images.

CHAPTER 1

Why Host a Medieval Celebration?

The popularity of recreating medieval events, celebrations, and feasts has been encouraged and promoted by Christmas madrigal dinners, hosted by many civic and church organizations across the United States, England, and Europe. Likewise, the popularity of the Medieval Times restaurant chain, the growth of medieval reenactment groups around the globe, and dozens of Renaissance fairs held throughout the United States have all helped broaden the appeal of selectively recreating the "Age of Chivalry." The more one sees of this long-gone age, recreated by people who are, by and large, just like the rest of us, the greater the appeal of visiting the Middle Ages for a day or two. Stepping into the past for a few hours is a great way to take a vacation to a far-off place without the hassle and expense of traveling thousands of miles. In fact, it is far more fun to take part in one of these medieval events than it is to attend them as a mere spectator.

Even if you have never hosted a party before and your knowledge of the Middle Ages is limited to a few old Robin Hood movies, this book is designed to guide you through every step necessary to help you host a medieval banquet that will make your party-planning skills legendary. And there are enough historical tidbits thrown into these pages that by the day of your banquet, you will sound like an authority on medieval history, customs, and lifestyle.

The truth of the matter is that with a little time and effort, a sense of adventure, and not much more money than it would cost to host any other type of party, you can successfully mount a beautiful and memorable medieval celebration. By taking your time and following the simple chapter-by-chapter guidelines provided in the following pages, you can host a medieval event that you and your guests will be talking about for years to come.

Defining the Middle Ages

The Middle Ages, in its greater historical aspect, is a vaguely defined period of time. Historians endlessly argue about when it began, when it ended, and even what, exactly, it was. For the sake of simplicity, we will define the Middle Ages as the period between 1066, when the Normans conquered England, and 1450, when the Renaissance and the rise of the nation-state brought an end to the feudal system that had dominated the political and social life of the medieval period. Basically, this gives us four wonderfully exciting centuries to play with. Since this book is in no way intended to be an historical treatise on medieval history, we are going to take the liberty of picking and choosing elements from this broad period that will help you create the most memorable medieval event possible.

For a variety of practical reasons, we will be using an amalgam of decorating styles, manners, and foods from this period to create our medieval feast. Because few written recipes from the early years of this period survive, we will extract our menu items primarily from cookbooks of the fourteenth and fifteenth centuries (the 1300s and 1400s). The clothing styles and decorative motifs covered in our chapters on costumes and decorating are taken primarily from the fourteenth century because they are far simpler, and therefore easier to reproduce, than those of the later Middle Ages. Our selection of music and dance comes from a variety of times and places throughout the medieval period. Similarly, while we will discuss specific customs from many different countries, we will mix and match those elements to guarantee that your guests have the greatest amount of fun possible during their short visit to the Middle Ages.

The variety of time periods on which we have drawn in compiling this book would undoubtedly drive a hard-nosed historian mad, and a visitor from the real Middle Ages would probably have no idea what was going on, but your feast and the activities surrounding it will be relatively simple to put together while still being based entirely in historical fact. If you are especially fond of a particular country, king or queen, historical event, or holiday, by all means build your medieval event around it. If all of the details are not exactly right, don't worry—we promise that no one from the distant past will show up to check on your historical accuracy.

Things to Consider

The major concern most people have when they contemplate recreating a medieval celebration has to do with preparing food for the banquet. "How hard is it to make these things?" and "Will anyone eat them when they are served?" are both legitimate concerns for anyone thinking about hosting a medieval feast. Most people, at most times throughout history, tend to eat foods with which they are familiar. When it's time to consider hosting a party, the guests' favorite dishes inevitably become potential menu items. No matter how much

effort you put into the preparation and presentation of your food, we understand that you don't want to ask your guests to be human guinea pigs for some weird, experimental cuisine. While many of the dishes listed on our menu may sound unfamiliar, the basic ingredients are all things that you and your guests eat on a regular basis; there is nothing here to be afraid of. The ingredients used in our recipes are all available without undue hassle or expense, and the necessary preparation does not require learning any new skills. Like all recipes, they only require that you follow the directions. To make your cooking experience as comfortable and stress-free as possible, a number of our recipes can be made well ahead of time and stored or frozen until the day of your event.

Likewise, the manners, customs, and decorations at most social events are not usually from some unaccustomed land or from a long-gone time period, and many people feel awkward and uncomfortable if they have to deal with strange customs and habits. We understand this and have taken it into account. Our goal is to help you and your guests enjoy a new, fun, and exciting experience without having to work at it. Throughout the course of this book we will guide you, the reader and the potential host of your own medieval event, through the ins and outs of medieval customs and cooking in such a way that you can host a party based on the habits and foods of six centuries ago while remaining completely confident that you and your guests will feel comfortable and at ease with the results.

Where Do I Start?

We have arranged this book in such a way that it can be equally useful to those readers who are planning a small dinner party, a large wedding, or a public event sponsored by a church, school, or charity organization. We will help you tailor your medieval celebration to the size of the space in which you are holding it, the number of people who will be attending, and your budgetary constraints. We will aid you in planning for the event, decorating your event space, and organizing your kitchen in such a way that preparing for your celebration and banquet are as worry-free as possible. Our hope is that when the big day comes, all of your guests will come to the feast ready to immerse themselves in the atmosphere of the Age of Chivalry.

We will also help you put together an information packet that will explain the day's events to your guests.

DICK CLARK

The packet should include a copy of the menu; exotic dishes often prove irresistible to those with an adventurous palate, but nothing will be so strange-sounding that any of your guests will be put off. You might want to photocopy the chapter on medieval table manners and include it in the information package to help your guests get into the proper mood. If your guests are expected to come in costume—and it is always more fun and authentic feeling if they do—they will need time to either make or rent appropriate clothing. You can provide copies of the clothing patterns in this book to anyone who expresses an interest in making his or her own costume.

If you are planning a medieval dinner in conjunction with a civic organization, such as a church, club, or

EUGENE SIREN

charity organization, it will probably be impossible to get everyone to come in costume, but everyone should be encouraged to dress for the occasion if they so desire. If you hold similar events in the future, you will almost certainly find that the number of people who come in costume will increase from year to year. The costumes may not be authentic, but it will show that people are willing to get into the spirit of things and are ready to join in and enjoy themselves.

In addition to recipes, decorations, and costumes, this book provides information and instructions on a wide variety of games, dances, songs, and other forms of entertainment that will keep your guests happy and busy for an evening or an entire day.

While all the basic information for hosting a medieval celebration, large or small, is contained in this book, for those of you who really want to go over the top or simply want to find more information about medieval celebrations, there is an extensive reference section and a bibliography at the back of the book. But even without referencing these additional sources, you should be able to prepare and host a medieval celebration and feast that will be remembered and talked about for years to come.

Allow yourself plenty of time to prepare for your event and feast. You will probably want to read this entire book several times before you actually begin making final plans. If you are going all-out, it can take two or three months of planning and preparation, followed by several weeks of hard work. Just take your time, don't panic, and above all, enjoy yourself. Be warned— medieval celebrations have a way of becoming a habit; soon after your first event, you will probably find yourself thinking up ways of doing it better the next time.

CHAPTER 2

A Brief History of Medieval Celebrations

There is no such thing as a "typical" medieval celebration. Celebrations and feasts during the Middle Ages were as different and varied as celebrations during any period of history, including our own. Then, as now, there were two basic types of festivities: public and private. Public festivities generally centered around the village church, both because many public holidays had a strong religious connotation and because the local priest or monks were willing to organize, and sometimes underwrite the cost of events for their parishioners. Private celebrations, with the exception of weddings, to which the entire village would invariably be invited, were normally limited to the households of the nobility and rich merchants. With the exception of the richest households no one had the time or money to waste on such frivolities.

Obviously the differences between celebrations among the village peasantry and those held by the high-and-mighty were significant. What might have seemed an immense and impressive celebration to village peasants would have been an appalling and miserable display to the eyes of the great nobility. Consequently, before recreating a medieval feast, it's a good idea to look at how these different levels of society celebrated.

The vast majority of the medieval population were peasants; certainly more than ninety percent of the population worked the land. While some of these peasants had incomes that were comfortable by the standards of the day, and others lived among the sophisticated denizens of cities and towns, peasant life was never grand nor sophisticated.

Most peasants lived in small villages which were owned by the local lord—a nobleman whom they may have never seen—or by a nearby monastic house. The peasants made their livings as sharecroppers, donating a portion of their labor and produce to the landowner to pay their rent and taxes. These villages were seldom more than a cluster of extended families held together by their social and economic isolation. With no means of transportation other than walking, it was a rare occasion when anyone left the village. Most people never traveled more than seven miles from the spot where they were born. Why seven miles? Because that is how far a person could travel on foot and safely return home by nightfall. Most peasants knew amazingly little about the world beyond their village, except that it was a physically dangerous place to be after dark; there were certainly thieves and murderous brigands out there, and the possibility of demons and monsters lurking in the woods was believed to be very real. In this unimaginably provincial world, everyone in the village knew everyone else and their business. Consequently, when anyone in the village had a reason to celebrate, the entire village joined in.

The backbreaking demands of subsistence farming and the constraints of the feudal system meant that feasts were few and far between. When they did take place, they probably lasted only one day, usually a Sunday, when most work was suspended in observance of the Sabbath. The only way more than one day could be taken off work was if the lord decreed a public holiday, but such occasions were rare. When a feast was planned by and for the villagers, everyone pitched in to make certain the festivities came together and to help guarantee that the day would be as memorable as possible. In most villages, bread and ale were plentiful, as were fish,

chicken, small birds, cheese, stew made of whatever vegetables were locally available and in season, and maybe the occasional pig or sheep, if the occasion was important enough. A cow was too valuable to kill just for a party, and wild game, with the exception of rabbits, was the exclusive property of the nobility.

Other than a church or chapel, there were few, if any, public buildings in a medieval village. Consequently, feasts and celebrations were normally held in the summer so they could take place outdoors. If anyone in the village knew how to play an instrument, he or she might provide music, but this, too, was fairly rare. Communal singing, on the other hand, was common and everyone knew the words to all of the songs; a new song was a rare treat. Most of the songs were either religious in nature or appallingly bawdy. The event being celebrated—and how much ale had been consumed—dictated what sort of song would be sung at any particular point during the day. Once the ale was gone and everyone had sung his song, told his story, or danced his dance—which everyone in the village had probably seen and heard a dozen times before—they all went

A wedding with early-sixteenth-century German Landskenect costumes illustrates the flamboyance of late medieval clothing.
DICK CLARK

home. They had little choice; they had to be up at sunrise, ready to go to work.

At the opposite end of the social spectrum was the world of the royalty, great nobles, archbishops, and bishops. Only on the rarest of occasions did the upper class have to cut their celebrations short because they had to go to work in the morning. In this rarefied society, great feasts, grand celebrations, glorious tournaments, and the presentation of lavish gifts were not only commonplace, they were also an important part of keeping a firm grip on power.

In the medieval world, hard cash, even among the most powerful, was almost nonexistent. Edward the Confessor, the last Anglo-Saxon king of England, reputedly kept the entire royal treasury in a wooden chest under his bed. Society functioned largely on barter, loyalty, feudal duty, and fear of punishment from God or the Crown. The only effective way to display wealth and power was to put up a good front, and hosting great feasts and tournaments was an ideal way of showing off. By bringing together political allies, potential allies, and even the occasional enemy who might be swayed or at least impressed, the nobility could reinforce and display their social and political strength. The more impressive the display, the greater the appearance of power.

Because travel during the Middle Ages was difficult at best, it was a rare occasion when a large number of noblemen and ladies had the opportunity to get together to strike political deals and relax. A gathering of nobles, whether it was for military or purely social purposes, was an opportunity to celebrate and provided an ample excuse for staging grand hunts, colorful jousts, dancing, and lavish feasts.

The guests at noble banquets were seated strictly according to rank and power. The highest-ranking personages, including the host, hostess, the most powerful guests, and the highest-ranking clergy, were seated around a "high table" strategically placed at the front of the great hall where they could be viewed by the assembled company. Chairs were traditionally placed on only one side of the high table so the rest of the room had an unobstructed view of the great and powerful. Some high tables were even placed on a raised platform, or dais, to improve the view of those seated there and to guarantee that the audience could see them. If there were guests of greater rank than the hosts, they would be granted the honor of being seated at the center of the high table. The most honored among the company were provided with massive, high-backed armchairs. Those next in rank would have armchairs with lower

backs, and toward the end of high table were chairs with no arms.

Other tables in the hall were usually arranged in long rows at a ninety-degree angle to the high table, so guests could look down the length of their table toward the high table. Even at these lower tables, seating was all-important; the closer a person was to the high table, the greater his or her rank and status. Those nearest the high table often had small, armless chairs; farther along were individual stools; and finally, at the far end of the hall, were common benches known as bankettes (from which the modern term "banquet" is derived). Beyond the tables was floor seating for musicians, entertainers, tradesmen, personal servants, and a few peasants who might have been invited to the feast as an act of Christian charity.

The food was also distributed according to rank. The best dishes, the greatest number of dishes, and the finest wines went to the high table, which was always served before the rest of the company. This allowed the guests to "ooh" and "aah" at the grandeur enjoyed by those of great rank.

Food was always served in a number of courses, called removes or messes (a term still used in the military). There might be three, four, or even five removes, and each remove was a mini-banquet in itself. The food was grand, gloriously prepared and presented, and seemingly available in endless quantity. The larger the occasion and the more powerful the hosts, the more impressive the spread was likely to be. When England's King Henry III threw a Christmas banquet in 1246, the shopping list included five thousand chickens, eleven hundred partridges, four hundred hares and rabbits, ten thousand eels, thirty-six swans, fifty-four peacocks, and ninety boars. All of this would have gone to the royal butchers and then to the kitchens, there to be transformed into hundreds of impressive dishes, and finally taken to the tables of the revelers in what was probably a series of at least four or five removes. Because no one could possibly eat the amount of food that flowed through the great hall, guests took small portions so as not to ruin their appetites for the removes yet to come.

Between removes there was entertainment, as well as toasts and speeches by those at the high table. Gifts were exchanged by the host and his most honored guests, and presentations were made to the nobility by those at the lower tables as a sign of gratitude for being invited to such a fine event. The presents were customarily held up for the entire audience to see, and murmurs of appreciation were an expected part of the display. At the end of the meal, there might be some form

The talents of a local recreationist group can add an exciting element of historical authenticity to your medieval event.

of theatrical performance, often of a religious or military nature, and finally, dancing to the accompaniment of court musicians. A lavish feast could go on for most of the day and well into the night. On important state occasions, such as a coronation, a royal marriage, or a visit from a foreign monarch or a cardinal sent as an emissary of the pope, rounds of feasting and reveling could stretch on for days or an entire week.

There were also instances when the nobility hosted feasts for the peasants and villagers who worked on their estates. Unless the lord was unusually generous, such largesse only took place when it was demanded by local custom or specifically decreed by king or church. The celebration of a successful harvest, the birth of a child into the noble household—usually a firstborn male—or the weddings of the lord's children, particularly the eldest son, all demanded some form of public revelry. On such occasions, the festivities were usually held on the grounds of the lord's estate, manor house, or castle. The amount of food provided to the populace depended entirely on the wealth and inclination of the lord. Ale and bread were basic requirements. These might be supplemented with cheese and meats, but on some oc-

casions, particularly if the lord was a cheapskate, the villagers were expected to supply themselves with anything beyond bread and ale.

Obviously, you will want to recreate something more impressive than a humble peasant feast, but it is unlikely that many of us can afford to put on a celebration as grand as those hosted by the medieval kings of England and Europe. For our recreated medieval celebrations we will follow in the footsteps of the third major social group in medieval society, the rich merchants and minor nobility, known at the time as "the middling sort." Like many of us in the modern world, this budding middle class tried hard to emulate the diet, customs, and manners of their social superiors but were constrained by the limitations of their purses. Consequently, the middling sort feasted on elaborate versions of foods they already knew and liked; foods they could be assured their guests would also like. Extra preparation time, a few rare and expensive herbs and spices to punch up the taste, and an impressive presentation guaranteed a warm reception at the table without the risk of overspending or producing a dish so exotic that none of the guests would eat it.

Most of the people in this class had access to a space large enough to accommodate their guests. Wealthy merchants would have rented their local guild hall, and the manor house of the petit nobility would have had a large enough dining hall to accommodate a few dozen guests. Like us, they were more likely to invite friends and business acquaintances they already liked, or wanted to get to know better, than to call in the entire village or potential military allies and their sometimes endless entourage. The middle classes did, however, strive to emulate royalty in the order of seating and strict adherence to social protocol.

No matter what a person's level of society might have been, there were certain holidays that were universally celebrated to whatever extent the individual's finances allowed.

With the advent of spring came three important festivals: Easter, New Year's Day, and May Day. Although Easter was primarily marked by religious observances, and its predecessor, Lent, was a time of fasting and prayer, Easter Sunday was also a time of gift giving among family members and friends at all levels of society. During the Middle Ages the New Year began on March 25, and it not only marked the beginning of spring planting, but was generally accompanied by revelry and tomfoolery even more intense than modern day New Year's celebrations. May Day, and the onset of summer weather, heralded the first trade fairs of the year and officially began the courting season. While young men and women of the peasant classes gathered on village greens to pick through the baubles offered by traveling merchants, dance around the maypole, and

The pageantry of tournament provided thrilling entertainment for royalty and noblemen throughout the Middle Ages.

SCARBOROUGH RENAISSANCE FESTIVAL, WAXAHACHIE, TX

sneak private moments alone, noble households held the first tournaments of the year and connived to marry off their children to families even more powerful than their own.

At the tournaments, young knights and squires had a chance to show off their martial prowess to fair maidens who, in turn, held Courts of Love where they would demand that their potential suitors make appropriately chivalric displays of love and declare their honorable intentions. While young noblemen were busy showing off their skill at arms and professing their love, their fathers struck bargains for politically and financially advantageous marriages.

Following the autumn harvest, most communities held harvest festivals, but these celebrations were obviously restricted to farming villages. The only part played in them by the nobility was the occasional day free from work and the possible donation of a keg of ale or a pig or ox that would be roasted and distributed among lucky villagers.

Last and most important in the medieval calendar of celebrations was Christmas. Not only was the Christmas holiday a celebration of the birth of Jesus, but it took place at an opportune time; during the dead of winter there was very little outside work that could be done, with the exception of feeding whatever animals were being kept over the winter and milking the family cow or nanny goat. This fortuitous combination of circumstances made Christmas an ideal time to gather family and friends for the biggest celebration of the year. Party decorations, as we think of them, did not exist in the Middle Ages, but Christmas was marked by decorating

the great hall or village church with any available evergreen plant, primarily pine, holly, and ivy; otherwise, it was a simple matter of putting out the best of everything you had. When important company was coming, the hosts displayed all their best pewter, silver, and, if they were really rich, gold plate. Heraldic flags and banners were hung from rafters and beams, and among those who could afford them, tapestries were hung on the walls. The idea was not only to make the house look festive, but also to show off the power and wealth of the hosts.

Beyond the specific celebrations mentioned above, most medieval holidays were religious in nature. The modern word holiday is, in fact, a corruption of the words "holy day." In addition to the requisite church attendance, major religious festivals were celebrated in much the same way as secular holidays, except among the clergy, who frequently used holy days as times of fasting and penance. The vast array of religious holidays that were regularly observed during the Middle Ages makes us wonder how the people got any work done at all. In practice, only the most important religious holidays were universally observed outside the monastic community. Families, villages, towns, and the nobility selected from among the rest to recognize their patron saints and days of particular personal or local significance.

In chapter 3 we provide a list of medieval holidays from which you can choose those that best suit the timetable for your own medieval celebration. In chapters 4, 5, 6, and 7 we offer in-depth details for celebrating a medieval Christmas, New Year's, May Day, and that most important occasion, a wedding.

A Calendar of Medieval Holidays

The medieval world revolved largely around the changing seasons and the activities and observances associated with each of them. Wheat and rye were planted in October, following the autumn harvest. By mid or late November animal fodder was running low, so excess livestock was slaughtered and the meat was salted or pickled to provide food over the winter. During the darkest days of winter, when no farming could take place because the ground was frozen, Christmas festivities provided a welcome break from the drudgery of plowing and planting. Where the weather allowed, spring crops were planted from early January through Easter. By the beginning of May, the first crops were available and the mud-clogged roads had dried out enough that the first traveling merchants reappeared on the roads. This provided an opportunity for May Day celebrations and spring fairs. But there were literally hundreds of other holidays which any given family or village might celebrate.

Below is a fairly complete list of the more important medieval holy days and secular holidays. For saints of local significance, we have included the patron saints of England, Scotland, Wales, Ireland, Spain, and France. Other nationalities had their own patrons, as did virtually every county, town, guild, church, school, and household. You may pick your favorite as an occasion to hold your own feast or celebration or, if there is no particular theme to your celebration, pick a saint whose special day falls near the time you want to hold your feast. If you wish to hold a Christmas, Twelfth Night, or New Year's celebration, or a medieval wedding, the next three chapters describe customs specifically associated with those particular occasions.

All the calendar dates below are based on the old Julian calendar, which was in use until 1582, when the Gregorian calendar came into official use, although many countries did not adopt the new calendar for decades or centuries afterward. After that time, many of the religious feast days were changed, so they will not all correspond with their modern counterparts.

Scattered throughout the calendar are days marked as Ember Days. These were days of particular dedication to fasting, prayer, and beseeching God for forgiveness of sins. Ember Days take place four times a year, each time on successive Wednesdays, Fridays, and Saturdays. The first group of Ember Days occurs during the week following the first Sunday in Lent, the next is in the week after Whitsun (derived from "White Sunday" and celebrated seven weeks after Easter), the third follows Holy Cross Day (September 14), and the last falls on the Wednesday, Friday, and Saturday following St. Lucy's Day (December 13).

January

1st. Circumcision of Christ. From 1582 onward, also **New Year's Day**. Prior to that time, the new year began on March 25. As part of the traditional New Year's festivities, dumb shows (mummer plays where no words were spoken) were presented in churches and at feasts in great halls.

6th. Twelfth Day, or **Epiphany**. The twelfth day after Christmas, this was marked by a major feast held on the previous evening, known as Twelfth Night. It formally brought the Christmas season to an end and was one of the most popular celebrations among all levels of medieval society.

7th. Plow Monday. Marking the advent of the coming spring's plowing season, Plow Monday was celebrated with plow races where the men of the village competed for the longest and straightest furrows. Children went from door to door begging for small coins and treats.

February

2nd. Candlemas, or **Purification of the Virgin Mary**. In Ireland, also the **Feast of St. Bridget**. Candlemas marks the day when Mary was allowed to reenter the temple after having given birth to Jesus. On this day, women traditionally proceeded to the local church carrying lighted candles. The traditional color for this festival was white, the symbol of purity.

14th. St. Valentine's Day. During the Middle Ages, as now, the occasion was a time of declaring one's love and praying to St. Valentine, patron saint of lovers. Local fairs and festivals were often held at this time, probably as a break from the long, dark months of winter, which were now coming to an end.

Variable. Shrove Monday. Falling on the day before Shrove Tuesday, Shrove Monday (six weeks and six days before Easter) was often marked by public sporting events in which entire communities took part. While the nobles held jousting tournaments, villagers participated in games including tug-of-war (usually across an obstacle like a fence, stream, or large mud hole), skipping contests, chasing a greased pig, marbles, climbing a greased pole, and "camping," the rules for all of which can be found in chapter 11. Bull and bear baiting and cock fighting were also popular entertainments now and throughout the warm months of the year. There was also a tradition that people who wished to change their luck would smash their pottery on this day.

Variable. Shrove Tuesday. Shrove Tuesday marked the last day before the beginning of the Lenten season. Because many people gave up meat, dairy products, other favorite foods, and sex during Lent as a sign of penance ("Shrove" is derived from "to be shriven," which means to be cleansed of all sin), Shrove Tuesday was often marked by feasting and revelry even in churches, where dinner was eaten from the altar. This tradition continues today in the custom of Mardi Gras, which literally translates from the French as "Fat Tuesday."

Variable. Ash Wednesday. The day after Shrove Tuesday, Ash Wednesday was the official beginning of Lent. All Christians attended mass, at which time the priest marked their foreheads with ashes in the sign of the cross. The Wednesday, Friday, and Saturday following Ash Wednesday were Ember Days, when good Christians were supposed to do particularly severe penance, giving up many foods and spending their time praying.

March

1st. St. David's Day. Observed in Wales only, St. David's Day, commemorating the patron saint of Wales, was celebrated with church services and local celebrations. The day was marked by the wearing of a leek (an onion-like vegetable) in the band of one's hat.

17th. St. Patrick's Day. Ireland only. Commemorating the patron saint of Ireland, St Patrick's Day was the high point of secular celebration in Ireland and rivaled Christmas for general merrymaking. St. Patrick's symbol is the shamrock, which is seen as representative of the Holy Trinity. The traditional color for the day was bright green.

18th. Feast of St. Edward the Confessor. In England, this was an important observance of the last completed reign of an Anglo-Saxon king prior to the Norman invasion. King Edward was the patron saint of England from shortly after his death until the mid-thirteenth century, when he was replaced by St. George.

21st. Feast of St. Benedict. Celebrated primarily among members of the Benedictine monastic order. St. Benedict was widely revered throughout Western Europe and England as the founder of the first monastic house in the Christian faith.

25th. Feast of the Annunciation and **New Year's Day** (prior to 1582 or later in many countries). The Feast of the Annunciation marked the day the Archangel Gabriel announced to the Virgin Mary that she would conceive Jesus. The traditional color for this feast was white, symbolizing Mary's purity. New Year's festivals were traditionally celebrated with public revelry centering around gift giving and the Feast of Fools. As part of the traditional New Year's festivities, dumb shows (mummer plays where no words were spoken) were presented in churches and at feasts in great halls.

Variable. Palm Sunday. The Sunday before Easter. This celebration commemorated Jesus' arrival in Jerusalem, when the citizens of the town strewed palm leaves in his path. Because palms were virtually nonexistent in northern Europe and England, parishioners proceeded to church carrying rushes or willow wands in their hands.

Variable. Good Friday. The Friday before Easter. Good Friday marked the day of Jesus' crucifixion. The day was spent in prayer and contemplation. The traditional color for this festival was yellow, the medieval color of mourning.

Variable. Holy Saturday. The day before Easter.

Variable. Easter Sunday. The first Sunday after the first full moon on or after March 21. If the full moon is on a Sunday, the next Sunday is Easter. Easter always falls sometime between March 22 and April 25. This holiday was celebrated by Christians everywhere as the day Jesus rose from the dead, bringing the possibility of salvation from sin. The traditional color for this festival was white.

Variable. Hocktide. The Sunday after Easter, Hocktide was a time of paying the taxes, tolls, and rents and collecting debts for the first quarter of the year. The name hocktide is related to getting out of hock, or debt.

April

1st. All Fools' (April Fool's Day). Celebrated since the second century, the custom of playing jokes and general tomfoolery associated with this day may have had its roots in the mocking of Jesus by Roman soldiers and the mob in Jerusalem prior to his crucifixion. Because the weather had usually turned fair by this time, martial sporting events were often held. Among the most popular were archery and quarterstaff contests. Other traditional observances for the feast included the fools' parade, where revelers disguised themselves with costumes and masks and paraded through the town or village, demanding entrance into homes. Not even the homes of

first time in months that the rough medieval roads were dry enough to be passable by the carts of traveling merchants. May Day was undoubtedly one of the most joyous and boisterous festivals of the year.

3rd. Holy Rood Day. This holiday celebrated the discovery of the cross on which Jesus was crucified, ostensibly by the mother of Roman Emperor Constantine during the third century. This was primarily a day of religious observance. A second Holy Rood Day occurs on September 14.

26th. Feast of St. Augustine. A religious observance celebrated primarily by members and followers of the Augustinian monastic order.

Variable. Rogation Sunday. Falling five weeks after Easter, Rogation Sunday was a time of asking God to forgive sins and bless the land for the coming growing season. The word rogation means beseeching or asking. During the ceremony, parishioners would march around the boundaries of the parish, bearing a cross and banners, asking a variety of saints to intercede with God on behalf of crops, livestock, and, in fishing communities, the bounty of the sea. As a sign of their sincerity, members of the procession would distribute alms to the poor and needy. At the end of the procession, they would assemble at the parish church for mass and communion.

Variable. Ascension Day, or **Holy Thursday.** This Thursday, forty days after Easter Sunday, marked the celebration of Christ ascending into heaven. In England, holy wells noted for their association with saints and

the great and powerful could be shut to the fools' parade, and once inside, the revelers would demand food and drink. This is not unlike the Halloween custom of trick or treating. All Fools' also traditionally marked the beginning of the spring planting season.

23rd. St. George's Day. Best known as the slayer of the dragon, St. George was the patron saint of soldiers everywhere and, after the displacement of St. Edward the Confessor in the thirteenth century, the patron saint of England. Public plays were often performed to tell the story of St. George and his victory over the dragon to rescue a maiden, who had been taken prisoner by the beast. The traditional color for this festival was blue.

25th. St. Mark the Evangelist.

May

1st. May Day. Feast of Saints Philip and Jacob the Apostles. As the beginning of summer, May Day was a time of great celebration, most of which was held outdoors. Spring flowers were woven into garlands and wreaths, which were tied to wagons and carts and worn around the heads of unmarried women, who traditionally danced around a Maypole erected in the center of the village green. Because the young maidens had thus consented to put themselves on display, May Day became the unofficial beginning of the courting season. The first market and trade fairs were held in early May, both because the first produce was available and because local tradesmen were anxious to sell the items they had made over the long, dark winter. It was also probably the

certain healing powers were decorated, or "dressed," with flowers. Bundles of willow wands tied with blue ribbons were carried to the local church.

Variable. Whitsun, or **White Sunday** (now Pentecost). Falling ten days after Ascension Day and fifty days after Easter Sunday, Whitsun commemorated the descent of the Holy Spirit on the Apostles. The Wednesday, Friday, and Saturday after Whitsun were Ember Days to be observed by prayer, penance, and fasting. After the solemnity of Whitsun, the following week became a time of public fairs and festivals, where Morris dancing and mystery plays were performed. A special Whitsun ale was often brewed and distributed or sold. Popular games were the same as those played on Shrove Tuesday. The traditional color for this festival was red.

June

24th. St. John the Baptist. Also **Rogation Sunday**. Based on the pagan holiday of Midsummer (the summer solstice), this holiday was supposed to mark the birth of St. John the Baptist, Jesus' cousin, who foretold Jesus' coming. Because St. John preached in the wilderness of Judea, people in many places decorated the outside of their houses with greenery. The traditional color for this festival was white. Despite the church's attempts to stamp out all pagan traditions, the lighting of a midsummer bonfire on midsummer's eve (the evening of June 23) survived in even the most staunchly Christian communities. At this time, the fairy folk and ghosts were believed to walk abroad, and the wildflower Saint John's wort was picked at this time as a charm against illness and bad luck. Surprisingly, the church seems to have tolerated these pagan practices with general good grace. As a rogation Sunday, this was also a time of collecting summer rents and taxes.

29th. Feast of Saints Peter and Paul the Apostles.

Variable. Trinity Sunday. Falling one week after Whitsun, Trinity Sunday was marked by contemplation of the Holy Trinity (God the Father, Son, and Holy Spirit) and the performance of miracle and mystery plays, which told stories of the Bible from the creation through Jesus' resurrection. The traditional color for this festival was white.

Variable. Corpus Christi. Celebrated on the first Thursday after Trinity Sunday, Corpus Christi gave thanks for the sacrament of Holy Communion. The day was celebrated with public festivities, including a procession through the streets of the town, during which the host (communion wafers) was taken through the streets and religious plays were performed by local guilds and monastic houses. In Coventry, England, a fair was also held in commemoration of Lady Godgifu (now known as Godiva), who rode through the town "clad only in her virtue" (stark naked) in protest of her husband, Earl Leofric, who brutalized and oppressed his subjects. The traditional color for this festival was red.

July

7th. Translation of St. Thomas the Martyr. A distinctly English holiday, this day marked the anniversary of moving the bones of Archbishop Thomas à Becket from their tomb to a shrine in Canterbury Cathedral, following his canonization (elevation to sainthood) in 1174, only four years after his murder.

15th. St. Swithin's Day. This holiday was not widely celebrated, but it was believed that the weather on this day would continue for the next forty days.

22nd. Feast of St. Mary Magdalene.

25th. St. James the Apostle and St. Christopher. St. James was the patron saint of Spain, where he is known as St. Iago. His day was widely celebrated throughout the country, but nowhere were the celebrations any larger or more devout than in Campostella, where the shrine of St. James is the heart of the cathedral and the culmination point of one of Christendom's most popular medieval pilgrimages. St. Christopher was the patron saint of travelers, and his feast date was particularly observed by those who were about to undertake

a long journey or who traveled habitually in the course of their work.

Thoughout July. July was the traditional time for the beginning of religious pilgrimages, and consequently, many outdoor religious services were held during this month to bless those who were undertaking pilgrimages.

August

1st. Feast of St. Peter in Chains (in Latin, St. Peter ad Vincula). Also **Lammas Day**. A commemoration of the miracle performed by God when the chains that bound St. Peter miraculously dropped away while he was imprisoned in Rome awaiting crucifixion. In Lammas Day (possibly derived from "Loaf Mass") celebrations, thanks was given for a successful wheat harvest; each household took the first loaf of bread baked from the new harvest to the local church to be blessed. During successful harvest seasons the blessing of the bread was customarily followed by a public feast.

5th. St. Dominic. Primarily observed by members of the Dominican monastic order in honor of their founder.

10th. St. Lawrence the Martyr. This saint's day was particularly popular in France.

15th. Assumption of Our Lady. The holiday marked the day when the Virgin Mary was carried into heaven. This was essentially a religious holiday, but there were occasional parades, particularly where the local church or monastery was dedicated to Our Lady.

24th. St. Bartholomew.

25th. St. Louis, patron saint of France and formerly France's King Louis IX. Although he died in 1270, by 1297 he had already been canonized and almost instantly became France's most popular saint. Celebrations were held throughout France in his honor.

28th. St. Augustine of Hipo. Celebrated primarily among members of the Augustinian monastic order in honor of their patron saint.

September

8th. Nativity of Our Lady. Ostensibly marking the Virgin Mary's birthday, this holiday was traditionally celebrated as a harvest festival. Harvesting was always blessed by the church, partly as a display of God's blessing on the crops, and partly because, by canon law, the church received one-tenth of the entire harvest. The final cartload of grain to be brought in from the field was

followed to the church with a great procession, accompanied by much singing and ceremony. At a public feast which signaled the end of the harvest in almost every rural community, tables were decorated with dolls made from wheat shafts, the dolls being burned after the feast was over. As the field workers blew off steam with reveling and drinking, harvest festivals obtained a reputation for being excessively rowdy.

14th. Exaltation of the Cross. A Holy Rood day. Supposedly the exact date of the discovery of the "true cross," this day was traditionally celebrated as a part of the harvest season festivities. The following Wednesday,

16

Friday, and Saturday were Ember Days, observed with fasting, prayer, and penance. The traditional color for this festival was red.

21st. St. Matthew the Apostle.

29th. Michaelmas, or the **Feast of St. Michael the Archangel.** Important to both church and laity, this feast signaled the end of the harvest and of the agricultural year. If the day fell on a Sunday, it was also a Rogation Sunday when the last rents of the year were traditionally collected, tithes were due, and accounts were settled. It was a time of great public celebration and feasting to mark the harvest. One of the most unique elements of this occasion was the appearance of "horn dancers," a troupe of men wearing or carrying sets of deer antlers, who danced in public marketplaces to the accompaniment of drums and pipes. The tradition of the horn dancers may date back to an ancient pagan custom celebrating the hunt.

October

9th. St. Denys' Day, patron saint of the city of Paris. St. Denys' Day was celebrated throughout France, but primarily in the capital, Paris, both at church services and with parades and festivals.

18th. Feast of St. Luke the Evangelist.

25th. St. Crispin's Day. Primarily remembered as the anniversary of the battle of Agincourt (1415), when England's King Henry V put the entire combined French army and cavalry, numbering in excess of thirty-five thousand men, to rout with a band of only seven thousand men. Thereafter, it was celebrated in England as a day of military victory. We can assume the French chose to ignore the occasion entirely.

28th. Saints Simon and Jude the Apostles.

31st. All Hallows' Eve. A time of spiritual unrest, when the souls of the dead, along with ghosts and evil spirits, were believed to walk the land. Church bells were rung and fires lit to guide these souls on their way and deflect them from haunting honest Christian folk. Barns and homes were blessed to protect people and livestock from the effects of witches, who were believed to accompany the malignant spirits as they traveled the earth. Although a rare few continued to divine the future, cast spells, and tell ghost stories in rural communities, woe to anyone who was denounced to the church for engaging in such activities. This may seem like innocent fun today, but it was deadly serious stuff during the Middle Ages.

November

1st. All Hallows' Day or **All Saints' Day.** The word hallow was simply another word for saint. This feast was dedicated to all the truly holy people in the history of Christianity. The traditional color for this festival was white.

2nd. All Souls' Day. A time when prayers were said for the souls of the dead and penance was done to help extricate the dead from purgatory.

20th. St. Edmund the King and Martyr. Another uniquely English celebration. St. Edmund had been a ninth-century king of Norfolk, which was then an independent kingdom of Anglo-Saxon England. He was martyred by the Danes in 870.

25th. St. Catherine's Day. Famous for surviving torture on a spiked wheel (the Catherine wheel) only to be beheaded, St. Catherine was the most popular female saint of the Middle Ages and was venerated by both men and women. Many guilds, churches, ships, and organizations were dedicated to her name. On her festival day, great processions were held in her honor throughout Europe.

Variable. Advent. Beginning the fourth Sunday before Christmas, Advent lasted through Christmas Eve. Missing Sunday services during this period would have been unthinkable.

December

6th. St. Nicholas' Day. Precursor to the Santa Claus tradition, the feast of St. Nicholas was observed by the presentation of gifts to children, accompanied by family-oriented merrymaking. Traditionally, the feast of St. Nicholas began more than a month of celebrations, worship services, and feasts revolving around the Christmas season. In cathedrals throughout England and Europe, "boy bishops" were elected in commemoration of St. Nicholas' compassion for children. From St. Nicholas' Day until the Feast of the Holy Innocents (December 28), these juvenile mock bishops were allowed to undertake all ecclesiastical duties except delivering the mass.

8th. The Conception of Our Lady. This day celebrated St. Anne becoming pregnant with the future Virgin Mary.

11th. St. Andrew's Day. Andrew is the patron saint of Scotland, where his celebration was widely observed with both religious services and traditional Scottish games such as the caber toss, throwing the stone, and displays of martial prowess.

13th. St. Lucy's Day. The next Wednesday, Friday, and Saturday after St. Lucy's Day were Ember Days.

21st. St. Thomas the Apostle.

25th. Christmas. The most joyous time of the year, Christmas marked the birth of Jesus and his message of salvation for all who believed in him. The season was celebrated with feasts, dancing, wassailing through the streets, and performances of religious and secular plays, all set amid garlands of holly, ivy, and evergreen.

26th. St. Stephen's Day. St. Stephen, a Roman soldier, is considered to have been the first Christian martyr.

28th. Feast of the Holy Innocents. Commemorating King Herod's slaughter of thousands of children in an attempt to kill the infant Jesus, this was a day of particular importance for pregnant women, families with sick children, and mothers who had lost children through disease, accident, or stillbirth, which included almost every family during the Middle Ages.

29th. Feast of St. Thomas the Archbishop and Martyr. This day celebrated the life and work of Thomas à Becket, archbishop of Canterbury, murdered on this date in 1169 on the order of King Henry II. Only four years after his martyrdom, Becket was canonized. His shrine in Canterbury Cathedral, Canterbury, England, became a place of pilgrimage for people throughout Europe, only exceeded in popularity by the shrines of St. Peter in Rome and St. James in Santiago de Compostela, Spain. The celebration of his feast day, however, was most popular among the English.

CHAPTER 4

Medieval Christmas Celebrations

Long before Europeans began recording their history, they celebrated a great winter festival. There were good practical reasons for having one last, great feast before the onset of the most severe weather. All the carefully preserved stocks of salted meats, dried fish, grain, and milled flour had been put aside, and any remaining fresh provisions needed to be consumed before they went bad. In this primitive world, the privations of winter were a very real threat to survival, and as an act of defiance against this long, dark season, people chose to celebrate. The human spirit was determined to live on until the next growing season, and to do so with bravery and good cheer.

But the winter festivals of pre-Christian Europe were far more than railing against the storm and snow that accompanied the final season of the year. A major element of the old pagan winter festivals was dramatizing the death of the old year and celebrating the beginning of a new one—what the Scandinavians called "iul" (yule), meaning "the wheel of the year." These celebrations undoubtedly had a vital religious aspect, because they were an affirmation of man's relationship with nature and an attempt to appease the angry gods who controlled it. The food consumed at the feasts was simultaneously a celebration and a sacrifice to the gods of nature. At the time of year when the sun appeared to decline in the sky, and deprivation threatened the very survival of the community, winter festivals were an attempt to appease whatever mysterious forces were responsible for bringing about the bleakness of the season, and to encourage the return of the sun and the fertility of the land. This aspect of the festival was connected to traditional pagan fertility rites.

In attempting to drive away the darkness of winter, lights and fires were important to these festivals; the fire attracted or called out to the sun, to hasten its return. Similarly, the use of evergreens, holly, and ivy to decorate homes was far more than an attractive adornment. Because these were the only plants that remained green when all else turned dead and brown, they were symbolic of the continuity of life. Another factor in the popularity of midwinter celebrations was that rural communities, which made up over ninety-five percent of the population of the ancient world, had plenty of spare time during this season and needed something to break the boredom. Farmers had little to do during the winter apart from milking and feeding the cows and tending the other livestock. The plow and other implements of cultivation had been put away until spring.

There were two distinct lines of winter holiday festivities in the later, classical world: those of the Germanic north and those of Romanized southern Europe. The later Roman Empire had three important midwinter festivals: Saturnalia, which began on December 17 and lasted an entire week; the Birthday of the Unconquered Sun, on December 25; and the Kalends, on January 1. Saturnalia was named for the early Roman god

Saturnus (Saturn), whose name meant "plenty" or "bounty," and his festival was characterized by revelry, feasting, and drunkenness. During the two weeks between the start of Saturnalia and the Kalends, which inaugurated the New Year and gave us the word calendar, buildings were brightly lit and decorated with evergreens, while holiday processions crowded the streets and families exchanged presents. Public and private feasts were presided over by a mock ruler, or a master of revels, and the normal social order was turned on its head: masters waited on their servants; pastimes which were forbidden at other times, such as gambling, were permitted; and men dressed as women or in animal skins, while the women dressed in men's clothes. There was even a special place in the Roman festival season for children, celebrated as the feast of Juvinalia.

In the midst of these weeks of revelry came a day set aside for the celebration of the sun, whose annual crisis at the winter solstice formed the heart of almost all ancient winter festivals. It was the occasion when the sun appeared, from the perspective of northern Europe, to stand low and still on the southern horizon during the shortest days of the year. With the passing of the solstice, the sun stopped receding and began returning northward toward the zenith. The sun briefly standing still was a noteworthy event for a heavenly body that brought life to the earth and was deified in many religions. Some early religious ceremonies were designed to ensure, by magic and sacrifice, that the sun would move back to the center of the sky rather than disappear completely. Although celebrated throughout the Roman world, the Day of the Birth of the Unconquered Sun, or Sol Invictus, was in particular the great feast day of Mithraism, a salvationist religion popular among soldiers in the Roman world, and a vigorous competitor with early Christianity. By the time Christianity became an established religion in the fourth century A.D., the winter solstice had been fixed at December 25.

The northern European festival of Yuletide had many similarities to its counterparts in the Roman Empire. There were the same sumptuous feasts, and the drinking and carousing among the Germanic tribes were as copious and boisterous as the revelry of the Romans. The practices of lighting great bonfires and burning the yule log were both ritual encouragements to the waning sun and bringers of festive cheer in the dead of winter. Also during the winter festival, Odin, or Wotan, the Nordic-Germanic god of war, was believed to hurtle across the night sky in a chariot pulled by two huge goats, bearing gifts for his faithful followers.

There was a peculiar northern European preoccupation with death and the dark forces of the night during Yuletide. Ghosts and demons were believed to roam freely through the vast forests of northern Europe on long winter nights. Among the darkest pagan customs was the tradition of selecting a "king of the bean" or a "yule lord" who would receive supreme power and authority for the season, after which he would be ritually sacrificed to appease the gods and the forces of darkness. The odd title "king of the bean" was derived from the custom of randomly choosing the unfortunate mock-monarch by hiding a dried bean in one roll out of an entire batch of biscuits. The man who received the biscuit with the bean inside was the winner—or loser, as the case may be.

In Scandinavia, the demigod Julebuk (Yule buck) appeared in a devilish horned mask, but strangely, like Odin, he brought gifts to children. In parts of Germany, legends of a similar hideous monster lived on into modern times as Klausauf, a companion to St. Nicholas during his seasonal visit to children.

One of the longest surviving features of the pagan mid-winter festival is the tradition of wassailing. The wassail pot was a large bowl, traditionally made of maple wood, which was filled with a mixture of warming drinks. Ale or cider, often heated, was the chief ingredient, to which were added spices, sugar, raisins, roasted apples, and any other pleasant ingredients available. It was, in fact, an early kind of punch. Wassail bowls were passed around by the host, who toasted his guests by raising the bowl and saying "waes hael" (meaning be well); the guests would answer "drinc hael" (drink and be well). The wassailing season lasted until the end of the winter festival and culminated in the wassailing of the apple trees—a blessing bestowed by pouring a little of the wassail onto the roots of the trees to appease the gods and ensure a good harvest in the coming year.

Early Christians did not celebrate the birth of Christ. The celebration of birthdays was deeply rooted in pagan traditions, and the Gospels said nothing about the actual date of Christ's birth. Possibly, because it was widely believed that Christ would return in the very near future, the exact date of his birth seemed unimportant. As Christianity developed, the concept of Jesus as both fully divine and fully human became accepted dogma. With the acceptance of Jesus as God in human form, there was an urgent desire to celebrate the occasion of his nativity. Jesus had to have an official birthday.

The need to celebrate Jesus' birth, the traditional pagan rites of the winter solstice, and other elements, including Saturnalia, all converged by the fourth century A.D., when Pope Julius I officially fixed the Christian Feast of the Nativity on December 25. Christmas is, in fact, a classic example of the Christian Church coming to terms with the traditional customs and rites of the people, superimposing a Christian holiday on a pagan festival.

In Anglo-Saxon England, the Christian festival fit easily into existing pagan practices, for December 25 was both the beginning of the Anglo-Saxon year and the time of the Yule festivities. Recognizing that people were not easily weaned from their comfortably familiar traditions, Pope Gregory the Great (540–604) became an enthusiastic advocate of converting pagans to Christianity by coming to terms with existing social and religious customs. He wrote to St. Augustine of Canterbury when the latter was embarking on his mission to England in 596, telling him how the old festivities of the "killing time" could be used by Christianity:

> Nor let them now sacrifice animals to the Devil, but to the praise of God kill animals for their own eating, and render thanks to the Giver of all things for their abundance; so that while some outward joys are retained for them, they may the more easily respond to inward joys. For from obdurate minds it is undoubtedly impossible to cut off everything at once, because he who strives to ascend to the highest places rises by degrees or steps and not by leaps.

Despite Pope Gregory's hopes, the pagan elements in the Anglo-Saxon midwinter feast probably remained stronger than the Christian aspects for the majority of early Anglo-Saxon Christians. The Viking invasions of England in the eighth and ninth centuries reinvigorated pagan traditions, while Christian priests were scarce and often as superstitious and illiterate as their flocks. Away from the influence of prelates and monasteries, it is likely that the Yuletide tradition remained strong and the midwinter feast in northern Europe remained substantially what it had been before the coming of Christianity: a time of heavy drinking and carousing among blazing yule logs in buildings adorned with evergreens. Many of the customs accompanying the festivities— the mummers' plays, whose usual theme was a dramatic presentation of death and resurrection, the wassailing (blessing) of fruit trees, and even the games that have become our blind man's bluff and leapfrog—were, consciously or unconsciously, derived from fertility rites.

From the beginning of its celebration, we find an ambiguity in the attitude of fervent Christians to the festive season. There is an emphasis on the fact that it is Christ's birthday and, along with Easter, the most important of festivals. There is, at the same time, an uneasy feeling that many aspects of the celebration are all too worldly. Early Christians were warned against "feasting to excess, dancing and crowning the doors [with evergreens]" and urged to keep "the celebration of the festival after an heavenly and not after an earthly manner." That the "true spirit of Christmas" and the central miracle of the Christian religion—God becoming man—were constantly in danger of being lost amidst the revelry of Saturnalia, or Yuletide, has been feared since Christianity first chose to celebrate the birth of its savior. Many a priest, prelate, and minister has preached to his congregation in similar vein, from A.D 389 to the present day.

The Medieval Christmas Celebration

During the Middle Ages, Christmas was observed in a variety of ways. Our word Christmas, which seems to have been first used in Britain on the eve of the Norman Conquest, is derived from the Middle English term for "Christ's Mass." Central to the celebration of the Nativity was the mass, which had been established by the year 600 and did not notably change throughout the Middle Ages (a complete twelfth-century Latin mass is found at the end of chapter 7). In medieval England there were, in fact, three masses celebrated on Christmas Day. The first took place at midnight prior to Christmas morning. Known as the Angel's Mass, this service proposed that the light of salvation had appeared at the darkest moment of the darkest date in the very depth of winter. The second, the Shepherd's Mass, came at dawn, and the third, the Mass of the Divine Word, during the afternoon.

The season of Advent, the forty days leading up to Christmas, was being observed in the Western Church by the year 500. Advent, combined with the twelve days of Christmas or in some cases, the forty days between Christmas and Candlemas, quickly supplanted earlier, pagan winter festivals as a time of great celebration. Why hold a series of parties that might last up to three months? There are many valid reasons, not the least of which had to do with the fact that travel was difficult and dangerous. It might take guests and relatives weeks to gather, and they were unlikely to undertake such an arduous journey for a simple evening meal.

Despite the best and most creative endeavors of the church, the essentially secular nature of Christmas celebrations persisted throughout the Middle Ages just as it does in the modern age. To some extent, Christmas can be seen as a contest between the dictates of the church and the popular culture of the people. The ecclesiastical hierarchy alternately viewed the sensual enjoyment of Christmas festivities as either a necessary indulgence to the weak and fallible nature of men or a dangerous distraction from serious worship.

The Twelve Days of Christmas were the main national holiday in medieval England and were popularly observed as a time for feasting, dancing, singing, sporting, gambling, and general excess and indulgence. Part of the cause for celebration undoubtedly arose from the security that came with winter. True, the weather could be harsh and cruel, and food and stores could be in short supply, but political enemies were unlikely to start a war or undertake a siege in such conditions. One was alive, safe from enemy threat, surrounded by friends and good company, and had enjoyed plentiful harvests and good hunting with which to cover the tables and fill the belly—by all means, celebrate.

Sharing this time of ease with the lowliest of society, generous lords gave their servants and retainers gifts of food, ale, new clothing, and firewood. From the great feasts that were an integral part of the upper-class Christmas, the entrails (the heart, liver, brains, pancreas, lungs, and other internal organs, known as "humbles") of the butchered animals were donated to the servants and villagers who used them in making what was known as "humble pie." Among those of the merchant class, small mince pies—made of chopped meat and suet, flavored with cinnamon, cloves and nutmeg (three expensive spices symbolizing the three gifts brought to Jesus by the Magi)—were baked in oblong or rectangular shells to symbolize the manger in which Jesus was laid at his birth.

St. Nicholas was a very popular medieval saint, and his feast day, which took place on December 6, was commemorated by giving gifts to children in the good saint's name. However, Nicholas did not evolve into Father Christmas or Santa Claus, the bringer of Christmas Eve gifts for everyone, until after the Reformation of the mid sixteenth century. During the Middle Ages, gift giving among adults generally took place not at Christmas but on Twelfth Night, at the end of the merrymaking.

Throughout the Christmas season, medieval royalty and nobility competed against each other in their displays of grand celebration. The feast hosted by King John of England at Christmas 1213 is supposed to have surpassed the most sumptuous and gargantuan banquets of any previous time, but the celebrations of his son Henry III were on an even grander scale. In 1252, Henry entertained a thousand noblemen and knights at York; the feast was so expensive that the archbishop of York alone gave six hundred fat oxen and the staggering sum of £2,700 toward the feasting. A century and a half later, Richard II provided two thousand oxen and two hundred barrels of wine for the ten thousand revelers who shared in the daily Christmas parties at the king's expense. It was incumbent upon kings, barons, and lesser magnates to dispense hospitality and provide good cheer to the greatest extent their resources would allow. Staging a magnificent feast was tantamount to mounting an army in the field; it was a wonderfully effective way to display wealth and power. After all, who but a great king could find, and afford, several thousand oxen to serve to his dinner guests?

These public displays of lordly wealth, generosity, and seasonal cheer were more than simple vanity; they were good politics. They enhanced the reputation of hosts, could bind together alliances and strengthen feudal bonds, and were probably essential to the survival of poor retainers and peasants during the bleakest time of the year. The size of the banquets obviously varied in sumptuousness according to the resources of the celebrants. The menu was varied, with soups and stews, birds and fish, beef and lamb, breads and puddings. A common element was the Yule boar—the entire beast for those who could afford it, with the head being served as a centerpiece to decorate the high table, or in merchant-class households, a meat pie shaped like a boar.

Churches, castle feast halls, public buildings, and houses were all decorated with ivy, mistletoe, holly, and anything that remained green. These decorations were put up during Advent and remained in place until the eve of Candlemas.

The types of entertainment people might have employed to keep from getting bored are succinctly summarized in a letter written by Margaret Paston on Christmas Eve 1459, describing how her Norfolk neighbor, Lady Morley, had conducted her household, which had been in mourning since the previous Christmas and the death of Lord Morley: "There were no disguisings [acting], nor harping, luting or singing, nor any lewd sports, but just playing at the tables [backgammon] and chess and cards. Such sports she gave her folk leave to play and no other." The "lewd sports" Paston mentions probably refers to the carol dance. The leader of the dance sang a verse of the carol, and a ring of dancers responded with the chorus. Carol dances were often suggestive of their pagan ancestors, where, for instance, holly and ivy had fertility associations with male and female. Further music for the celebration of the season was provided by hymns, sung in Latin or French.

Another important aspect of medieval Christmas festivities was that they provided a release from the strict medieval social order and allowed authority to be symbolically overturned. The old Saturnalia customs of dressing in the clothes of the opposite sex or putting on the skins of animals continued to be associated with Christmas, as did gambling and the practice of role reversal, where superiors waited on those of inferior rank, a custom which survives to this day in the British Army. The reign of "Lords of Misrule" in castle feast halls and the elections of "Boy Bishops" in cathedrals are both customs which appear to have become popular in the tenth century.

Perhaps it was a combination of viewing Jesus as an infant, the role-switching aspects of Roman Saturnalia, and the association of St. Nicholas with children that gave rise to the curious medieval custom of appointing a boy to the position of bishop for the Christmas period. St. Nicholas, whose feast day falls on December 6, was bishop of Myra, in modern Turkey. Among Nicholas' roles was that of the patron saint of children. The unsavory story that tied Nicholas to children claims that during a time of famine an innkeeper, short on food, killed three schoolboys, pickled their flesh, and stored it in a barrel. When Bishop Nicholas happened by, he restored the three boys to life. In medieval representations of St. Nicholas, the saint is often portrayed standing next

to a cask from which three boys are emerging. A play covering the St Nicholas story is included in chapter 14.

Boy Bishops were found in England by the first quarter of the thirteenth century and the custom continued until 1559. At Salisbury Cathedral, to cite one specific case, the Boy Bishop was chosen by the cathedral's youth choir from among their members on St. Nicholas' Day and performed his pseudo-Episcopal office, which included everything except delivering the mass, for just over three weeks, until the night of the Feast of the Holy Innocents. Following his election and investiture, the Boy Bishop, like a true bishop, would set out with his attendants on a visitation throughout his bishopric, imposing correct doctrine and discipline as he traveled. The visitation of the Boy Bishop and his retinue to ecclesiastical establishments and noble households in the vicinity might last several weeks and involved much gift giving and lavish entertainments. Many of the gifts would later be sold to cover expenses. The whole carnival of the Boy Bishop was splendid entertainment; it was sometimes irreverent and unruly, but it suited its era by allowing ritual protest against the rigid authority structure that was integral to maintaining social order in an unstable and violent world. In a similar tradition, the Lord of Misrule was a random member of the populace who was selected to serve as Lord or King for the duration of the seasonal festivities of peasant villages. As such, he presented a serious upheaval to an otherwise stagnant social order. The customs of Boy Bishops and the Lord of Misrule were undoubtedly medieval incarnations of the violent pagan customs of the "king of the bean" and the "yule lord" mentioned earlier.

While the Church reinterpreted many old customs, the most important part of its effort to popularize the more pious aspects of Christmas celebrations was telling the story of Christ's birth in terms accessible to the common people. Knowing that visual interpretations of religious stories had more impact than recited texts, particularly if the text was read in Latin and the general populace had no way of understanding it, the church instituted the tradition of the Nativity play. Nativity plays began as seasonal embellishments to the liturgy, and eventually passed from churches to the streets and from the clergy to the laity, losing the Latin dialogue in the process.

The commoners had their own plays as well, generally of pagan origin. These annual performances, known as mummers plays, are probably the oldest surviving feature of the Christmas festivities and put all the rest into proper perspective. They present, in dramatic

Carol singing, although considered more secular than religious, was a popular part of medieval Christmas celebrations. EUGENE SIREN

form, the contest between the powers of light and darkness. The basic plot is always the same; the powers of darkness fight with the hero and give him a mortal wound. As he lies dying, a frantic call goes up for a doctor, who comes in and heals the expiring hero with a magic elixor. The dark figures steal away, and the hero rises renewed and triumphant. In some versions, the plot has become so confused that it is difficult to tell which are the good guys and which the baddies, but someone is always brought back to life from apparently certain death. Two such plays are included in chapter 14.

Another frequent character in the mummers play is a rather pathetic figure hung with ten or twelve tiny cloth dolls representing his numerous children. This character, traditionally named Johnny Jack, is important, for he explains how the mumming plays have managed to survive. He is unashamedly a beggar. Entering toward the end of the play, he recites a speech that reveals the mumming plays for what they became: a means by which the poor obtained Christmas charity from the rich. It was the custom for village mummers to make the rounds of the great houses in the district and perform their play in the great halls. At each they would

collect gifts of cash or food. Considering the lucrative pickings available in castles and great houses around Christmastime, it is hardly surprising that the rural poor kept the plays alive for so many centuries. A Johnny Jack play is included in chapter 14.

Although it had far more ancient roots, one of the better-known features of the medieval Christmas celebration is the tradition of wassailing. By the Middle Ages, the fertility aspect of wassailing was slowly dying out, and the revelers simply carried the wassail bowl around the village, greeting friends, encouraging them to join in the singing, and sometimes collecting money for the church. The wassailing season lasted from Christmas Eve until Twelfth Night.

To a large extent, carol singing slowly replaced wassailing, but the object remained the same—to spread cheer and collect money. Today, carolers range from small children who stumble through one verse and then knock at the door to efficiently organized parties from the local church choir who perform for shut-ins, the elderly, and charities. Carols were not originally confined to Christmas as they now are; there were, for instance, Easter carols, some of which may be found in modern church hymnals. The first carols specifically written for Christmas appeared around the fourth century, and by the thirteenth century the tradition of Christmas carols sung in the native language, rather than in Latin, had taken hold throughout Europe. By 1426, the first collection of twenty-five Christmas carols appeared in printed version in English. Carols were also sung at the Feast of All Saints, also known as All Hallows. When All Hallows became secularized and popularized as Halloween, the tradition of going from door to door begging for gifts survived, but adults were replaced by children, and singing was lost in favor of calling out "trick or treat."

The carol itself originated in popular French dance songs which were condemned by the church as lustful and pagan. Originally associated with Christmas only by the season in which they were sung, carols eventually evolved into a form that was primarily religious and was therefore acceptable to the church. While carols became specifically religious in nature, they remained quite commonplace in subject, as with this fourteenth-century English example:

Iesu, swete sone dere!
On porful bed list thou here,
And that me greveth sore;
For thi cradel is ase a bere,
Oxe and asse beth thi fere;
Weepe ich mai tharfore.

Translation:
Sweet, dear baby Jesus,
Your bed is so poor,
And I grieve for you;
Because your cradle is in a cow barn,
The oxen and asses are your companions;
Therefore, I weep for you.

The rural poor were profoundly affected by the concept of a prince born into poverty, who was attended by shepherds and surrounded by beasts that miraculously fell on their knees before him. In the Middle Ages, country folk firmly believed that on Christmas Eve, bees sang in their hives and oxen knelt in their stalls, their heads bowed toward Jerusalem in the east.

As well known as the wassail bowl and carol is the Yule log. A Yule log once burned on every hearth at Christmas. The log was not brought into the house until Christmas Eve, and once lit, the fire was not allowed to go out until the log was entirely consumed. It had associations with the Christmas candle, which was also a common feature of medieval Christmas festivities. Both log and candle were lit at the same moment. Placed on the table at the beginning of the feast, the Christmas candle was not to be moved, blown out, or snuffed out during the meal. The Yule log and candle symbolize Christ as the "light of the world" and man's spiritual triumph over darkness of the spirit through salvation.

Prince Albert, the husband of Queen Victoria, is usually given the credit for introducing Christmas trees to England in 1847 from his native Germany. Certainly from that time their popularity increased rapidly, but there are records of such trees in London streets in the Middle Ages, and at the same time Germans paraded through the streets carrying small pine trees adorned with paper flowers.

Although there are no records of Christmas trees being lit in medieval great halls, boughs of holly and pine brought color and fragrance to the dreary interiors, while the Yule log and candles provided warmth and light to help revelers forget about the cold and dark which waited outside. In fact, the idea behind the Christmas tree is the same as the idea behind bringing evergreen cuttings into the house; they both symbolize the survival of life in a frozen world.

Mistletoe, because of its pagan associations, was forbidden in most churches, with the notable exception of York Minster Cathedral in York, England. Mistletoe featured prominently in Norse mythology as the plant by which the hero Baldur was slain. It was also sacred to the old Celtic religion and was cut with much ceremony by the Druids. The practice of kissing under the mistletoe is very ancient, and in countries where mistletoe was scarce, there was a tradition of making a kissing bush of other evergreens and decorations, to be suspended from the ceiling.

Holly has usually been a permitted Christmas decoration, although in ancient times it was considered to be the home of woodland spirits. It is even today occasionally regarded as a witches' tree, and the belief that it is unlucky to bring holly into the house before Christmas Eve still survives. Ivy was likewise an acceptable Christmas evergreen. On the Isle of Man, sweet cicely, which the Manx people called myrrh, was said to blossom for one hour on Christmas Eve. It is an amazing fact that on or about Christmas Day, the great thorn tree at Glastonbury Abbey in Somerset, England, inexplicably bursts into flower, though some years it waits until the original Christmas Day, January 5. In either case, there is no doubt that it does flower in midwinter, something no thorn bush should do under any circumstances.

Sprigs of pine, holly, and ivy add a seasonal touch of brightness and cheer to a medieval Christmas celebration. STEVE LUND

Religion as well as custom can be credited with the extravagant celebrations associated with the Christmas season, but the basic tenet of Christmas was that people should be merry and hospitable; if they were also inclined to be prayerful, all the better.

Our Christmas celebrations today owe quite a bit to ancient and medieval Christmas traditions. Our odd ritual of cutting down an evergreen, bringing it into our home, and decorating it with lights as though it were on fire reaches back to a time long before our medieval ancestors. Santa Claus's sleigh, drawn through the skies by reindeer, evolved from Odin's chariot. When Odin and his kind were banished by Christian rulers, his place was taken by St. Nicholas, and he eventually evolved into the jolly man in the red suit. The exchange of presents is most likely a holdover from the gifts exchanged by the Romans on Kalends. The generosity of the gift exchange was reinterpreted under Christian doctrine to be a reenactment of the gifts of gold, frankincense, and myrrh brought to the baby Jesus by the wise men. Decorations of holly, mistletoe, and ivy are borrowed from Celtic and Nordic tribes. Wassailing has been inherited from ancient fertility rites, and carol singing started as little more than institutionalized begging.

For all the rules and regulations that bound medieval society, there was no absolute standard about when the Christmas season was to end. Most people ended the revelries with Epiphany, popularly known in the Middle Ages as Twelfth Night (hence the Christmas carol "The Twelve Days of Christmas"), but many carried it through February 2, the Feast of the Purification of the Virgin, then known as Candlemas. During Candlemas, in one of the most elaborate processions of the year, all parishioners proceeded to mass carrying a penny and a candle, both of which were offered to the priest as part of the parochial dues of the faithful. The candles were blessed and taken away to be used during thunderstorms or to give comfort to the sick and the dying. These candles were thus important for giving people a light of solace in the face of hostile forces and stressful events. Candlemas marked the end of the long season, commencing with Advent, which drew medieval Christians to concentrate on the miraculous birth of Christ and his promise of salvation, while still leaving ample space for fun, feasting, and socializing.

CHAPTER 5

Medieval New Year Celebrations

Welcoming in the new year has always been accompanied by fun, festivities, and frivolity, but during most of the Middle Ages knowing exactly when to hold those revels was a matter of almost constant debate.

Virtually all ancient cultures celebrated the beginning of the year near the time of the vernal equinox, which can fall on either March 20 or March 21. In those societies where adherence to the calendar and attention to detail had replaced stargazing in social importance, the beginning of the new year was eventually fixed at April 1. In either case, dating the beginning of the year in the spring was a perfectly sensible approach during a time period when our work and lifecycle was tied to the rhythms of nature and farming. Under this ancient system, the new year heralded a time of planting the fields and helping domesticated animals through the process of giving birth to their young. A new year meant new life.

In 46 B.C., Julius Caesar introduced a new calendar that placed the beginning of the year at January 1. For the urbanized Romans, the new year had more to do with the practicalities of keeping accounts and records than observing the cycles of nature. The new Julian calendar worked fine until Christianity became the dominant social force in European society and a series of popes and ecumenical conclaves decided the year should begin on a date of theological importance. Some insisted the year should begin on the date of Jesus' birth, Christmas. Some opted for the supposed date of Jesus' circumcision, which allowed New Year's Day to remain on January 1 and still have a religious significance. Still others firmly backed Easter, which caused a serious problem because the date of Easter is tied to the cycle of the moon and changes every year. By early in the twelfth century most of Europe had agreed that March 25 was an acceptable date for the year to begin. It may not have been at the beginning of a month, but it marked the Feast of the Annunciation, placed the beginning of the year back at the start of the planting season, and was only six days from the old traditional New Year's date of April 1. It was hardly an ideal solution, nor was it universally adopted, but for four and a half centuries March 25 marked the beginning of the new year for England and the majority of Europe's kingdoms and principalities.

Eventually the lack of agreement over the date of New Year's led France's King Charles IX to set the date back to January 1, and twenty years later in 1582, Pope Gregory XIII instituted a new calendar that also placed New Year's Day on January 1. Not everyone complied immediately—the British did not officially adopt the Gregorian calendar until 1752—but eventually the western world agreed that the year would start exactly when Julius Caesar had said it should.

While the precise date of New Year's Day had no bearing on the type of celebrations enjoyed by our medieval ancestors, it does give you the option of holding your own recreated medieval New Year's celebration on either March 25 or the more familiar date of January 1. Fortunately, during the centuries of mass confusion over when the year began, the manner in which it was celebrated changed very little.

Among family members, New Year's, especially during the centuries when it was celebrated on March 25, was a time of gift giving. There had been no such occasion since the Christmas season, when gifts were exchanged on Twelfth Night, and fair weather brought an opportunity for gifts of spring flowers and baby animals to add to the family's herds and flocks.

Throughout this same period, the more public celebration of the new year centered around the notori-

ously bawdy Feast of Fools. Like the curious Christmas custom of electing a Boy Bishop and a Lord of Misrule, the Feast of Fools had its roots in the Roman holiday of Saturnalia. It probably dated from the earliest years of Christianity and the Julian calendar, when New Year's Day was observed on January 1. When New Year's Day was transferred to late March the customary celebrations migrated along with it, and the remnants of pagan Saturnalia and the more recent customs of Boy Bishops and the Lords of Misrule were reincarnated as the Feast of Fools.

Like Saturnalia and the Boy Bishop celebrations, the Feast of Fools saw a temporary dislocation of social rules and roles. Servants and peasants were allowed time off work, villagers and townspeople elected their own mock leaders, and the laity assumed satirical versions of positions of authority in the church. Inevitably, as the ale flowed and merriness spread, the celebrations got out of hand—a problem which seems to have been particularly widespread in France. There, each town elected a king from among the mock church officials, who was referred to as the *Abbe de la Malgouverne* (Abbot of Bad Government) for the six-day duration of the festival. French priests often allowed the counterfeit clergy to perform shocking parodies of church services and sometimes participated in these services themselves. Priests are known to have worn masks while performing satirical versions of the mass, and at those points in the service where clergy and congregation normally answered with a solemn "Amen," the refrain was replaced by a "Hee-Haw," like a donkey's bray.

Outside of France, the Feast of Fools was celebrated with equal enthusiasm, if with slightly less sacrilegious overtones. Scottish towns elected an Abbot of Unreason and English villages declared a King of Fools, Lord of Misrule, or King of the Bean. In each case the master of revels had the authority to incite the locals to various kinds of chaotic and riotous behavior, which often included singing bawdy songs and dancing in the sanctuary of the local church. Unlike in France, this did not extend to mocking the mass, and while the clergy may have tolerated the goings-on, they did not participate in them.

Not surprisingly, such revelry eventually drew the condemnation of church officials, nobility, and staid merchants alike. Not only was the Feast of Fools sacrilegious, it often threatened to spill over into full-fledged public rioting and destruction of property, and it posed a very real threat to the fragile maintenance of order that existed throughout the Middle Ages. As the arbiters of moral authority, church leaders were never overly pleased with the ribald nature of the Feast of Fools and were every bit as distressed by its pagan overtones as by its threat to public order. As early as 1199 the Bishop of Paris tried to impose limitations on the celebrations in his district, particularly at Paris's Notre Dame Cathedral. Under the new regulations, the Lord of Misrule was allowed to carry his staff of office into the cathedral until dusk, when it was time to celebrate the first vespers service of New Year's Day. At that time he was required to hand over the staff to a church official, who acknowledged that the Lord of Misrule had "put down the mighty from their seat." It was an honest attempt to allow the ancient public celebration to continue while simultaneously curbing its worst offences. Unfortunately, small gestures seldom work.

By the beginning of the fifteenth century, observance of the Feast of Fools had become so widespread, so riotous, and so sacrilegious that it had become a full-blown public embarrassment for the church. One of the many issues considered during the church's Council of Basle (1431–35) was the future of the Feast of Fools. Taking into account that no previous attempts to dampen the celebration had produced any noticeable effects, the church fathers decided the celebration had to be outlawed entirely. Those who failed to obey the edict would be subject to the most severe penalties the medieval church could impose. Although it took nearly a century to entirely eradicate this most unruly of all medieval celebrations, by the middle of the sixteenth century the outrageous, boisterous Feast of Fools had become no more than a disquieting memory. Some cultural historians argue that a small remnant of the insanity that once marked the Feast of Fools still lingers in the form of April Fools jokes.

SCARBOROUGH RENAISSANCE FESTIVAL, WAXAHACHIE, TX

CHAPTER 6

Medieval May Day Celebrations

Ancient Origins of May Day

Like many holidays, the joyous, lighthearted May Day festivals of the Middle Ages had their roots in rituals that had been practiced since ancient times. In the pre-Christian world most pagan religions celebrated the end of the planting season and the onset of summer. To the Celts this late spring festival was known as Beltane and the Germanic tribes called it Walpurgis Night, but for both cultures it was a celebration of nature's renewed fertility and reverence was paid to the woodland spirit known either as the Green Man or the Horned god, who was similar to the Greek and Roman god Pan. The Romans, who always seemed ready for a good time, adapted this tradition into the festival of the goddess Maia, the mother of Mercury, and in whose honor the first month of summer was named May. For all of these ancient and classical cultures May Day represented not only the onset of summer, but the time of year when girls officially became women, ready to take their place in the reproductive cycle of life.

May Day Among Medieval Common Folk

As the Christian religion replaced pagan beliefs, the church overlaid this holiday with a more acceptable significance. May was officially dedicated to Mary, the mother of Jesus, and the first day of the month was declared the feast of Saints Philip and Jacob. This reorientation allowed the people to continue with their customary revelries while eliminating the pagan overtones. By the end of April the spring planting had been completed and the loss of a day or two of work would not have any adverse consequences, so May Day celebrations began on the last evening of April and continued through the night and throughout the next day. As they had done for centuries, at nightfall on April 30th young men and women ran into the woods and meadows to collect armloads of wildflowers, freshly sprouted greenery, and budding hawthorn branches in a ceremony that became known as "bringing in the May" or "going a-Maying."

On the morning of May 1 the young people proceeded back into their towns and villages, led by a gaudily costumed version of the ancient Green Man— now known as Jack O'the Green—and went from door to door, decorating the houses and shops with flowers and greenery. If a young man of the company wanted to declare his interest in a special girl he might lay a hawthorn branch, decorated with flowers and ribbons, at the door of her parents' house. Other men among the crowd would carry a tree trunk, stripped of its branches, into the village square, where it would be decorated with flowers and ribbons before being set up to serve as the maypole. By this time the entire village was busily preparing for the day's celebration, decorating animals and carts with flowers and weaving floral crowns for the young women to wear during the day's celebrations.

One contemporary account of these preparations gives us a feeling of the happy excitement that preceded the day's festivities:

All the young men and maids, old men and wives, run gadding overnight [in]to the woods, groves, hills and mountains, where they spend all the night in pleasant pastimes; and in the morning, they return, bringing with them birch and branches of trees, to deck their assemblies withal.

While many of the May Day festivities were sponsored by the local church, for obvious reasons the church fathers frowned on the idea of dozens of unchaperoned young girls being out all night in the company of excitable young men. One churchman, Philip Stubbes, described this scandalous custom: "I have heard it credibly reported by men of great gravity and reputation, that of forty, three score or a hundred maids going into the wood overnight, that there have scarcely the third part of them returned home again undefiled." While this fact was not lost on the locals, they were far less shocked than the clergymen and laughingly referred to the very obvious grass stains on the backs of the girls' dresses as "the green gown."

Despite the occasional awkward moment caused by such glaring evidence of the previous night's amorous

Brightly colored tents, fluttering banners, and a crowd of costumed revelers help to give an outdoor May Day event an authentic medieval atmosphere.

Above: *A mixed party of costumed and uncostumed revelers enjoy a medieval May Day celebration in a park. Outdoor settings work for all time periods and remove the necessity of elaborate decorations or finding an architecturally appropriate space.* DICK CLARK Right: *The Green Man*

adventures, everyone was generally too excited by the upcoming celebrations to allow a little illicit love-making to ruin the fun. Central to the day's activities was the character of Jack O' the Green. Throughout most of Europe, this later-day incarnation of the Green Man served as the day's Lord of Misrule and master of ceremonies, running around the village, exhorting the cooks to hurry with the food, urging the setting up of the maypole, poking fun at the village elders, and clearing a path for the grand parade that would soon make its way through the narrow streets and toward the village green, where the maypole would serve as the centerpiece of the remainder of the day's frivolity.

Curiously, in England the character of Jack O' the Green was often replaced by a man dressed as Robin Hood, and in many English villages May Day became known simply as Robin Hood's Day. Wherever Robin replaced the Green Man as master of ceremonies, he and the previous year's May Queen—dubbed Maid Marian for the day—led the parade through the village. Whether the parade was led by Robin Hood or Jack O' the Green, those who followed them always included laughing young women dressed in white and wearing garlands and crowns of flowers, troupes of dancers and musicians, and farm wagons and carts pulled by placid oxen, all decked out with flowers. As they moved toward the maypole the assembly sang "Summer is a-Coming In" (which can be found on page 126). When they reached the village

A well-costumed maypole dance can serve as the centerpiece for a May Day revel and feast.

square the parade broke up and everyone's attention began focusing on the maypole.

As the centerpiece of the day's celebrations, the maypole was a grand affair. It stood between fifteen and twenty feet tall, and the top of the pole was decked with a wreath of flowers from which hung brightly colored ribbons long enough that their ends lay in piles on the ground. The May dancers held the ends of these ribbons and wove intricate patterns around the pole as they executed the steps of the maypole dances. There were any number of maypole dances and the steps varied from area to area. Normally there were some dances intended for females of mixed ages, some for young women only, some for both young men and women, and some just for children. Like so many aspects of May Day celebrations, the maypole dance had begun as a pagan fertility rite but by the Middle Ages its significance had shifted to nothing more than general fun. (Instructions for building a maypole are at the end of this chapter, and several maypole dances are included in chapter 16).

When the maypole dances had all been done and the exhausted participants had quenched their thirst, a new May Queen was elected from among the most eligible young women of the village. As in beauty contests throughout history, the runners-up became her court and attendants. Decked with garlands of flowers and crowned with a fresh floral crown, the May Queen was seated on her throne before being hoisted into the air and paraded around the square and through the streets. After her coronation, the May Queen presided over the afternoon's sporting events and awarded prizes to the winners. (Many outdoor games appropriate to a May Day celebration

can be found in chapter 13. Those who include Robin Hood in their May Day celebration might consider performing the Robyn Hode play included in chapter 14).

May Day Among the Nobility

While the peasants were rolling in the hay and dancing around the maypole, the nobility had developed their own celebrations to observe the first holiday of the summer season, most which centered on the knightly virtues of chivalry and courtly love.

According to medieval tradition, to be truly chivalrous a knight or nobleman must swear to protect the church, the overlords to whom they owed service, and those who were unable to defend themselves, and to always honor and serve titled ladies. Even a cursory reading of history tells us that most members of the medieval warrior class fell far short of these lofty goals, but like so many virtuous standards throughout history the code of chivalry was always given lip service, and never more so than on May Day.

Even a hurriedly assembled maypole dance with both costumed and uncostumed dancers has the feel of a real medieval celebration. CATHY RICH

Integral to the concept of chivalry was the idea of courtly love. This was supposedly the chaste love which a knight felt for a lady of higher social station than his own. Because of her elevated position the lady could not return these feelings (at least not publicly), but she could always encourage the young man to ever greater feats of courage and valor. This rather peculiar tradition originated around the time of the First Crusade (1095–99) in the noble courts of the Aquitaine, Provence, Champagne, and Burgundy areas of France. Initially finding its voice in the songs and lyric poems of minstrels and troubadours, the concept of courtly love extolled the idea of "love for love's sake" and the spiritual qualities of unrequited love for a lady who would always remain unattainable. The troubadours who wrote and performed these songs sometimes described the un-named woman in question as a lady in a far-away land, possibly a lady the smitten man had never even seen but only heard described by others who were equally stunned by her grace and beauty. Courtly love has been described as "a love at once illicit and morally elevating, passionate and disciplined, humiliating and exalting, human

and transcendent." Not surprisingly, this completely contradictory view of love was designed as the first known form of entertainment intended to appeal specifically to bored women of the privileged class, who often had nothing to occupy their time except gossip.

If these poems and songs had any appeal to young men it was because they held out the promise—no matter how vague and futile—that a man might be able to advance his career if a lady of high rank convinced her husband to elevate the young man's social status or, just as desirable and just as unlikely, if the lady might actually pay attention to the young man.

The possible dangers inherent in the concept of courtly love were obvious in some of the earliest stories of King Arthur, which also originated in France during this same period. While good, hard-working King Arthur was off fighting his enemies, his queen, Guinevere, wound up having a torrid affair with his most trusted knight, Lancelot. The outcome of this liaison was the destruction of Arthur, Guinevere, and Camelot itself. Still, the romantic possibilities inherent in courtly love appealed deeply to noble women whose lives were often crushingly dull and whose marriages had been arranged for their families' political advancement rather than because of any mutual affection.

Because all of medieval noble society was based on complicated rules of behavior, so was the course of courtly love, as described in the lyric poems. The progress of courtly love went something like this:

> The young lover is smitten by a beautiful lady
> He worships her from afar
> He declares his devotion to her
> The lady rejects his advances
> Undaunted, he swears his devotion and insists
>   he will die without her love
> He goes off to war, or on a quest, to prove his love
> When he returns the lady gives in and they
>   make love
> They spend the rest of their lives trying to keep
>   the affair secret

One of the earliest proponents of courtly love was Christine de Pisan (1365–1434), an Italian noblewoman who spent most of her life in France. At first, de Pisan popularized courtly love through the writings of her personal chaplain, Andreas Capellanus, but later she took up the pen herself and became the first woman in Western history to earn a living as an author.

Like many before and since, de Pisan considered love to be a sort of a game and, like any game, love must

May Day was the traditional beginning of the courting season for young people of all social classes. Among the upper classes courting was as highly formalized and ritualized as the mating dances of birds. EUGENE SIREN

have its rules. Some of these rules are amazingly sensible and ring true even after seven centuries; others seem cruel and politically incorrect in the extreme, particularly when you consider that the rules listed below were written by a woman. Do bear in mind that the Middle Ages were a violent time; jealousy taken to its violent conclusion was an accepted part of life, and women were as much to blame for this as men. If men loved to pull swords on each other to show how macho they were, women loved to taunt and tease them into doing so. Bearing these things in mind, here are Christine de Pisan's rules for courtly love:

1. The state of marriage does not properly excuse anyone from loving.
2. He who does not feel jealousy is not capable of loving.
3. No one can love two people at the same time.
4. It is well known that love is always either growing or declining.
5. Whatever a lover takes against his lover's will has no savor.
6. A male does not fall in love until he has reached full manhood.
7. A mourning period of two years for a deceased lover is required by the surviving partner.
8. No one should be prevented from loving except by reason of his own death.
9. No one can love unless compelled by the eloquence of love.
10. Love is an exile from the house of avarice.
11. It is unseemly to love anyone whom you would be ashamed to marry.
12. A true lover does not desire the passionate embraces of anyone but his beloved.
13. Love that is made public rarely lasts.
14. Love easily obtained is of little value; difficulty in obtaining it makes it precious.
15. Every lover regularly turns pale in the presence of his beloved.
16. On suddenly catching sight of his beloved, the heart of the lover begins to palpitate.
17. A new love drives out the old.
18. A good character alone makes someone worthy of love.
19. If love lessens, it soon fails and rarely recovers.
20. A man in love is always fearful.
21. The feeling of love is always increased by true jealousy.

22. When a lover feels suspicious of his beloved, jealousy, and with it the sensation of love, are increased.
23. A man tormented by the thought of love eats and sleeps very little.
24. Everything a lover does ends in the thought of his beloved.
25. A true lover considers nothing good but what he thinks will please his beloved.
26. Love can deny nothing to love.
27. A lover cannot have too much of his beloved's consolations.
28. A small supposition compels a lover to suspect his beloved of doing wrong.
29. A man who is troubled by excess lust does not usually love.
30. A true lover is continually and without interruption obsessed by the image of his beloved.
31. Nothing forbids one woman being loved by two men, or one man by two women.

Among the topics Christine de Pisan addressed in her writings was the curious Court of Love, and this became one of the favorite May Day pastimes of the medieval nobility.

While cynical older men—mostly the ladies' husbands—were off celebrating May Day by hunting, the senior ladies would hold a court of love for young male courtiers. During the court, the men would state their case and explain why the object of their desire (who was never publicly named) should succumb to their advances. To prove how chivalrous and worthy they were, the young men might be told to engage in mock combat, a joust, or other physical contests, or to compose love songs or poems on the spot and recite them in front of the assembled court. (A number of appropriate competitive sports are described in chapter 13).

If one of the sought-after young ladies chose to make herself known, she might demand that her young man declare his undying love in such a forceful way that he would convince the judges to bestow their blessings on the couple's love. If the young man won his love's approval and acknowledgement, but the judges still demanded that he engage in physical competition to prove himself, his lady-fair might give him a "favor"—a token such as her handkerchief or scarf—that he would wear during the assigned activity.

Throughout these proceedings, the young men, the available young ladies who watched each scenario

With spring in the air, a medieval May Day event can even make grownups fall victim to the sting of Cupid's arrows. EUGENE SIREN

unfold with bated breath, and the older, wiser (and often bitter) women who sat in judgment would all engage in flirtatious word games filled with double entendres and hidden, but discernable, sexual references. Proceedings of the court of love might be lighthearted or serious, but they must never descend into nastiness or crude language.

The entire concept of courtly love, with its inherent temptation for engaging in adulterous affairs, was as widely condemned by the church elders as was "going a-Maying" and the "green gowns" of the May Day festivities of the less privileged classes. Predictably, these condemnations were generally ignored by both highborn and lowborn.

Constructing a Maypole

1. The pole

a) Select a sturdy wooden pole or straight tree trunk 18 to 22 feet in length. To guarantee that your pole is sturdy enough, select one that is no smaller than 2 inches in diameter at the top, which should be the narrowest point.

b) If your pole is a tree trunk, we suggest a straight pine, fir, or other conifer.

c) Remove the branches as close to the surface of the trunk as possible.

d) Alternately, you may use a metal pole (like a flagpole) but make sure there is a large enough hole in the top of the pole that you can drive a wooden plug at least 2 inches in diameter into it.

2. The streamers

a) Select an even number of ribbons in two contrasting colors. You should only have as many ribbons as you are guaranteed to have dancers; extra ribbons will only cause confusion. Ideally, you should have between eight and twenty-four dancers, and if you are planning on dancing the Three Strand Dance (described in chapter 16), your total number of ribbons must be divisible by three (twelve, eighteen, or twenty-four ribbons). If you are going to be doing this dance you may want to use three colors of ribbon rather than just two. The ribbon should be either 1 or 1½ inches wide.

b) For eight to sixteen dancers, cut the ribbons to the same length as the pole (This will make them about 3 feet longer than the pole once it has been mounted in the ground). For eighteen to twenty-four dancers, add an additional 3 feet of ribbon.

c) Stack the ribbons on top of one another, alternating the colors (i.e., gold, green, gold, green, gold, and so on).

d) Place the stacked ribbons against the top end of the pole and drive a large-headed nail through the stack of ribbons and into the pole. A 2- or 2$^{1}/_{2}$-inch-long roofing nail is ideal for this purpose. The nail should be driven into the pole at least 1$^{1}/_{2}$ inches, but not so deeply that the head is tight against the ribbons.

e) If you are using a metal pole, whittle a wooden plug large enough that you have to tap it into the opening at the top of the pole with a hammer, and attach the ribbons to the plug.

f) Spread the ribbons into a circle so they fan out around the entire diameter of the pole. When the ribbons are evenly spaced, drive the nail firmly into the pole. Small nails or a staple gun can be used to secure each ribbon into place so they do not shift from their intended position.

3. The wreath

If you desire, you can construct a large wreath (3 to 4 feet in diameter) from straw or fresh reeds, fill it with flowers, and attach it to the top of the maypole. Expert maypole dancers sometimes keep the wreath suspended only by the tension of the ribbons, allowing it to descend as the ribbons are wrapped around the pole during the dance. For beginners we recommend attaching the wreath to the top of the pole; dealing with a dozen or more trailing ribbons will probably provide all the challenge you want.

4. Erecting the pole

a) With a post-hole digger, dig a hole at least 3 and no more than 4 feet deep, large enough to stand the pole in. If you know someone with a tractor with an auger bit for drilling fencepost holes, it will make this job a lot less painful.

b) Gather 4 or 5 feet of the loose ends of the ribbons, place them in a plastic bag, and secure the bag about 6 or 7 feet above the bottom end of the maypole. This will protect the ribbon from becoming dirty while the pole is being erected.

c) Stand the pole in the hole.

d) Fill the space around the pole with dirt, tamping it firmly into place after every 6 or 8 inches of dirt that is shoveled into the hole. If you are erecting the pole several days ahead of time, wet the soil and allow it to dry for several days. Alternately, you can fill the area around the pole with cement or concrete if you have three or four days to allow it to harden.

5. Preparing for the dance

a) Remove the plastic bag from the pole and the ribbons from the bag.

b) Spread the ribbons on the ground, around the pole. Keep them from becoming tangled and arrange them in their proper order according to the alternating colors.

6. The dance

a) See the maypole dance steps in chapter 16.

b) Allow your dancers several hours to rehearse the dances before performing in front of the assembled company.

CHAPTER 7

Medieval Wedding Celebrations

The marriage ceremony as we understand it today is essentially an invention of the Middle Ages. Until well after the end of the first millennium, marriage was an entirely secular rite. Prior to A.D. 1100, most marriages had no religious ceremony connected to them. If the church was involved at all, it was only because a priest had been invited to witness the ceremony as a reliable member of the community who could verify, in writing if necessary, that the marriage had taken place. In rural communities and among the urban poor of this period, there were almost no formalized marriage rituals of any sort. The public exchange of a kiss and the announcement that a couple were married, followed by the act of consummation, were enough to satisfy the community of the legitimacy of the marriage. If a formal ceremony did take place, it was more likely to be celebrated by the couple joining hands over the anvil of the local blacksmith and swearing their good intentions than it was to take place in a church.

It was not until the Fourth Lateran Council in 1215 that the church included marriage in its list of holy sacraments. Once marriage became an official rite of the church, prelates everywhere were quick to encourage people to legitimize their marriages with religious ceremonies. Not only did this put the church's stamp of approval on the nuptials but it was usually a guarantee of extra income for the local church. In 1220, Bishop Richard de Marisco of Durham, England, declared:

We enjoin that marriages be celebrated decently, with reverence, not with laughter and ribaldry, not in taverns or at public drinkings and feastings. Let no man place a ring made of rushes or of any worthless or precious material on the hand of a woman in jest that he may more easily gain her favours, lest in thinking to jest the bond of marriage. Henceforth let no pledge of contracting marriage be given save in the presence of a priest and of three or four respectable persons summoned for the purpose.

This is not meant to indicate that marriage was taken lightly before it became a sacrament of the church. There were still rules that had to be followed. The couple had to have reached the legal age of consent: twelve for girls and fourteen for boys. Under no circumstances could women be forced to marry against their wishes and still be bound to uphold the marriage contract. At least, they could not be *legally* forced into marriage; in politically-motivated marriages among the noble classes, selling a daughter for financial or political gain was far from uncommon. Even in relatively poor rural communities, both families tried to ensure that their children's marriage would be advantageous for all concerned. To a large extent, this meant that marriages were arranged. Parents, grandparents, elder siblings, village elders, and even the groom might all be involved in the prenuptial negotiations. The bride was almost universally excluded from determining her future husband. She did, however, have the legal right to refuse to marry anyone who did not suit her, and she could appeal to both the church and civil authorities to be saved from a bad marriage proposal. The church, in particular, was very unhappy about young girls being taken advantage of by being forced to marry elderly men.

Once a match was arranged, negotiators began dealing with the most important detail of the marriage: the settlement of a proper dowry. Contrary to popular belief, both sides had to contribute to the dowry, not just the bride's family. The size and value of the dowry were determined by the social positions and wealth of the marrying parties. Assuming that both of the betrothed were of comfortable, merchant-class status, the bride's dowry might include property such as money, gold, plate, horses, possibly some land, and even her clothes. These all became the uncontested property of the groom once the marriage had taken place. For his part, the groom had to promise that his wife would be taken care of should he precede her in death. He would guarantee that she would receive a certain portion of his income, usu-

ally between a third and a half, as long as she lived. When a widow died or, in many cases, married again, the property reverted to the groom's family. There were sometimes clauses in dowry contracts demanding that the dowries be returned if the bride died within a specified period after the wedding, usually one or two years. As long as the bride survived her first pregnancy or two and did not contract one of the many incurable diseases that were rampant during the Middle Ages, it was a good arrangement for the groom and his family.

Once the dowry was agreed upon, the betrothal was publicly announced. This announcement, known as "publishing the bans," was in many senses the most important part of the medieval wedding. Bans were published several months prior to the date of the wedding. This advance notice gave time for anyone with a legitimate objection to the marriage to come forward and present his or her case. Once the bans had been published, the families of the newly engaged couple hosted a feast that rivaled the actual wedding feast. As a symbol of his honorable intentions, the groom presented the bride with a ring, traditionally engraved with both of their names. This was essentially an engagement ring. The

A fully costumed period wedding can bring the romance of the Middle Ages dramatically to life. PETER SAMWORTH

bride presented the groom with a sleeve from one of her garments, one of her stockings, or both. This may seem a strange custom today, but in the Middle Ages, these "favors" were considered honored gifts. A heraldic device known as a "maunch," which appears on many medieval coats of arms, is a stylized form of a woman's sleeve. Certainly these portions of clothing suggested that the groom was getting closer to undressing his new bride. Just as certainly, he didn't have long to wait for the real thing.

Many medieval betrothal feasts ended with the happy couple being sent off to bed to begin a cohabitation that often lasted right through the wedding itself. Living together as man and wife during the betrothal period enabled a prospective groom time to ensure that his wife-to-be was not barren. As long as she was able to conceive during the betrothal period, the marriage would probably be a fruitful one. But because any child born prior to the actual wedding would legally be a bastard and denied rights of inheritance, it was important that the marriage take place before the child was born. If, however, the bride-to-be did not become pregnant, the marriage could always be called off; once again, good for the groom. As cold and businesslike as this all may seem, it does illustrate two important points: Living together is hardly a modern phenomenon, and medieval weddings were primarily the ceremonial aspect of a business deal.

Assuming that the prenuptial period went well and everyone was happy with the arrangements, the date for the wedding would be set, and preparations for the big day would begin in earnest.

The wedding feast could take place at the home of either party's family and was usually hosted by the family with access to the largest feasting hall. A portion of the expenses might have been taken out of the bride's dowry, but the rules seem to have been flexible. What we do know is that throughout the Middle Ages, there were no decorations or clothes specifically designed for weddings. Weddings were simply one more occasion for which everyone brought out the best silver and put on his or her best clothes. In the case of the nobility and the very rich merchant class, new clothes probably would have been ordered, but they were not any different in design than the best fashion of the day, except for the fact that as far as we know, the bride never wore white. There are, however, records of a few grooms dressed in white. Considering the cost of good clothes, it was imperative that they be something that could be worn more than once.

If the couple was of high enough status, members of the groom's party often dressed in matching livery—clothes with the colors or coat of arms of the groom's family. For the 1234 wedding of France's nineteen-year-old King Louis IX and thirteen-year-old Marguerite Berenger, the king's party were all dressed in purple, scarlet, and green robes trimmed in ermine. Their belts were enameled in gold, and on their heads they wore "cloth of gold" caps trimmed with peacock feathers. No record seems to survive as to what Marguerite wore, but then, she was just the daughter of a count, not of a king.

The more important the celebrants, the grander the procession to the church. For King Louis's and Marguerite's nuptials, the wedding party rode in procession from the king's hunting lodge at Fontainebleau to the cathedral in Paris. While the number and splendor of this wedding party may have been particularly grand, the

Even a small family wedding can easily capture the feeling of the Age of Chivalry with adequate planning, a sunny day, and an attractive setting. VALERIE ROWE/FANTAYSIA LIMITED

The church may not be medieval, but the iron chandeliers and arched Gothic windows provide an evocative setting for this recreated medieval wedding. BRIAN EDWARDS/COURTESY SEAN AND INGRID COULTER

order in which the guests rode would have been the same at the wedding of any notable couple. The parade was led by a troupe of minstrels playing flutes, viols, trumpets, drums, and bagpipes. Behind the musicians came the bridal couple, followed by their parents. Usually the groom's family rode ahead of the bride's. In this case, Louis's mother, the dowager queen, rode ahead of the bride's parents. In instances where the bride's family was of much higher status than the groom's, this order would probably be reversed. If there was a best man, a tradition more popular in Italy and Spain than elsewhere in Europe, he would probably ride between the bride and groom and their families. The positioning of the best man in the wedding procession was dictated by the reason for his existence. He was the "best" man because he was the best swordsman the groom could find—often a hired position—and it was his job to see to it that no one decided to make a last-minute attempt to stop the wedding.

At last the grand parade reached the church, and everyone dismounted, the gentlemen helping the ladies off their horses. As the party re-formed on the walkway leading to the church, the bride was escorted by her father or guardian, and the groom was joined by the best man, just to be sure nothing nasty happened. As the parties approached the church doors, the priest, bearing the wedding ring, came outside and waited under the portico for everyone to approach. The church doors were usually closed behind him; the entire ceremony would take place outside the church.

When the bride, the groom, and their attendants stood in front of the priest, he began to question them. Were they old enough to legally marry? Did they swear that they were not related in such a way that it would legally prevent them from marrying? Did their parents consent to the marriage? Had they published the bans of their marriage, and had an appropriate time elapsed since the publication of the bans to allow anyone who objected to step forward? Did they both freely enter into the marriage? The last two of these questions are largely ceremonial today, but during the Middle Ages, this was the last chance to stop what might be an illegal or forced marriage.

With the legalities out of the way, the church provost, a lawyer, or the groom himself would read aloud the list of dowry arrangements: what the bride was bringing, what the groom was offering, and the terms and arrangements for payment. With the dowry having been read, the groom presented the bride with a small bag of coins, usually thirteen in number, which she would later distribute to the poor. This was not a symbolic act of buying the woman, but showed that she was empowered to act in financial matters on her new husband's behalf.

The bride's father then relinquished hold of his daughter, and the groom took her right hand in his as they began to repeat their vows or, as it was known, "plight their troth." The troth plighted by Sir William Plumpton in 1450 was strikingly similar to modern wedding vows: "Here I take thee, Jhennet, to be my wedded wife, to hold and to have, at bed and at board, for fairer or lather [uglier], for better or worse, in sickness and in health, to death us depart, and thereto I plight my troth."

After the groom had completed his vow—the bride traditionally remained silent throughout the ceremony—the priest delivered a short sermon on the sanctity of marriage and how it is the natural state in which man and woman should live their lives. References were often made to idyllic Biblical marriages and to the fact that the pairs of animals that went into Noah's ark were actually married in the sight of God, and that is why they, rather than other animals, were spared from the flood. The priest would then bless the ring, which he or an assistant had been holding, and hand it to the groom, who slipped it, one by one, on the first three fingers of the bride's left hand. As the ring moved from finger to finger, the groom said: "In the name of the Father, and of the Son, and of the Holy Ghost, with this ring, I thee wed." The use of the third finger on the left hand is explained in a sermon that has survived from the fourteenth century. Bear in mind that this speaker considered the thumb a finger, so the ring finger is called the fourth finger, rather than the third. The sermon says that the ring must be "put and set by the husband upon the fourth finger of the woman, to show that a true love and cordial affection be between them, because, as doctors say, there is a vein coming from the heart of a woman to the fourth finger, and therefore the ring is put on the same finger, so that she should keep unity and love with him, and he with her." A bride did not present a ring to her husband until the sixteenth century. With the completion of the ring ceremony, the civil portion of the ceremony was concluded.

The vows having been said, the bride distributed the coins to the poor or gave them to the priest to distribute as he saw fit, the church doors were thrown open, and the wedding party entered the church for mass. The fact that the vows took place outside the church showed that although the wedding was sanctified and legitimized by the clergy, it was still primarily a civil rite. It was the public acceptance and acknowledgment of the marriage that was of utmost importance.

Inside the church, everyone took his or her place in the pews while the bride, groom, two attendants, and the best man (if there was one) followed the priest to the altar. As the couple knelt in front of the priest, the attendants opened a large cloth over their heads to form a canopy, which would remain in place throughout the mass. The best man stood to the side of the groom. When the mass was finished, the canopy was removed from above the couple, and the priest gave the groom the "kiss of peace," which the groom then transferred to his new wife. The priest closed the service with a blessing for the new couple. One such blessing that survives goes as follows: "Let this woman be amiable as Rachel, wise as Rebecca, faithful as Sarah. Let her be sober through truth, venerable through modesty, and wise through the teachings of heaven." As the couple proceeded out of the church, the choir traditionally chanted the "Agnus Dei." (Since modern-day couples will probably want to exchange their vows inside the church rather than outside the front door, they might consider using the Agnus Dei as the processional rather than the modern Wedding

Attendants hold a canopy above the bride and groom during a wedding mass.

March. Music and words for this song are included in chapter 15.)

Following the conclusion of the mass, the members of the wedding party remounted their horses and followed the musicians as they wended their way to the wedding feast. (The feast hall was laid out in the same manner as described in chapter 2, "A Brief History of Medieval Celebrations" and chapter 8, "Decorating in the Medieval Style.") Among the rushes that were usually scattered on the floor of the hall were strewn flowers, especially roses and lilies. Not only did the flowers add a festive flair to the room, but each time they were trod on, their scent was released into the air. The flowers and the long tables set with the finest silver and pewter the family owned were all fine and grand, but as with all medieval banquets, the center of attention was the food. At the 1376 wedding feast of wealthy, forty-year-old Italian merchant Francesco di Marco Datini and his sixteen-year-old bride Margherits Bandini, the shopping list included 406 loaves of bread, 250 eggs, 100 pounds of cheese, 2 quarters of oxen and 16 of mutton, 37 capons, 11 chickens, 2 boar's heads, and innumerable pigeons and waterfowl, as well as wines imported from Provence, France, and Chianti from Tuscany. Based on the quantity of food listed here and the probability that the wedding feast lasted the traditional three days, we can assume that the wedding party must have numbered between fifty and sixty people.

At their wedding feast, the bride and groom were normally allowed the honor of the central seats at high table, even though, in most cases, their parents would have outranked them. The feast was formally opened by the bride and groom drinking from a goblet especially commissioned for the occasion. The groom drank first, then passed the cup to his bride to finish. They were the only two people who ever drank from this cup, which was to be used only this once. Traditionally, this cup had two handles on it—not unlike a modern trophy—and came to be known as a "loving cup" or "love cup."

Between food courses, the entertainments were interspersed with rounds of gift giving. Guests would present the newlyweds with gifts in much the same manner as they do today, although it was traditional for female members of the groom's family to present the new bride with rings. Not only was jewelry an appropriate gift in a time before electric blenders and pop-up toasters, but the rings also symbolized the bride's being welcomed into the family of the groom. In many instances, the same rings were passed on to new brides generation after generation as a symbol of the continuity of family

unity through successive generations. The guests often expected to receive gifts in return. Although seldom more than tokens of appreciation, these gifts had to reflect the social status of the recipient, not the giver.

During Italian wedding receptions, it was customary to place a gold florin (a coin) in the shoe of the new bride and a baby in her arms. Both of these tokens symbolized the families' hopes for the bride's future fertility. At the end of the first day's feasting, when everyone had wished the new couple many years of happiness filled with innumerable children, their future connubial bliss was given a proper inauguration by the entire company. Once the marital bed was made ready by the servants and sprinkled with rose petals, the company escorted the couple to their bedchamber. In separate anterooms, the bride and groom were undressed by their closest friends or by servants and dressed in their best nightclothes. When they were ready, they were ushered into their bedchamber and put into bed in front of as many family members and friends as could squeeze into the bedroom. The priest then blessed the bed and the happy couple in a ceremony that would hopefully ensure fertility and remove any taint of premarital promiscuity from the bride (male offenses didn't seem to count). In most instances, the priest then said a benediction and the company withdrew to leave the couple to consummate their marriage in private, but there were exceptions to every rule. Occasionally, even among the nobility, wedding-night sex became a public spectacle.

During the Middle Ages, as in any period, wedding customs varied according to regional, local, and family traditions. The above should, however, provide you with a good overview of the complicated process through which a betrothed couple had to make their way to complete their wedding ceremony. Some of the movies listed in the filmography section (page 203) contain weddings; they are marked with an asterisk (*) for easy reference. Do not assume that they are accurate representations of a medieval wedding, but they may offer some ideas.

For more information on planning your own medieval wedding, please refer to chapter 18, "Organizing Your Medieval Celebration." Here we have included general information on organizing events and specific information on the suggested order of events for a recreated medieval wedding. Other elements of your medieval wedding are covered in the chapters corresponding to particular aspects of the big day; for example, information on wedding dinners is found in chapters 10, 11, and 12.

The Twelfth-Century Mass

The mass below includes staging directions, very much as it would have been performed during the Middle Ages. This is the *Sarum* mass used in England, not the post-Reformation Roman Catholic mass. Although it is no longer practiced, it is still an official form of the mass and should be acceptable as a part of any church ceremony, including a wedding. Consult your local priest as to specific proprieties.

The performance of the mass requires two persons. Here they are listed as the priest (P) and a monk (M), as they would have been in the Middle Ages. Your priest will know the appropriate substitution for the part of the monk.

Remember that church Latin is completely phonetic. For example, Tuum is pronounced "too-um."

Priest and monk proceed toward altar.

P ASPERGES ME DOMINE, HYSSOPO ET MUNDABOR   Purge me, Oh Lord, with hyssop and I shall be clean.
   LAVABIS ME, ET SUPER NIVEM DEALBABOR   Thou shall wash me and I shall be whiter than snow.

M MISERERE MEI DEUS,   Have mercy on me, Oh God,
   SECUNDUM MAGNAM MISERICORDIAM TUAM   after Thy great goodness.

P GLORIA PATRI ET FILIO ET SPIRITUI SANCTO   Glory to the Father, the Son, and the Holy Spirit.

M ASPERGES ME DOMINE, HYSSOPO ET MUNDABOR   Purge me, Oh Lord, with hyssop* and I shall be clean.
   LAVABIS ME, ET SUPER NIVEM DEALBABOR   Thou shall wash me and I shall be whiter than snow.

P OSTENDE NOBIS DOMINE MISERICORDIAM TUAM   Show Thy mercy unto us, Oh Lord.

M ET SALUTARE TUUM DA NOBIS   And grant us Thy salvation.

P DOMINE EXAUDI ORATIONEM MEAM   Give thanks unto the Lord.

M ET CLAMOR MEUS AD TE VENIATE   And let my cry come unto Thee.

P VIDI AQUAM EGREDIENTEM DE TEMPLO   I saw water issuing out of the temple
   ALATARE DEXTRO   at the right hand side
   ALLELUIA   Halleluia
   ET OMNE AD QUOS PER VENIT AQUA   and all to whom that water came
   ISTA SALVI FACTI SUNT ET DICENT   were made whole and shall say
   ALLELUIA, ALLELUIA   Halleluia, Halleluia.

*Hyssop was an herb believed by medieval physicians to have great cleansing properties.

Priest then goes to altar, picks up bowl of holy water, takes sprinkler and sprinkles bride, groom, and congregation, then turns to altar, bows, and sprinkles altar. When he has finished, he puts holy water and sprinkler on the altar, bows, and crosses himself.

M VENI CREATOR SPIRITUS	Come, Holy Spirit, inspire our souls
MENTES TUORAM VISITA	and light them with celestial fire.
IMPLE SUPERNA GRATIA	Thou art the anointing spirit
QUAE TU CREASTI PECTORA	who imparts thy sevenfold gift.
QUI PARACLETUS DICERIS	Thy blessed gift from above
DONUM DEI ALTISSIMI	is the comfort of life and the fire of love
FONS VIVUS IGNIS CARITAS	to enlighten with perpetual light
ET SPIRITALIS UNCTIO	the dullness of our blinded sight.

While the monk has been chanting, the priest has been putting on the chasuble, a sleeveless outer vestment.

P EMITTE SPIRITUM TUUM	Come, Holy Spirit
M ET RENOUABIS FACIEUM TERRE	and renew the face of the earth.
P DEUS CUI OMNE COR PATET	Oh Lord, to whom all hearts are open,
ET OMNIS VOLUNTAS LOQUITUR	all desires known,
ET QUEM NULLUM LATET SECRETUM	and from whom no secrets are hid,
PURIFICA PER INFUSIONEM SANCTI SPIRITUS	cleanse the thoughts of our hearts
COGITATIONES CORDIS ET DIGNE	by the inspiration of thy Holy Spirit.
LAUDARE MEREAMUR	
P PSALMUS QUADRAGINTA DUO JUDICA ME DEUS	Pass judgment on my side, Oh God.
M *(Reads Psalm 42 in English)*	*(Reads Psalm 42 in English.)*
P GLORIA PATRI ET FILLIO ET SPIRITUI SANCTO	Glory to the Father, the Son, and the Holy Spirit.
M SICUT ERAT IN PRINCIPIO ET NUNC	As it was in the beginning, is now,
ET SEMPER ET IN SECULA SECULORUM	and shall be ever more,
AMEN	Amen.
P KYRIE ELEISON, CHRISTI ELEISON, KYRIE ELEISON	Lord have mercy, Christ have mercy, Lord have mercy.
M KYRIE ELEISON, CHRISTI ELEISON, KYRIE ELEISON	Lord have mercy, Christ have mercy, Lord have mercy.
P KYRIE ELEISON, CHRISTI ELEISON, KYRIE ELEISON	Lord have mercy, Christ have mercy, Lord have mercy.
OREMUS	Let us pray.

P   PATER NOSTER   Our Father
     QUI ES IN CAELIS   who art in heaven
     SANCTIFICETUR NOMEN TUUM   Hallowed be thy name
     ADVENIAT REGNUM TUUM   Thy Kingdom come
     FIAT VOLUNTAS TUA   Thy will be done
     SICUT IN CAELO ET IN TERRA   on earth as it is in heaven
     PANEM NOSTRUM COTIDIANUM DA NOBIS HODIE   Give us this day our daily bread
     ET DIMITTE NOBIS DEBITA NOSTRA   And forgive us our trespasses
     SICUT ET NOS DIMITTIMUS DEBITORIBUS NOSTRIS   As we forgive those who trespass against us
     ET NE NOS INDUCAS IN TENTATIONEM   And lead us not into temptation
     SED LIBERA NOS A MALO   But deliver us from evil.
     AMEN   Amen.

M   AUFER A NOBIS DOMINE DEUS   Take from us, Oh Lord God,
     CINCTAS INIQUITATES NOSTRAS   the sins which encompass us;
     UT AD SANCTA SANCTORUM PARIS MENTIBUS   that with untroubled minds
     MEREAMUR INTROIRE   we may be worthy to enter the Holy of Holies;
     PER CHRISTUM DOMINUM NOSTRUM   through Christ our Lord.

P   CONFITEOR DEO OMNIPOTENTI   I confess to God,
     BEATI MARIA SEMPER VIRGINI   the Blessed Holy Virgin Mary,
     BEATO MICHAELI ARCHANGELO   and the Blessed Archangel Michael

P   BEATO JOANNI BAPTISTAE   Blessed John the Baptist,
     SANCTI APOSTOLIS PETRO ET PAULO   Holy Apostles Peter and Paul,
     OMNIBUS SANCTIS ET TIBI PATER   to all the saints and to You, Father,
     QUIA PECCAVI NIMIS COGITATIONE   that I have sinned in thought,
     VERBO ET OPERE   word, and deed.

Priest strikes breast three times, saying,

P MEA CULPA, MEA CULPA, MEA MAXIMA CULPA   I have sinned, I have sinned, I have most grievously sinned.

P IDEO PRECOR BEATAM MARIAM SEMPER VIRGINI   Therefore, I pray the Blessed Mary, ever Virgin,
    ET TE PATER ORARE PRO ME AD DOMINUM   and You, Father, to pray for me to the Lord
    DEUM NOSTRUM   our God.

Priest turns to face congregation and then crosses himself.

P MISEREATUR VESTRI OMNIPOTENS DEUS   May Almighty God have mercy on you
    ET DIMISSIS PECCATIS VESTRIS   and deliver you from your sins,
    PERDUCAT VOS AD VITAM AETERNAM   and bring you everlasting life.
    AMEN   Amen.

Priest makes sign of cross in the air, turns to the altar, then turns to a second monk carrying an incense burner, who has moved forward. Priest bows to the incense bearer, who bows back. Priest then moves to one side, and incense bearer incenses the altar to the right, left, middle, and back to the right again.

Priest goes to altar and kisses altar top.

P AB ILLO BENEDICARIS IN CUJUS HONORE   May you be blessed by Him in whose honour
    CREMABERIS AMEN   you shall be burned. Amen.

The Gloria, below, can be sung.

M GLORIA IN EXCELSIS DEO	Glory be to God on high
ET IN TERRA PAX	and in earth, peace,
HOMINIBUS BONAE VOLUNTATIS	goodwill toward men.
LAUDAMUS TE	We praise Thee,
BENEDICIMUS TE	We bless Thee,
ADORAMUS TE	We worship Thee.

M GLORIFACAMUS TE	We glorify Thee,
GRATIA AGIMUS TIBI	We give thanks to Thee
PROPTER MAGNAM GLORIAM TUAM	for Thy great Glory.
DOMINE DEUS REX CAELESTIS DEUS	Oh King of heaven, Lord God,
PATER OMNIPOTENS	Father Almighty,
DOMINE FILI, UNIGENITE JESU CHRISTE	God the Son, the only begotten Jesus Christ,
DOMINE DEUS AGNUS DEI	the Lamb of God,
FILIUS PATRI	Son of the Father,
QUI TOLLIS PECCATA MUNDI	who takest away the sins of the world,
MISERERE NOBIS	receive our prayer and have mercy on us.

P QUI TOLLIS PECCATA MUNDI SUSCIPE	Thou that takest away the sins of the world,
DEPRECATIONEM NOSTRAM	receive our prayer.
QUI SEDES AD DEXTRAM PATRIS	You who sit at the right hand of God the Father,
MISERERE NOBIS	have mercy upon us.
QUONIAM TU SOLUS SANCTUS	For You alone are holy,
TU SOLUS ALTISSIMUS JESU CHRISTE	You alone Jesus Christ, are most high
CUM SANCTO SPIRITU IN GLORIA DEI PATRIS	with the Holy Spirit in the Glory of God the Father.
AMEN	Amen.

Monk now reads a Collect, a call to worship that changes with the particular holy day or saint's day, in English.

P DOMINUS SIT IN CORDE TUO ET IN LABIIS TUIS	May the Lord be in your heart and upon your lips
UT DIGNE ET COMPETENTER ANNUNTIES	that you may worthily proclaim
EVANGELIUM SUUM	His evangelic greatness.

Monk bows to altar, puts on a long vestment called a cope, takes Bible, and walks to other side of room, escorted by the incense bearer. At far end of room, the incense bearer incenses Bible and monk. Monk makes sign of cross in air over Bible.

M SEQUENTA SANCTI EVANGELII SECUNDUM   The gospel according to (insert Gospel name here).

Monk now reads a selection in English from one of the Gospels, then says,

M GLORIA TIBI DOMINE   Glory be to Thee, Oh Lord.

Monk crosses self, walks back to altar, bows, places Bible on the altar, removes cope, and returns to his place. Everyone turns to face altar.

P CREDO	I believe.
CREDO IN UNUM DEUM PATREM OMNIPOTENTEM	I believe in one God, Father almighty,
FACTOREM COELI ET TERRA VISIBLIUM	maker of heaven and earth
OMNIUM, ET INVISIBILIUM	and all that is invisible,
ET IN UNUM DOMINUM JESU CHRISTI	and in one Lord, Jesus Christ,
FILIUM DEI UNIGENTUM	the only begotten Son of God,
ET EX PATRE NATUM ANTE OMNIA SECULA	and begotten of his Father before all worlds.
DEUM DE DEO	God of God,
LUMEN DE LUMINE	light of light,
DEUM VERUM DEO VERO	very God of very God,
GENITUM NON FACTUM CONSUBSTANTIALEM	begotten, not made, of one substance
PATRI PER QUEM OMNIA FACTA SUNT	with the Father by whom all things were made,
QUI PROPTER NOS HOMINES ET PROPTER	who for us and our salvation
NOSTRAM SALUTEM DESCENDIT DE COELIS	came down from heaven

Entire congregation kneels. Priest should allow thirty seconds before continuing.

P ET INCARNATUS EST DE SPRIITU SANCTO	and was made incarnate by the Holy Spirit
EX MARIA VIRGINEE ET HOMO FACTUS EST	of the Virgin Mary and was made man.
CRUCIFIXUS ETIAM PRO NOBIS SUB PONTIO	He was crucified under Pontius Pilate,
PILATO PASSUS ET SEPULTUS EST	suffered, and was buried,
ET RESUR EXIT TERTIA DIE	and rose again on the third day
SECUNDUM SCRIPTURAS	according to the Scriptures.

P ET ASCENDIT IN COELUM

He ascended into heaven

   SEDET AD DEXTERAM PATRIS

and sitteth at the right hand of the Father

   ET ITERUM VENTURUS EST CUM GLORIA

and He shall come again with Glory

   JUDICARE VIVOS ET MORTUOS

to judge the quick and the dead.

   CUIUS REGNI NON ERIT FINIS

His Kingdom shall have no end.

   ET IN SPIRITUM SANCTUM

And in the Holy Spirit,

   DOMINUM ET VIVIFICANTEM

the Lord and giver of life

   QUI EX PATRE FILIOQUE PROCEDIT

who proceedeth from the Father and the Son,

   QUI CUM PATRE ET FILIO SIMUL ADORATUR

who with the Father and Son is worshipped

   ET CONGLORIFACTUR

and glorified,

   QUI LOCUTUS EST PER PROPHETAS

and spoken through the prophets,

   ET UNAM SANCTAM CATHOLICAM ET

and in one Holy Catholic and

   APOSTOLICUM ECCLESIAM

Apostolic Church.

   CONFITEOR UNUM BAPTISMA IN REMISSIONEM

I acknowledge one baptism for the remission

   PECCATORUM

of sins,

   ET EXPECTO RESURRECTIONEM MORTUORUM

and I look for the resurrection of the dead

   ET VITAM VENTURI SECULI

and of the life of the world to come.

   AMEN

Amen.

Everyone stands up.

P SUSCIPE SANCTA TRINITAS HANC OBLATIONEM

Receive, Oh Holy Trinity, this oblation

   QUAM EGO MISER ET INDIGNUS OFFERO

which I, an unworthy sinner, offer

   IN HONORE TUO ET BEATE MARIA PERPETUE

in Thy honour and in that of the Blessed Mary,

   VIRGINIS

ever a virgin,

   ET OMNIUM SANCTORUM TUORUM

and all the saints,

   PRO PECCATIS MIES ET PRO SALUTE VIVORUM

for my sins and for the salvation of the living

   ET REQUIE OMNIUM ET PRO SALUTE VIVORUM ET

and the repose of all the faithfully departed;

   REQUIE OMNIUM FIDELIUM DEFUNTOREUM

   QUI VIVIS ET REGNAS

Who lives and reigns for ever and ever.

M IN SPIRITUS HUMILITATIS

In the spirit of humility

   ET ANIMO I CONTRITO SUSCIPIAMUR

and with a contrite heart, may we be accepted,

   DOMINE A TE

Oh Lord, by Thee

   ET SIC FIAT SACRIFICIUM NOSTRUM UT A TE

and cause our sacrifice to be accepted as worthy

   SUSCIPIATUR HODIE UT PLACEAT TIBI

in Thy sight that it may please Thee,

   DOMINE DEUS

Oh Lord God.

From this point, a plus sign (+) means that the speaker crosses himself.

A bowl of water and a towel are now brought forward. The priest washes his hands and dries them on towel. The bowl is then removed.

P DOMINUS VOBISCUM

The Lord be with thee,

M ET CUM SPIRITU TUO

and with thy spirit.

P SURSUM CORDA

Lift up your hearts,

M HABEMUS AD DOMINUM

We lift them to our Lord God.

P GRATIAS AGIMUS DOMINO DEO NOSTRO

Let us give thanks to our Lord God.

M DIGNUM ET JUSTUM EST

It is meet and right so to do.

The Sanctus, below, is sung.

P SANCTUS SANCTUS SANCTUS
   DOMINE DEUS SABAOTH
   PLENI SUNT COELI ET TERRA GLORIA TUA

Holy, holy, holy
Lord God of Hosts,
Heaven and earth are filled with Thy Glory.

M HOSANNA IN EXCELSIS

Hosanna in the highest.

P BENEDICTUS QUI VENIT IN NOMINE DOMINI

Blessed is he that cometh in the name of the Lord.

M HOSANNA IN EXCELSIS

Hosanna in the highest.

P TE IGITUR CLEMENTISSIME PATER
   PER JESUM CHRISTUM FILIUM TUUM
   DOMINUM NOSTRUM
   SUPPLICES ROGAMUS AC PETIMUS UTI ACCEPTA
   HABEAS ET BENEDICAS HAEC DONA (+)
   HAEC MUNERA (+) HAEC SANCTA (+) SACRIFICIA
   ILLIBATA IN PRIMIS QUAE TIBI OFFERIMUS
   PRO ECCLESIA TUA SANCTA CATHOLICA
   QUAM PACIFICARE CUSTODIRE ADUNARE
   ET REGERE DIGNERIS TOTO ORBE
   TERRARUM UNA CUM FAMULO TUO PAPA NOSTRO
   (insert Pope's name)
   ET ANTISTE NOSTRO (insert local Bishop's name)
   ET REGE (insert name of monarch or president)
   ET OMNIBUS

Therefore, most merciful Father
through Jesus Christ thy Son,
our Lord,
we humbly pray Thee to accept
and bless these gifts (+)
these presents (+) these holy (+) unblemished sacrifices
which we offer to Thee
on behalf of Thy holy Catholic Church,
which you promise to keep in peace
and govern throughout the whole world
together with Thy servant, our Pope
(insert name),
our Bishop (insert name),
and our King (name of monarch or president),
and all

P ORTHODOXIS ATQUE CATHOLICE ET APOSTOLICE
FIDEI CULTORIBUS
MEMENTO DOMINE FAMULORUM
FAMULARUMQUE TUARUM
(here insert names of bride and groom)
ET OMNIUM CIRCUMSTANTIUM QUORUM TIBI
FIDES COGNITA EST NOTA DEVOTIO
PRO QUIBUS TIBI OFFERIMUS. VEL QUI TIBI
OFFERUNT HOC SACRIFICIUM LAUDIS PRO SE
SUISQUE OMNIBUS
PRO REDEMPTIONE ANIMARUM SUARUM
PRO SPE SALUTIS ET INCOLUMITATIS SUAE
TIBI REDDUNT UOTA SUA
ETERNO DEO VIVO ET VERO

who are Orthodox, and who hold the Catholic
and Apostolic faith.
Remember, Oh Lord, Thy servant
and Thy handmaiden
(*insert names*)
and all here present whose faith is approved
and whose devotion is known to Thee
on behalf of whom we offer unto Thee
this sacrifice of praise for themselves
and all theirs,
and the redemption of their souls
for the hope of their salvation and their security,
who make these vows unto You
the eternal, living God.

M COMMUNICATNES ET VENERENTES
IN PRIMIS GLORIOSAE SEMPER VIRGINIS MARIA
GENITRICIS DIE ET DOMINE NOSTRI JESU CHRISTI
SED ET BEATORUM APOSTOLORUM AC
MARTYRUM TUORUM PETRI, PAULO ANDREAE
(*here add the names of any saints who are special to the
couple or the saint whose feast day is nearest*)
ET OMNIUM SANCTORUM TUORUM QUORUM
MERITIS PRECIBUSQUE CONCEDAS UT IN OMNIBUS
PROTECTIONIS TUAE MUNIAMUR AUXILIO
PER EUENDEM CHRISTUM DOMINUM NOSTRUM
AMEN

In communicating and reverencing
with the glorious and ever virgin Mary,
Mother of our God and Lord Jesus Christ
and also of Thy blessed apostles
and martyrs Peter, Paul, Andrew,
(*add saint names*)

And all Thy Saints through whose prayers
and merits Thou grant that in all things
we may be defended by the aid of Thy protection
Through the same Christ our Lord.
Amen.

P HANC IGITUR OBLATIONEM SERVITUTIS NOSTRAE
SED ET CUNCT FAMILIAE TUAE QUAESUMIS
DOMINE UT PLACATUS ACCIPIAS DIESQUE
NOSTROS IN TUA PACE DISPONAS
ATQUE AB ETERNA DAMNATIONE NOS
ERIPI ER IN ELECTORUM TUORUM JUBEAS

Therefore, Oh Lord, graciously accept this oblation
of our service and of Thy whole family,
we beseech Thee, Oh Lord,
dispose our days in Thy peace,
and that we may be delivered from eternal damnation
and be numbered among the flock of Thine elect

P GREGE NUMERARI PER CHRISTUM DOMINUM
NOSTRUM
AMEN

Through Christ our Lord.

Amen.

P QUAM OBLIATION TU DUES IN OMNIBUS
QUAESUMUS
BENEDICTAM (+) ADSCRIPTAM (+)
RATAM RATIONABILEM ACCEPTABILEMQUE
FACERE DIGNERIS UT NOBIS CORPUS (+)
ET SANGUIS (+) FIAT DILECTISSIMI FILII
DOMINI NOSTRI JESU CHRISTI

Which oblation, we beseech Thee,
Oh God
to bless (+) approve (+)
ratify and make reasonable and acceptable,
that it may become to us the body (+)
and blood (+) of Thy most dearly beloved Son,
our Lord, Jesus Christ

Priest bows to altar, bends knee, and kisses altar top.

P QUI PRIDIE QUAM PATERETUR ACCEPIT, Who, the day before he suffered,
PANEM IN SANCTAS ET VENERABLIES MANUS SUAS took bread into His holy hands,
BENEDIXIT AC FREGIT DEDITQUE DISCIPULIS SUIS blessed it, broke it and gave it to His disciples
DICENS saying:

Priest picks up Host on paten and raises above his head. Monk rings bell three times. Priest places Host on altar and puts hands over Host.

P ACCIPITE ET MANDUCATE EX HOC OMNES HOC Take and eat ye all, of this,
EST ENIM CORPUS MEUM for this is My body.

Monk rings bell three times.
Priest bows to altar, then pours wine into chalice, which is sitting on right side of altar.

P SIMILI MODO POSTEA QUAM CENATUM EST Likewise, after supper,
ACCIPIENS ET HUNC PRAECLARUM CALICEM taking the chalice
IN SANCTAS AC VENERABILIS MANUS SUAS in His holy and venerable hands
ITEM TIBI GRACIAS AGENS BENEDIXIT (+) and giving thanks to Thee He blessed it (+)
DEDITQUE SUIS DICENS and gave it to His disciples saying:

P ACCEPITE ET BIBITE EX EO OMNES Take and drink ye all, of this

Priest raises chalice above head, replaces chalice on altar, and places hands over chalice.

P HIC EST ENIM CALIX SANGUINIS MEI NOVI For this is the cup of My blood of the new
ET ETERNI TESTAMENTI and everlasting testament,
MYSTERIUM FIDEI QUI PRO VOBIS ET PRO MUTIS the mystery of faith which shall be shed for you
EFFUNDETUR IN REMISSIONEM PECCATORUM and for many for the remission of sin.
HAEC QUOTIES CUMQUE FECERITIS As oft as ye do these things,
IN MEI MEMORIAM FACIETIS do them in remembrance of Me.

Monk rings bell three times.

P PER IPSUM (+) ET CUM IPSO (+) ET IN IPSO (+) Through Him (+) and with Him (+) and in Him (+)
EST TIBI DEO PATRI (+) OMNIPOTENTI all honour and glory (+) is to Thee,
IN UNITATE SPIRITUS (+) SANCTI OMNIS HONOR God the Father almighty (+) in the unity of the Holy
ET GLORIA PER OMNIA SECULA SECULORUM Spirit, for ever and ever.
AMEN Amen.

M PRECEPTIS SALUTARIBUS MONITI	Taught by saving precepts,
DIVINA INSTITUTONE FORMATI	and divine institution,
AUDEMUS DICERE	we dare to say:
PATER NOSTER	Our Father
QUI ES IN CAELIS	who art in heaven
SANCTIFICETUR NOMEN TUUM	Hallowed be Thy name
ADVENIAT REGNUM TUUM	Thy Kingdom come
FIAT VOLUNTAS TUA	Thy will be done
SICUT IN CAELO ET IN TERRA	in earth as it is in heaven
PANEM NOSTRUM QUOTIDIANUM DA NOBIS HODIE	Give us this day our daily bread
ET DIMITTE NOBIS DEBITA NOSTRA	And forgive us our trespasses
SICUT ET NOS DIMITTIMUS DEBITORIBUS NOSTRIS	As we forgive those who trespass against us
ET NE NOS INDUCAS IN TENTANTIONEM	And lead us not into temptation
SED LIBERA NOS A MALO	But deliver us from evil.
AMEN	Amen.

Priest takes Host in hands, breaks it in half, puts one part on paten, then takes the other half and again breaks it in half.

P HAEC COMMIXITIO ET CONSECRATIO CORPORIS	Let this most holy mixture and consecration of the body
ET SANGUINIS DOMINI NOSTRI JESU CHRISTI	and blood of our Lord, Jesus Christ,
FIAT ACCIPIENTIBUS NOBIS IN VITAM AETERNAM	be for us to receive it for everlasting life.
AMEN	Amen.

Priest takes one quarter of the Host, puts it in chalice with wine, eats other quarter, then strikes breast three times.

M AGNUS DEI QUI TOLLIS PECCATA MUNDI	Lamb of God that taketh away the sins of the world,
MISERERE NOBIS	have mercy on us.
AGNUS DIE QUI TOLLIS PECCATA MUNDI	Lamb of God that taketh away the sins of the world,
MISERERE NOBIS	have mercy on us
AGNUS DEI QUI TOLLIS PECCATA MUNDI	
DONA NOBIS PACEM	and grant us Thy peace.

Priest gives Host to bride and groom, saying,

P CORPUS CHRISTI	Body of Christ
DOMINUS VOBISCUM	Lord be with you
M ET CUM SPIRITU TUO	and with thy spirit.
P ITE MISSA EST	Go, the mass is ended.

Priest turns to the congregation to give blessing.

P BENEDICAT VOS OMNIPOTONS DEUS PATER	May almighty God, Father,
ET FILIUS ET SPIRITUS SANCTUS	Son, and Holy Spirit, bless you.
AMEN	Amen.

Priest makes sign of cross in the air. Wedded couple depart, followed by priest and monks. Everyone genuflects before leaving.

CHAPTER 8

Decorating in the Medieval Style

During the Middle Ages, like today, the grandeur of a home's public spaces made an important statement about a family's wealth and social position. To host a proper medieval feast, you must either have access to an appropriately medieval great hall in which to hold it or, alternatively, create the feel and mood of a feast hall in your home or whatever rented space happens to be available to you. Drawing on websites, illustrations in books, and movies you have seen, create in your mind's eye the feast hall of a medieval castle. Start by visualizing the empty space—a huge, cavernous room with walls reaching up toward massive rafters of dark, ancient oak. As you walk across the floor made of heavy tiles or wide planks, the echo of your footsteps rolls softly around your ears.

Now, begin to fill in the furnishings. At the far end of the room stands a massive table nearly as long as the room is wide. At its center are two high-backed armchairs, flanked by several smaller chairs on either side. Along one side wall may be a heavily carved sideboard piled high with pewter and silver platters, bowls, and mugs. With the exception of a few long, high-backed benches standing against one wall and one or two trunks or chests, the room is nearly devoid of furnishings. The walls are hung with an assortment of rich tapestries and banners decorated with coats of arms. Interspersed between the tapestries and banners are brightly painted shields and arrangements of primitive, vicious-looking weapons. A soft light filters through narrow windows positioned along one wall but the primary light comes from clusters of large candles set in tall, wrought-iron candelabra that stand in each corner of the room and massive, wrought-iron chandeliers suspended from the ceiling beams by heavy chains. In the distance, you can hear the nasal piping of medieval music.

Unfortunately, this magnificent room only exists in your mind. For your feast, you will have to transform whatever space you have available into a reasonable facsimile of this imaginary medieval banquet hall. If you are working with your own dining room, you are pretty well locked into the available floor space and ceiling height. A basement or garage might offer more room, however, and if you have access to a barn, it can be made to look far more medieval than any modern space. If you are considering a rented space, try to locate one that has the feel of a medieval building. This is not as hard as it might seem. Many towns have one or more Victorian Gothic churches, National Guard armories, or other buildings with appropriately grand assembly halls that owners are glad to rent out; the price is often surprisingly reasonable.

Alternatively, you might opt for an outdoor setting. During the Middle Ages many feasts were held in huge tents and open-air pavilions. This same feel can be achieved by renting a marquee tent from a company that supplies tents for wedding receptions or by contacting a local park and reserving a pavilion for your feast.

Above: *A large marquee tent can provide a splendid setting for your medieval event at a fraction of the cost of hiring a meeting hall.* VALERIE ROWE/FANTAYSIA LIMITED Right: *An actual medieval great hall as it would have appeared around 1400. Note the painted tapestry on the wall at the right of the picture.* BARLEY HALL, YORK, ENGLAND

Even if no appropriately medieval space is available in your area, we will walk you through every step you need to take to make even the most mundane-looking space appear very passably medieval. No matter how modern the space you begin with might be, making it look and feel properly medieval will only require a little bit of time, judicious planning, ingenuity, and a few days' work. If you are good with decorative crafts, or can recruit one or more artistic friends to help you, all the better.

Start by planning the overall feel of the room in which your feast is going to be held. If the room already has a decorative scheme, select properly medieval colors that will enhance the impact of the space. To get a feel for medieval color schemes, look at the pictures of medieval rooms reproduced throughout this book. Medieval decorating colors were rich and vibrant: ruby reds, emerald greens, brilliant oranges, and bright gold. Blues were rare in the medieval world, as blue dyes and paints were scarce and unable to hold their color over time.

Wall Decoration

Banners

No medieval feast hall is complete without great tapestries to adorn the walls. Armorial banners and wall hangings can be made to decorate your feast hall with as much or as little effort as you feel like putting into them. Banners will help hide plain-looking walls or wallpaper with inappropriately modern designs. Banners will also give an open-air pavilion an added degree of privacy and, when hung on both the inside and outside of a rented marquee tent, make it look grand enough to host noble knights and ladies attending a medieval tournament.

The easiest way to adorn your space with banners is to buy flat panel curtains with large rod loops attached to the top edge. The cheapest place to buy these is either your local Ikea or Walmart store. Purchase drapes in a length that will allow them to hang from near the ceiling to as near to the floor as possible. Buy as many panels as you need to cover large, blank spaces of wall, but there is no need to cover every inch of the walls—just use enough panels to give a feel of the medieval to the space. We suggest using more than one color so you can alternate bright-colored panels with dark-colored panels. Alternating panels in combinations of gold and red or gold and green are both good medieval combinations but you may want to coordinate the colors to suit your event, especially if you are having a wedding with a specific color scheme. To get a visual image of how this will look, turn to the photograph on page 55 of Barley Hall, a recreated medieval house in York, England. Depending upon your space, you may also want to buy inexpensive curtain rods to hang the banners on.

If you choose to make the banners yourself, the best choice of material is bright, plain-colored upholstery fabric. Leave the fabric in its full width and cut it into

A nineteenth-century church assembly hall, decorated with painted banners and filled with guests dressed in homemade medieval costumes, makes for a surprisingly convincing medieval setting.

lengths that will extend from about six inches below the ceiling to about one or two feet above the floor. Begin making the wall hangings by hemming all four edges of the tapestry. Along the top, sew a rod pocket, drapery rings, or lengths of cloth ribbon to attach the tapestry to wooden rods or inexpensive drapery rods. Decorative finials on the ends of rods will add to the visual effect. If you are using a space where you cannot, or do not wish, to attach drapery rods to the walls, fabric panels can be tacked directly to the wall with small nails or thumbtacks without inflicting noticeable damage to the walls. If you are using a rented space be sure to ask permission before tacking anything to the walls.

If you are holding your feast in a space where there are exposed beams or open rafters, additional banners can be suspended from the ceiling for a strikingly medieval look. If possible, these banners should be confined to the long sides of the room and should be hung at a ninety-degree angle to the wall. Unlike modern flags, which are often hung horizontally from ceiling beams, medieval banners were always hung vertically. This will also add to the visual height of the room. If your ceilings are less than ten feet in height, however, such banners may actually reduce the visual height of the room and should be avoided.

Painted Wall Hangings

Kings, princes, and popes spent small fortunes to adorn their walls with embroidered or woven tapestries, but people of more modest means added visual richness to otherwise plain hangings and banners by decorating them with painted designs ranging from simple coats of arms to elaborate scenes of court life and battle.

The easiest and simplest approach to producing your own decorated hangings is to paint coats of arms on the lighter-colored panels that you will be hanging in your medieval feast hall. A two-page selection of coats of arms can be found on pages 58–59. Be sure the designs you choose to reproduce are suitable to your level of artistic skill; for beginners, coats of arms are much safer than taking on a complex scene involving people, castles, and running horses. These can be just as impressive as wall-size paintings and are far easier to make. You also have the advantage of being able to ask friends to paint one or two panels without overwhelming anyone.

Sketch the designs, full-size, on brown wrapping paper, newsprint, or butcher paper until you are happy with them. Remember to keep your designs large. Don't be afraid to make them nearly as wide as the banner on which they will be painted. When the design is sketched

out, you are ready to transfer it to the canvas. Position the drawing on the canvas, and pin it in place so it does not shift during the transfer process. Take a piece of paper and rub a very soft-leaded pencil across one side of it until the entire surface of the paper is covered. This will act as carbon paper to transfer the image from the paper to the canvas. Slide the "carbon paper," carbon side toward the canvas, between the drawing and the canvas. Trace over the drawing carefully with a ballpoint pen to transfer the image to the canvas.

When the transfer is complete, paint in the image with latex-based interior wall paint or acrylic artist's paints. When the painting is finished, be careful not to fold the banners because the paint can crack if it is creased. Instead, roll your banners around a large-diameter cardboard tube of the type used for rolls of carpet.

For those with a flair for the artistic and a few days to dedicate to a more elaborate project, you might consider painting a wall hanging with a medieval scene adapted from a manuscript illumination or tapestry. For pictorial reference, do an Internet search using the key words "medieval manuscript illuminations images," "medieval tapestry images" or "medieval wall painting images." These searches will lead you to literally hundreds of images from which to choose. Alternately, your local library may have one or more books with pictures of medieval artwork. Remember, the more elaborate the design, the more time it will require to transform it into a painted wall hanging. When you have located a suitable image, download or photocopy it. You may want to make several copies as these will be essential in transferring the design to your canvas.

Next, decide how large you want your wall hanging to be—but remember that it should be dimensionally proportionate to your photocopy. If your photocopy is 4 inches high and 5 inches wide, the full-sized canvas should have a relative proportion of 4 to 5.

From lightweight canvas, a painter's drop cloth, or any fine-textured heavyweight cotton fabric (even bedsheets would work in a pinch), cut banners of a size appropriate to the room in which they will hang, so that they cover a large section of a wall. Hem the edges to prevent fraying, and sew a rod pocket or attach loops of fabric along the top if they are going to be hung on a rod. When all four edges have been hemmed, prime the finished cloth with a coat of artists' gesso or interior-grade latex primer.

Either of two methods can be used to transfer the design to the canvas. If you have access to an opaque projector you can project the image directly from your

Coats of Arms

Facing page and above: *Coats of arms like these can be adapted for use on banners and shields to decorate your feast hall. These designs are original medieval coats of arms from England, Ireland, and Germany but the colors have been changed.*

photocopy onto the canvas and trace around the images with a pencil. Alternately, you can enlarge the image by means of a grid transfer. On one of your photocopies, draw a grid pattern that divides the image into 3/4-inch (20mm) or 1-inch (25mm) squares. The size of the grid you will need is determined by the size and complexity of your original design; the smaller the design, or the more detail it contains, a smaller the grid pattern should be. For a visual guide to gridding your image and paint-

ing your wall hanging, please refer to pages 60–61 for four step-by-step photos of a painted wall hanging.

Next, make a paper facsimile of your blank canvass using either butcher paper or newsprint. Divide the paper into a grid pattern that corresponds to the number of squares on your photocopied image. If the photocopied image is 4 inches high and 5 inches wide and is divided into one-inch squares, your paper facsimile should be divided vertically into 4 equal sections and

Making a Painted Wall Hanging

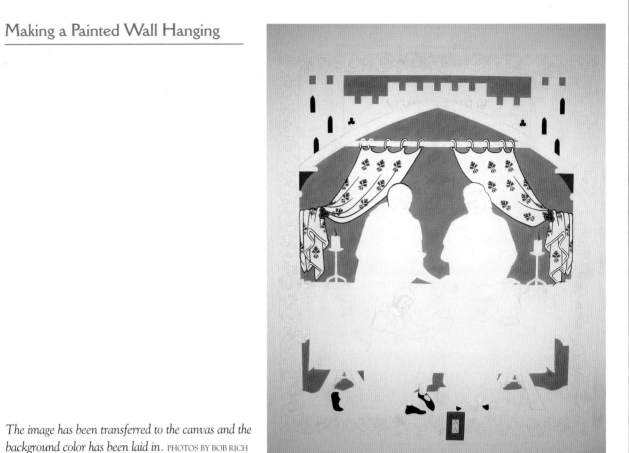

The image has been transferred to the canvas and the background color has been laid in. PHOTOS BY BOB RICH

Smaller items are shown in various stages of completion. Note that some pieces of tableware only have the basic color painted in, while others like the pewter pitcher have been given shadows and a complete outline.

The gray ground color of the figure on the left has been overlaid with the final brown color and the colors on the other two figures have been laid in and outlined.

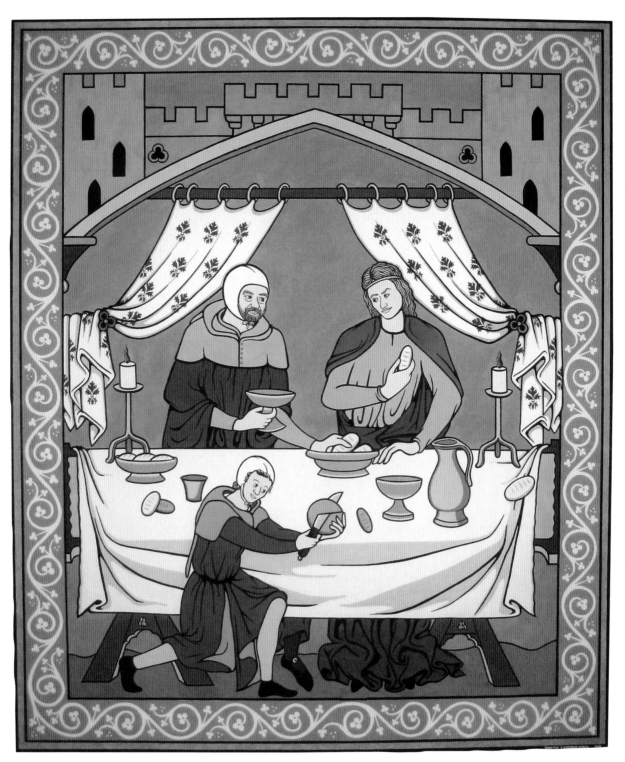

Here is the completed wall hanging with all the details completed, including shading and outlines. Note that the outlines around small details, such as faces and hands, are narrower than the lines around large items such as the tablecloth and clothing. BOB RICH

horizontally into 5 equal sections. When the paper has been marked out into a grid, reproduce the picture in the photocopy, one square at a time, onto the paper. Pay close attention to the places on the grid where the image lines cross from one square into another.

When the image has been completed, prick holes along all of the lines in the drawing with a small, sharp object like a toothpick or knitting needle. Space the holes about 1/2 inch (13mm) apart. You now have a stencil of your finished image.

Next, construct a pounce bag from a piece of fine linen, muslin, or other fine-weave fabric about 3 or 4 inches (7 1/2 to 10 cm) square. Into the center of this cloth square pour a spoonful of carpenter's line-marking chalk (available at any hardware store). Draw the cloth firmly around the chalk and tie it shut with a piece of string to form a small, tight bag.

Beginning at the left side of your canvas, tape one section of your stencil over the canvas, hold the stencil firmly against the canvas with your hand, and tap the pounce bag over the perforations in the area immediately around your hand. Repeat this process until you have covered the entire first section of the stencil. When the first section has been thoroughly pounced, remove the paper and connect the dots with a pencil to reproduce the outline of your drawing. Proceed to the next section of the stencil and continue the process until the entire drawing has been transferred to the canvas. Make sure to connect the dots on each section of the drawing before proceeding to the next section so the chalk dust is not accidentally smeared or rubbed off as you work. To make the pencil lines bold enough to see clearly, use a 00 size artist's brush and go over them with gray or gray-green paint. If you have not already done so, once the entire picture has been outlined, it is best to hang the canvas on a wall before you begin painting in the large areas of color. Once the large areas have been painted in, you can give your painting a three-dimensional look by painting in highlights and shadows similar to the ones that appear in the original photocopy. Details of this shadowing process are shown in the step-by-step photos. Highlights and shadows can be applied using lighter and darker shades of the base color used in each area of the painting. The process of applying shadows and highlights takes some practice but the results are well worth the effort.

Final details on painted wall hangings, as on medieval manuscript illuminations, are usually limited to dark, cartoon-like outlines around all of the figures or small areas of bright color. The outlines should vary slightly in width depending upon the size of the area they are defining; smaller areas like faces, hands, and other small objects should be outlined with finer lines than those used for large areas like clothes and architectural details.

When the painting is finished, allow it to dry overnight before removing it from the wall. Be careful not to kink or crease the canvas, as this can cause the paint to crack, peel, or chip. If you are going to store your painting or move it from one place to another, roll it around a large-diameter cardboard tube of the type used for rolls of carpeting.

You are now ready to insert a stout pole or curtain rod through the rod pocket at the top of your canvas or tack it directly to the wall. Your painted medieval wall hanging will add a real touch of the Middle Ages to your event.

Tapestries

For those with more refined tastes and larger budgets, there are marvelous copies of medieval and Renaissance tapestries available from companies specializing in historical reproductions, such as Design Toscano, Schumacher Wallcoverings, Braunschwig & Fils Wallcovering, and other companies, which can be found online by doing a search for "reproduction medieval tapestries." These can be purchased for prices from under $100 for small tapestries to several thousand dollars for larger, more elaborate ones.

In those places on the wall of your recreated medieval feast hall where there are gaps between wall hangings, or where walls are entirely exposed, remove any existing pictures, mirrors, and framed paintings, all of which were unknown during the Middle Ages and will make your feast hall look less authentic.

Other Wall Decorations

Because the vast majority of the men in upper-class medieval families were soldiers, it was common for them to decorate the walls of their homes and castles with the tools of their trade. Swords, battleaxes, shields, breastplates and helmets help give a room a medieval feel and eliminate those awkward blank spots between banners and wall hangings. Reproductions of medieval arms and armor can often be rented through local costume shops and are available for purchase through online merchants whose names will come up under a web search for "medieval armor and weapons." Obviously if there are no costume shops near you and you find that purchasing reproduction weaponry and armor gets a bit pricey, you can

A painted wall hanging behind the feast table adds tremendously to the historical feel of this medieval event. EUGENE SIREN

always opt for cutting shields out of 1/4-inch plywood or cardboard and painting them with brightly colored coats of arms. Toy stores, both at the local mall and online, sometimes offer plastic swords and shields that can look perfectly passable from a distance, especially if you paint the handles and scabbards of the swords black and pick out any designs on the shields with paint.

Window Decoration

Most medieval windows were left bare. The only means of shutting out light and cold was by closing heavy wooden shutters. So leaving the windows in your recreated feast hall undecorated is entirely appropriate. If you want draperies, however, they should be made of a heavy fabric and as free of designs as possible. If you want patterned draperies, select a heavy damask where the design is picked out in various shades of a single color. Winter-weight bedspreads often have surprisingly medieval-looking damask patterns and can be adapted as window coverings with very little effort. Otherwise, panels of heavy upholstery fabric will work just as well. Choose

your colors to correspond with one of the colors in your wall hangings and banners. Once in place, swag the draperies to one side with heavy tiebacks or open them on an existing curtain rod. By all means, remove lace curtains and sheers, both of which are Victorian inventions and were unknown during the Middle Ages.

Alternately, you might consider turning your windows into "stained glass" works of art, keeping in mind that these are effective only if your dinner is to take place in the daytime. Stained-glass painting kits, complete with bright-colored glass paint and artificial lead, are available at many craft and hobby stores. Select an attractive coat of arms or scene from a medieval manuscript or from a stained-glass pattern book. If you do not want to paint directly on your windows because of the hassle of removing the paint, use a piece of single-strength Plexiglas that can be hung or screwed in place over the window frame and removed later. An easy and inexpensive way to get a stained-glass window effect is to use permanent markers on waxed paper, which can be removed and discarded after your event.

Another idea for window treatment is to replicate the heavy wooden shutters that usually covered the interior surface of castle windows. Using sheets of plywood, or perhaps even cardboard, cut panels to size and pierce them with an arbalestina, a cross-shaped arrow slot specifically designed to accommodate the use of crossbows during times of danger. This cutout will allow a small amount of light to enter the hall while masking any modern distractions outside the window.

Floors

Floors in medieval feast halls were either great slabs of stone, glazed tile, or wooden planks. Though few homes today have flagstone floors, many have hardwood. If your home has natural wood floors, by all means roll up the area rugs and leave the floors bare. But if your dining room is carpeted, don't worry; the room will be so impressive when it is fully decorated that no one will notice. If your feast is being held in a space with a tile floor, and the tiles are laid in a checkerboard pattern, it already has a passable medieval look and can be left as is and will provide a perfect surface for practicing medieval dance steps, which are explained in chapter 16 of this book.

The floors of feast halls in the Middle Ages were often strewn with hay, rushes, and sweetgrasses to help keep the room warm and fresh smelling. Though this is not recommended for use on a carpeted floor, if you are holding your feast in a space with a linoleum or concrete floor, a light covering of hay will add significantly to the medieval atmosphere. If you choose to use hay on the floor, be sure to purchase fresh hay, not straw, and only bring it in from outdoors a few hours before the feast to ensure that it does not dry out and become dusty, which increases the risk of fire. Sprinkling some potpourri around in the hay will add a pleasant scent to the room. Be careful to keep hay and any other combustible material well away from open flames, fireplaces, and candles.

Feast Tables

The most important visual element in recreating the medieval feast is having proper-looking feast tables. Variations in the arrangement of tables in the feast hall were almost endless, but in all cases there was a designated high table, where the host, hostess, and the highest-ranking visitors were set apart from the guests. Some high tables were placed on a raised platform, giving the guests a good view of the nobility and their fine clothes and refined manners. Chairs were placed only on one

side of the high table so everyone there would be in full view of the rest of the room. The highest-ranking guests were seated in the middle of the high table. Those of highest rank would be seated in high-backed armchairs, those next in rank would have armchairs with lower backs, and toward the ends of the table were chairs with no arms.

Other tables in the hall were arranged in long rows, at a ninety-degree angle to the high table, so guests could look down the length of their tables toward the high table. Even at these lower tables, seating was all-important. Those nearest the high table had small, armless chairs, farther down the tables were individual stools, and at the ends of the tables were common benches.

The variety of seating used during the Middle Ages makes it all the easier to reproduce the feel of the medieval feast. Standard dining room chairs can serve as the seating at the high table. If your chairs have high backs and are fairly simple in design, so much the better. If you have carver chairs with arms, these can be the seats of honor at the center of the table. Seating at the lower tables can be a mixture of folding chairs (wooden ones look better than metal) placed nearest the high table and picnic benches farther down the tables.

For these "lower" tables, use rented folding tables. For serious do-it-yourselfers, old doors, heavy planks, or thirty-inch-wide sheets of three-quarter-inch plywood set on sawhorses all make good period substitutes. If you are in a situation where your recreated feast hall comes with picnic tables, such as a pavilion in a public park, it is best if the tables have separate benches so you can seat people on one side only. If your picnic tables have attached seats on both sides of the table you have the option of seating people on one side and leaving the other empty or using both sides for seating. The worst that will happen is that some of the guests will have to turn around to view any entertainment that you might have planned.

If you have a large room for your feast, try to approximate the seating arrangement of the medieval feast hall by placing the lower tables at right angles to the high table. Depending on the size of your feast, one row of additional seating can be placed directly in front of the high table, so the two tables form a T arrangement (see table diagram A). The top bar of the T should always serve as the high table. An alternative version of the T-shaped arrangement is the L. By moving the lower tables off to one side of the high table, the majority of the floor space in the room is left open for dance and theatrical performances that might take place before or after the meal and between courses.

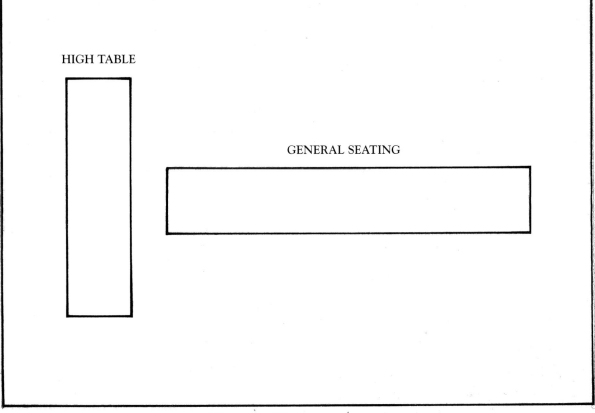

TABLE DIAGRAM A

TABLE DIAGRAM B

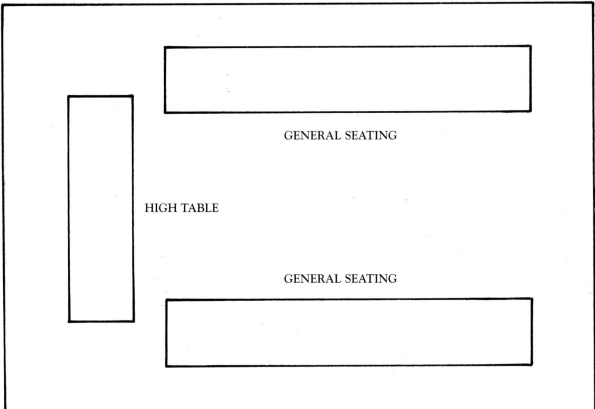

If you are having a really large feast, arrange three lines of tables in a U shape (see table diagram B). The bottom of the U is the high table, and two additional rows of tables extend from either end. This arrangement is particularly nice because it allows the presentation of the food, as well as any entertainment, to take place in the center of the U, in full view of the entire company. If you use the U-shaped arrangement, you can have seating at one or both sides of the lower tables. If there is seating only along one side of the lower tables, everyone in the hall will be offered an unobstructed view of all the guests as well as the entertainment. If you have seating on both sides of these tables, as long as everyone can see those at the high table, you have a satisfactory medieval arrangement. Under no circumstances should there be seating on both sides of the high table.

If your room is too long and narrow to allow for a T- or U-shaped arrangement, seat your guests at one long table or several short tables placed end-to-end. Seat everyone along one side and at both ends of the table, with the seats of honor being in the middle of the table. If necessary, people may sit on both sides of the table, but the area directly across from the "nobility" should be left open. The seats of these nobles can be distinguished by overlaying the main tablecloth with a secondary, contrasting cloth at the places of honor. The secondary cloth should hang over the front edge of the table at least as far as the primary tablecloth.

No matter what the physical arrangement of the tables, the table coverings should be selected so that the high table or seats of honor always stand out from the others. One type of cloth may be plain and others patterned, or one white and others colored. Traditionally, a white cloth with a heavily decorated over-cloth would be used on the high table. Play off the colors already in the room, and consider the materials and colors in your recreated wall hangings and tapestries when you select the over-cloth for the high table.

Other Furniture

Medieval decorating was spare and functional. Other than tables and chairs, great halls in castles were almost entirely bare and manor houses had only one main piece of furniture, the "cup board." Similar to Victorian sideboards, the cup board had a chest-type base with doors or drawers, above which was a shelf unit for the display of pewter and silver platters, plates, and goblets. If you have a traditional sideboard with open shelves, so much the better. Remove china and glassware from the shelves and replace them with pewter and silver, or silver-colored, metalware. Stainless serving platters, wooden bowls and plates, and pewter tankards or silver-plated stemware all make for a grand display. Incidental furnishings like small side tables, knickknack shelves, and china cupboards should be removed, as such things did not exist during the Middle Ages.

A few trunks or wooden chests may be brought into the room to serve as appropriately medieval decoration and also to provide additional seating space along the walls. Chests and trunks were an ever-present part

A mixture of wooden, pewter, and earthenware plates, bowls, and goblets will provide a convincing medieval table setting.
EUGENE SIREN

of medieval life and were used to store everything from clothing to written records to jewelry.

If you are going all-out in recreating the few, necessary pieces of medieval furniture, you can either build them yourself by following the instructions in either *Constructing Medieval Furniture* or *Medieval Furniture: Plans and Instructions for Historical Reproductions,* both published by Stackpole Books. If you are short on time and have ample funds, you can order fine-quality reproduction medieval furniture from a number of online craftsmen.

Lighting

Lighting in the medieval hall came from several sources. Narrow windows along one side of the hall, the crackling fire on the hearth, torches in iron wall brackets, and candles in great, floor-standing candelabra and chandeliers all played their part in brightening the vast, dark halls of castles and manor houses.

While we don't recommend that you have live torches hanging on the walls, a fire in the fireplace, if you are lucky enough to have one, is a great mood enhancer. The primary source of light for your recreated feast, however, should be candles. The most authentic-looking candles will be two or three inches in diameter and either white or natural beeswax color. Candles should be placed not only on the dining tables, but also throughout the room to spread a soft, diffused light. If you have, or can obtain, floor-standing candlesticks or candelabrum, they will make the ideal feast hall decoration.

Place drip catchers under any floor-standing candelabras. The best drip catcher is a large, sand-filled tray that covers the entire area beneath the candelabra; this will guarantee that neither hot wax nor flame falls on carpeting, hardwood floors, or hay. Make sure not to place open flames close to draperies, banners, or wall hangings.

If possible, avoid the use of ceiling lights unless you have chandeliers with lights that look like candles. In that case, use only fifteen or twenty-watt bulbs, preferably flame-shaped, which will provide an adequately soft light without overpowering the candles on the table. Another alternative to electric lights is to use a few strategically placed kerosene lamps. Although these lamps are certainly not medieval, the shimmering glow of a live flame is vastly preferable to electric lighting.

Christmas Decorations

During the Middle Ages, Christmas decorations as we know them did not exist. There were, however, efforts made to make the great hall look appropriately festive for the occasion and to help dispel the gloom of winter. So if your medieval feast is to take place over the Christmas holidays, here are a few extra things you should do to prepare.

When your feast hall has taken on a properly medieval look, it is time to add a few special trimmings appropriate to the holiday season. Not only did the addition of greenery bring a festive air to the great hall, but its scent freshened the musty air that was an inevitable result of large numbers of unwashed people living in cramped quarters. Mistletoe, with its supposed powers of love, brought the promise of new birth and spring, while the prickly holly leaves reminded the revelers of Christ's crown of thorns and the true reason for their celebrations.

Branches of evergreen or premade pine roping can be draped in large swags from ceiling cornices and beams and around door and window frames. Even the most unmedieval-looking ceiling lights can be draped with pine bows to disguise their presence. Additional greenery can be laid on dining tables and buffets as inexpensive centerpieces that add greatly to the primitive atmosphere of the medieval hall. Long-needled evergreens such as Austrian pine make the best decoration; not only do they provide the greatest amount of foliage for the money, but they have the most pungent scent and shed less than the short-needled variety. Mix sprigs of mistletoe, holly, ivy, and boxwood among the pine bows to provide visual texture. The bright red berries of holly are particularly effective punctuation to the greenery and should be used liberally. "Deck the hall" to your heart's content.

Surprisingly, the manger scene, with Joseph, Mary, the baby Jesus, shepherds, and wise men, was in common use during the Middle Ages, and the presence of a Nativity scene in a medieval setting is not at all out of place. Usually made of carved wood or fired clay, the figures used in medieval nativity scenes were normally left unpainted. Further information on Christmas decorating and traditions is given in chapter 4, "Medieval Christmas Celebrations."

Medieval Table Manners

Popular myth, heavily influenced by Hollywood, often envisions medieval feasts as debauched bacchanalias where bones were thrown on the floor to be eaten by the dogs and drunken brawls were an expected part of the evening's entertainment. Little could be farther from the truth. Medieval society demanded strict adherence to codes of chivalry in war and peace, absolute respect toward women, and the proper observation of religious duties at all times—not a social structure likely to sanction drunken orgies at the dinner table. Medieval table manners, if not as complex and rigid as those of the Victorians, were certainly more tightly structured and demanding than our own.

The Table Setting

To a great extent, table manners in any culture are established by the utensils with which food is served and consumed. In the broadest sense, the tableware available to medieval cooks, servers, and diners was not a great deal different from that used today, although the differences that did exist were fairly major. But before discussing table service and how it was used, let us look at the dinner table as it appeared to the arriving guests.

At the center of the high table, in front of the highest-ranking person or couple, was the salt cellar, which served as a symbol of status and hospitality. In use, the salt cellar held table salt, which was dispensed onto the food with a tiny spoon. Salt cellars usually took the form of a large, ornate cup, but some were made to look like small chests, animals, or even ships. Elsewhere at the table, between each pair of seats, was a large goblet and a small, luncheon-sized plate that was reserved for fruits or the occasional vegetable; two people normally shared one of these small plates and a goblet.

In front of each individual seat was a soup bowl made of wood or pewter, and a large dinner plate made of a similar material. On top of these dinner plates were placed thick slices of stale bread, known as a trencher, usually placed with the crust downward against the plate. Trencher loaves, either round or square, were allowed to go stale for four or five days before being used. If the trencher loaf was round, it would be cut horizontally into two round "dishes." The rounded surface of the top crust sometimes had to be cut away to allow the trencher to rest on the plate without rocking. The top halves of the trencher loaves were always served to the most noble among the company, and from this practice came the term "upper crust" as a reference to the wealthy elite. From these trenchers, solid foods like roasts, thick stews, and meat pies were eaten. If you use rectangular loaves, after allowing the bread to go stale, slice the loaf into one-inch-thick slices. Place five slices on each plate, with four slices arranged into a square and the fifth placed on top to keep the food and juices from dripping between the slices. Small pizza shells, large pita bread, or Indian naan breads can also be used as trenchers.

Recreating the Medieval Table Setting

Your table settings should begin with tablecloths; cover all of the tables with a white or light-colored cloth and add a contrasting cloth that hangs as far over the front of the table as the bottom hem of the undercloth on the high table in front of the seats of honor. There should also be a salt cellar for every six or eight guests, the grandest salt cellar being at the center of the high table, and more humble ones on each of the lower tables. Between each pair of seats should be shared plates for fruit and bread. Provide each individual with large plates and trencher bread, a soup bowl, possibly a spoon, a drinking goblet, and a cloth napkin. Each table should be provided with several loaves of bread and bowls of butter mixed with herbs or honey (see chapter 10 and chapter 11 for recipes). Bread and butter were served as appetizers at medieval banquets and were already on the table before the guests took their seats. Sometimes the bread and butter were augmented by a selection of cheeses.

Table Manners

Medieval dinner guests were traditionally divided into pairs, who shared more than just a salad plate. Like plates, drinking vessels fell into the category of shared property. Until well into the eleventh century, nobles and commoners alike frequently slept together on the

A table setting for two as it might have appeared in the fourteenth century. Note the aquamanile wine pitcher; bread trenchers set on wooden plates; individual soup bowls; a shared plate for fruit, cheese, and vegetables; and a shared goblet. The spoon on the left is made of pewter, the one on the right is horn. The knife on the left is a gentleman's belt knife and on the right is a lady's table knife, sometimes also worn on the belt. All of these items are modern and can be found in specialty stores, or online through dealers in medieval reproduction goods.

A variety of leather, wooden, and pewter tankards, along with wooden bowls, can make even a modern table appear medieval.
STEVE LUND

floor of the great hall, so shared drinking vessels did not seem like sharing too much. After drinking, a person wiped the rim of the cup with his or her napkin before replacing it on the table. Wine was consumed from heavy-stemmed goblets usually made from pewter or silver, although there are surviving examples made of earthenware, horn, and even glass. Beer was drunk from tankards, also known as jacks, made from pewter, earthenware, leather, or wood. For your recreated feast, metal (pewter, silver, or a modern alloy) or pottery will make the best presentation. If suggesting that your guests share goblets seems like carrying togetherness a little too far, it is perfectly all right if everyone gets his or her own. Similarly, medieval diners often shared a napkin that ran the entire length of the table. Again, this may be too unwieldy or impractical for your event.

Surprisingly, until well into the fourteenth century, even spoons were shared. Because only the richest households were likely to have enough spoons on hand for all the guests at a large banquet, guests either had to share whatever spoons were available or bring their own. When bringing a spoon to a feast became commonplace, people began competing to own the grand-est spoon. Some were even encrusted with jewels and worn around the neck like jewelry. Whether or not spoons were provided, everyone was expected to bring their own table knife. Small knives were constantly worn on the belt of every medieval person, regardless of social position. These "belt knives" (not to be confused with the larger daggers worn only by men) were the primary eating utensil of medieval society. To give your medieval banquet an air of authenticity, your guests could be encouraged to bring their own knives and spoons. Relate to them the above story and suggest that people decorate their spoons to see who can achieve the most elaborate results while still being able to eat with it. For belt knives, any standard hunting knife will suffice.

If there hasn't been any mention of medieval forks, it's because there weren't any. The fork did not become popular in most of Europe until nearly 1500, and not in England until nearly 1600. Although there were attempts to introduce forks into northern Europe from both Byzantium and Spain, where they had been widely popular for centuries, the northern Europeans thought the idea of putting an eating utensil into the mouth was a filthy habit practiced only by barbarians.

Those seated at the high table are constantly on display and their manners and courtliness are expected to set an example for the rest of the guests. CARA McCANDLESS

bowls, and towels moved from diner to diner, starting with the high table, allowing each guest to wash his or her hands. Additional washings between courses were not unusual, and a final washing at the end of the meal was absolutely mandatory. The water with which guests wash should be scented with fragrant oils (a bit of mint or vanilla extract will do nicely) and decorated with rose petals, violets, or fresh mint leaves.

Because of the importance of religion in medieval life, it was inevitable that a short service, or at least a prayer, would precede a special meal. If one of the guests at your recreated feast has come dressed as a monk or nun, having him or her read or recite the medieval Latin *Pater Noster* (the Lord's Prayer) would not be out of order. Below is the *Pater Noster* in twelfth-century church Latin. Latin is phonetic, so every letter is pronounced. For instance, each u in the word *tuum* is pronounced, making the word read "too-um." The prayer should properly be preceded by having the reader make the sign of the cross in the air, with the index finger and middle finger of the right hand extended upward. When making the sign of the cross, say, "Et nomine patre, et filis, et spitirtus sancti . . ." ("In the name of the Father and of the Son and of the Holy Spirit . . .")

Pater Noster, que es in calis,
sanctificúe nomen tuum.
Adveniáte regnum tuum.
Fiat volúntas tua, sicut in caelo et in terra.
Panem nostrum cottidiánum da nobis hódie.
Et dimítte nobis débita nostra, sicut et nos
  dimíttimus debitóribus nostrus.
Et ne nos indúcas in tentatiónem:
sed líbera nos a malo.
Amen.

After the opening ceremonies, the time has come to serve the first course, or remove. Those at the high table are always served first, and never served from behind—the risk of assassination was too high to ever allow a server to get behind a noble lord or lady. If necessary, serve other guests from behind, but not those at the high table; the servers for high table should stand in front of the table, where no one is seated, with their backs to the room, and serve the honored guests by extending the platters of food across the table. When the "nobles" have been served and the servers move away from the seats of honor, they must be certain not to turn their backs to the hosts; in the Middle Ages, this was cause for immediate dismissal from service, or at least a

Seating and Serving

At the appointed signal, usually a sign from a servant or a herald, the guests at a medieval feast all gathered at the tables and stood behind their seats. When those at the high table had seated themselves, they signaled the beginning of the feast by inviting their guests to "take their ease," at which time the guests seated themselves.

When everyone at your feast is seated, wine, beer, and other drinks should be brought to the table so the guests can refresh themselves. For best period effect, serve the drinks from large earthenware pitchers—which were known as flagons, jacks, or aquamanailes, depending on their size, shape, and contents—and serve all the drinks at room temperature. Of course you have the option of using ice, but during the Middle Ages ice was only available during the winter when it was too cold to want ice in your drinks.

Once the diners have their drinks, the next order of business is for guests to wash their hands. The most common and universal eating utensil used during the Middle Ages was the fingers, so hand washing was raised to a near-ritual level of importance. Pages with pitchers,

Both pages and gentlemen are expected to wait on the ladies. When new dishes are brought to the table, the pages will offer the first serving to the ladies. Once the plate has been placed on the table the gentlemen are expected to anticipate their ladies' needs and be ready to fulfill them. EUGENE SIREN

good beating. Once the high table has been served, food is served to the other tables. If the remainder of the guests are seated on only one side of the table, serving should be done from the open side of the table as it was at the high table, but if guests occupy both sides of the lower tables they should be served in the traditional way with platters of food being placed on the tables by reaching between two of the guests.

Those who brought the food into the hall were never allowed to serve it directly to the guests; they only placed the dishes on the table. Just as diners were paired to share utensils, they were also expected to assist each other in the serving process. Gentlemen serve their ladies, younger diners serve elder partners, and pages and squires serve their masters. Such courtesy extended to carving meat from a fowl or roast. Two fingers were used to hold the meat steady on the platter, known as a charger, while the belt knife was used to carve away pieces of meat, which were then served to the dining partner, after which the server served him or herself. The chargers can then be passed among the diners at will. At actual medieval feasts, those at the high table were rou-

tinely served better food and more courses than the rest of the guests, but this would probably be considered rude at a recreated feast.

Small Courtesies

With the medieval emphasis on social position and courtliness juxtaposed with the fact that so much food was consumed with the fingers, it is easy to see that great emphasis had to be placed on good manners. Medieval etiquette dictated that "diners not spit on, nor across, the table, nor belch or break wind while seated . . . or pick your nose nor finger nails while dining."

Although food was cut both on the serving platter and on the trencher with the belt knife, under no circumstances was it put into the mouth on the end of a knife blade. Food was cut into bite-sized pieces on the trencher and then eaten with the fingers. Men alone had the option of placing one end of a large piece of meat in the mouth, holding it firmly between the teeth, and cutting it free just in front of the lips with the knife. For your feast, it is a lot safer for guests to cut the food on their plates and put it in their mouths with their fingers than to risk someone inflicting severe damage to his lips.

The broth from soups was drunk from the bowl as though it were a cup, and the solids were eaten with the fingers or a spoon. Be certain that your soup bowls do not have sloping sides or wide lips. Small bowls with straight or inwardly curving sides are best or they will be almost impossible to drink out of.

Between Courses

Between courses, or removes, a short period of relaxation should take place to allow the food to settle and give diners time to excuse themselves briefly from the table, although during the Middle Ages it was considered rude to leave the table, and small containers were discreetly set beneath the table for taking care of nature's call. During these idle periods, the company can exchange toasts. Toasts to the host, hostess, honored guests, the occasion that brought the company together, and the cooks are all in order. The company may also

wish to sing songs or play some of the games designed for the dinner table (see chapters 13, 14, and 15).

At the end of the feast, just prior to the start of the evening's main entertainment, if any is scheduled, the steward, butler, or cook presents the pièce de résistance, the grand subtlety. Subtleties are fantastical desserts made of candies, pastries, and cake. The idea is to create an edible fantasy for the entertainment of the guests. (Complete directions for creating your own subtleties are given in chapter 11.)

An integral part of courtly manners and religious duty was the practice of almsgiving. Alms was a polite name given to food left on the table at the end of the meal. The leftovers, including the trencher breads, were collected in a large bowl by the almoner, who was also usually the household priest, monk, or chaplain, and distributed to the poor who gathered at the castle gate. While we no longer pass out leftovers to the less fortunate, you can explain the practice to the guests and have either the person who said the prayer, the head waiter or the host, pass a bowl among the guests to take up a collection to be given to a local charity. This should probably be done prior to serving the grand subtlety, so

With the right setting, costumes, tableware, and food, even a small, intimate gathering can provide the illusion of a grand feast.
EUGENE SIREN

Once they develop the necessary skills, youngsters can be made to feel part of a medieval feast by helping to serve their parents.
EUGENE SIREN

the company has not begun to break up before they have a chance to contribute. If you are holding a play (such as one from the selection found in chapter 14, "Mummers' Plays") at the end of the meal, this can also be a good time to collect money for charity; pleas for money are often included at the conclusions of the plays.

Kids And Medieval Manners

As much fun as most people have trying to eat medieval style, you may find youngsters reluctant to take part. Kids have enough trouble trying to remember ordinary din-ing etiquette and trying to adapt to new and strange rules can be more than they can deal with. We find that children often enjoy playing the part of peasants at me-dieval feasts so they don't have to dress as fancy or sit at the same tables as their parents, who appear determined to embarrass their offspring by dressing in funny clothes and acting abnormally. Let the youngsters sit at their own table, or on the floor, at the far end of the hall, and, as peasants, they will not be expected to have all the manners of the gentry, giving them a little latitude to be-have in ways not normally acceptable at a medieval din-ner. This extra freedom will help make the celebration much less stressful for everyone.

CHAPTER 10

Planning
The Medieval Feast

For a period of history not usually noted for its recordkeeping, descriptions of medieval feasts are surprisingly numerous and detailed. From precise shopping lists in royal account books to fanciful descriptions in such works as Chaucer's *Canterbury Tales*, food and feasts seem to have been almost as important to our medieval ancestors as were courtly love and glorious battles. The reason for this food obsession is simple: Feasts were powerful symbols of social position in a world where many, if not most, people lived on the verge of malnutrition or, if the harvest was bad, outright starvation.

The variety and elaborateness of the dishes served at medieval banquets were limited only by the wealth of the host and the creative talents of the kitchen staff. Generally, the higher in the social order a household was, the more the diet tended toward a preponderance of red meat and red wine. Vegetables were only served cooked and were usually considered beneath the palates of the nobility. This was particularly true among men of the warrior classes.

Although the clergy enjoyed a more balanced selection of foods than any other social class, priests warned people against eating salads, and many physicians advised their patients to avoid eating raw fruit. But then, like now, the well-intentioned advice of clergymen and doctors was generally ignored.

At major feasts, every effort was made to provide the broadest and most interesting variety of dishes that the season and the host's pocketbook would allow. Holiday menus, even in midsize manor houses and small castles, could be astonishing in both abundance and complexity. Four or five courses, called removes, each containing ten to sixteen dishes, were not uncommon. When Henry IV was crowned king of England in 1399, his coronation banquet must have been impressive, even for its time. The entire meal was dutifully recorded by Jean de Froissart in his *Chronicles*.

First Remove
Meat in pepper sauce, Viaund Ryal [a crustless cheese and ale quiche], Boar's head and tusks [mostly as a decoration for the high table], Grand Chare [a meat dish], Cygnets [baby swan], Fat Capon [a type of chicken], Pheasant, Heron, Lombardy Custard [custard with dried fruit], Sturgeon, a Subtlety [an elaborate dessert].

DICK CLARK

Second Remove

Venison in frumenty [a wheat custard], Jelly [a cold, jellied meat, probably jellied eel], Stuffed Boar, Peacocks [probably redressed in their own feathers before being served], Crane, Roast Venison, Coney [rabbit], Bittern [a marsh bird], Pullets [half-grown hens], Great Tarts [probably a meat and fruit pie], Fried Meat, Leech Custard [date paste with wine syrup], and a Subtlety [dessert].

Third Remove

Quince in comfit [quinces probably stewed in wine], Egrets, Curlews, Partridge, Pigeons, Quails, Snipes, Small Birds, Rabbits, Glazed meat-apples [meatballs], White meat leche [poultry stewed in wine], Glazed eggs [probably hard-boiled and painted with an edible glaze], Fritters [similar to doughnuts, sometimes made with ground meat in them], Doucettes [a custard and bone marrow pie], Pety perneux [quiche tarts with currants and dates], Eagle, Pottys of lylye [unknown], a Subtlety.

As seems obvious by this mind-boggling selection of food, medieval feasts were intended to last throughout the day, or over the course of several days, and during those periods when food was being served, guests were expected to take only small helpings of those foods that appealed to their particular palates, while declining the rest. The prodigious amounts of leftovers were then offered to the servants or given to the poor as a sign of the noble lord's charity.

Every good banquet—or in the case above, at the end of each remove—culminated with the presentation of a grand subtlety. Subtleties were extravagant desserts, shaped to look like something other than what they really were, such as dragons sculpted from marzipan, ships made from cake, forests of spun honey, or even four-and-twenty blackbirds slipped inside a baked pie shell and presented for the amusement of the guests. Ice sculptures, gingerbread houses, and scantily clad ladies jumping out of cakes are the nearest modern equivalent to the medieval subtlety.

It is obvious from the menu above that not all of the foods served at a medieval feast would appeal to modern appetites, nor are all the ingredients readily

Menu

FIRST REMOVE

Bread
select one: parsley bread
barley bread

Butter
herb butter and honey butter

Cheeses
a selection of cheeses

Soup
select one: squash in broth
pea soup
tredure soup

SECOND REMOVE

Presentational, for the high table only
select one: Boar's head
Cockentrice

Fish or poultry
select one: fruit and salmon pie
chicken with milk and honey
haddock with roses and almonds

Salad
select one: herbs with vegetables and flowers
compost
orange salad
(We suggest serving the orange salad with the
salmon pie, the compost with the chicken, and
the herbed vegetables with the haddock.)

Side dish
select one: lemon rice with almonds
chestnut torte
herb fritters
(We suggest serving the lemon rice with the salmon
pie, the fritters with the chicken, and the chestnut
torte with the haddock.)

Subtlety
select one: pears in compost
candied violets
cherry potage
(We suggest serving the pears with the salmon, the
candied violets with the chicken, and the cherry
pottage with the haddock.)

THIRD REMOVE

Meat
select one: pork in spicy syrup
pumpes with almond sauce
game pie

Vegetable
select one: cabbage with marrow
ember day tarts
turnips baked with cheese
(We suggest serving the cabbage with the pork,
the tarts with the pumpes, and the turnips with
the game pie.)

Side dish
select one: frumenty
mushroom tarts
applesauce with pears
(We suggest serving the tarts with the pork, the
frumenty with the pumpes, and the applesauce
with the game pie.)

FOURTH REMOVE

Grand subtlety
select one: live frog pie
gingerbread castle

EUGENE SIREN

EUGENE SIREN

obtainable at the local market. Therefore, the menu suggested on page 77 has been selected to suit today's palate and product lines. Our recreated medieval feast will be offered in three removes, followed by a grand subtlety, with a variety of options for each dish in each remove. Choose your combination of dishes in each remove carefully to achieve a balance in color, taste, and texture. Of course, if you find choosing from among the suggested dishes too limiting you can follow the lead of King Henry IV: prepare everything on the list and allow your guests to choose for themselves.

Because some of the combinations of ingredients and procedures may be unfamiliar to modern cooks, it is best to try all of the recipes before serving them to guests. Also review the ingredients list carefully; some, like bone marrow and a few of the spices, may require ordering ahead. If your local grocer can't supply some of the ingredients, check with gourmet food stores or specialty butcher shops or do an online search for hard-to-find items. Wherever possible, make the dishes ahead of time and reheat them just before serving. Bread, soup, and the

grand subtlety can all be made days ahead and frozen until the day of the feast. And remember, a good microwave oven can do just as much work as four assistant cooks in a steamy medieval kitchen could ever hope to accomplish.

When preparing the dishes for delivery to the table, remember that most medieval food was never portioned onto plates. Solid foods were served on great platters called chargers, while soups were served from tureens, and guests could take as much or as little as they pleased. But caution your guests that there will be a vast number of dishes served over the course of the meal so they should avoid taking too much of any one thing no matter how yummy it looks and smells.

If you want to let your guests know ahead of time what they are going to be eating, write out the menu on the menu border provided on page 191, have it color copied, and send it out with your invitation or information packet.

Full ingredient lists and complete cooking instructions for all of the dishes listed below are provided in the next chapter.

CHAPTER 11

Recipes

First Remove

Bread. As an alternative to baking your own bread, you can substitute store-bought bread. If you opt for bakery bread, we suggest buying round or oval-shaped loaves rather than those baked in loaf pans. For the high table, select a white bread like French or Italian; for those next in line, choose a light brown, whole-grain bread; and for those at the end of the hall, serve a pumpernickel or rye. Of course, you also have the option of serving two or three different types of bread at each table.

PARSLEY BREAD

2 pkgs. ($1/2$ oz.) dry yeast (active)

$13/4$ c. warm water

6 Tbsp. honey

8 c. (or more) all-purpose unbleached white flour (not self-rising)

6 eggs

1 egg yolk

$2/3$ c. chopped dates or softened currants

$12/3$ Tbsp. salt

6 Tbsp. oil

$11/2$ tsp. rosemary

$11/2$ tsp. basil

$2/3$ c. finely chopped fresh parsley

$11/2$ tsp. cinnamon

Sprinkle yeast in $1/2$ cup warm water and stir in the honey. Let stand for 5 minutes. Add remaining water to the yeast; beat in 3 cups of flour. Cover with damp cloth, place in a warm place, and allow to rise for 45 minutes, or until the dough doubles in size. Knead the mixture down.

Beat together 5 eggs and 1 egg yolk. Stir in the currants. Beat in the salt and oil. Mix combined ingredients into the dough.

Crush together the dried herbs and the fresh parsley. Stir in the cinnamon, and then add to the dough and beat well. If the parsley is fresh, the bread will take on a pale green color. Stir in the remaining flour a spoonful at a time, until the dough comes away from the sides of the bowl.

Place the dough onto a lightly floured work surface, and knead until the dough is smooth and elastic, about 10 to 12 minutes, adding the occasional sprinkle of flour if necessary.

Clean out the mixing bowl and grease the sides. Return the dough to the bowl, cover with a damp cloth, and set in a warm place until it doubles in size, about 1 hour. For a finer-textured bread, give the dough an additional kneading and rising.

Knead down the dough, and place it on a greased cookie sheet. Cover with a damp towel, and set in a warm place to rise until doubled in size, about a half hour.

During the final rise, preheat the oven to 425° F. When the bread has risen, beat the remaining egg white and brush it on the surface of the loaf. Bake the loaf for 45 to 50 minutes, or until the surface is nicely brown and the crust sounds solid when tapped. Remove from oven and cool. The bread can be made ahead of time and frozen for up to two months; allow a full day for frozen bread to thaw before serving. Each loaf serves 6 to 8. (Adapted from *Fabulous Feasts*)

BARLEY BREAD

1 lb. 3 oz. whole-meal flour

8 oz. barley flour (2^1/4 cups)

^{1}/2 tsp. salt

2 pkgs. (^{1}/2 oz.) dry yeast (active)

^{1}/3 c. dark brown ale

2 c. warm water

2 tsp. honey

Mix the dry ingredients in a bowl and set aside. Mix the yeast and a little brown ale until it becomes creamy, then add 1^1/2 cups water and the honey to the yeast mixture. Set aside for 5 minutes.

Stir the yeast mixture into the dry ingredients until it forms a firm dough, adding a little extra water if needed. Place the dough onto a lightly floured work surface, and knead until the dough is smooth and elastic, about 10 to 12 minutes, adding the occasional sprinkle of flour if necessary.

Clean out the mixing bowl and grease the sides. Return the dough to the bowl, cover with a damp cloth, and set in a warm place until it doubles in size, about 1 hour. For a finer-textured bread, give the dough an additional kneading and rising.

Divide the dough into two round loaves, place them on greased cookie sheets, cover with a damp towel, and set in a warm place to rise until doubled in size, about a half hour.

During the final rise, preheat the oven to 425 degrees F. Bake the loaf for 45 to 50 minutes, or until the surface is nicely brown and the crust sounds solid when tapped. Remove from oven and cool. Makes 2 loaves. Each loaf serves 6 to 8. The bread can be made ahead of time and frozen for up to two months; allow a full day for frozen bread to thaw before serving. (Adapted from various sources, as found in *The Medieval Cookbook*)

HONEY BUTTER

1 lb. butter

^{1}/3 c. honey

Allow the butter to come to room temperature. Blend the butter and honey together thoroughly. Shape into a mound or spoon into small cups. Chill before serving. Can be made ahead of time and stored in the refrigerator for up to two weeks. One batch serves 12 to 14.

HERB BUTTER

1 lb. butter

^{1}/4 c. dried herbs or ^{1}/2 c. finely chopped fresh herbs
(equal parts basil, thyme, and parsley)

Allow the butter to come to room temperature. Blend the butter and herbs together thoroughly. Shape into a mound or spoon into small cups. Chill before serving. If you are using dried herbs, allow at least 8 hours for the herbs to soften in the butter before serving. Can be made ahead of time and stored in the refrigerator for up to one week. One batch serves 12 to 14.

CHEESES

Serve a nice selection of both hard and soft cheeses. We suggest such soft cheeses as Brie and Camembert and such traditional hard cheeses as Cheddar and Stilton. If possible, place large wedges or entire small wheels of cheese on a large platter to allow guests to serve themselves. Can be prepared ahead, wrapped in plastic wrap or stored in airtight containers and kept in the refrigerator for up to one week.

SQUASH IN BROTH

2 lbs. pumpkin or butternut squash

4 to 6 c. beef, pork, vegetable, or chicken stock
(bouillon can be substituted)

3 to 4 onions, minced

1/2 lb. ground pork

1 Tbsp. brown sugar

2 Tbsp. minced parsley

1/2 tsp. salt

1/4 tsp. ginger

1/4 tsp. cinnamon

1/8 tsp. nutmeg

Skin, seed, and cube the squash; set aside. Brown the pork and onion, with salt, in a skillet. Drain off the fat. Place the stock in a soup kettle, and add pork and onions, squash, spices, brown sugar, and parsley. Simmer covered about 10 minutes, until squash is tender but still firm. Serve hot. Can be made ahead, frozen, and reheated. If you plan to freeze this soup, slightly undercook it so the squash will not become mushy when it is reheated. Serves 8 to 10. (Adapted from *Two Fifteenth-Century Cookery Books*, as translated in *To the King's Taste* and *The Forme of Cury*, as found in *Pleyn Delit*)

PEA SOUP

3 lbs. green peas, fresh or frozen

4 c. vegetable stock or bouillon

3 onions, peeled and minced

1 Tbsp. brown sugar

1/2 tsp. salt

1/2 tsp. saffron

fresh, coarsely ground pepper

Bring stock to a boil in large saucepan or kettle. Add remaining ingredients to the broth, cover, and simmer 15 minutes or until peas are quite soft. Puree the soup in a blender. Return the soup to the pot and reheat. Garnish with pepper. Serves 6 to 8. Can be made ahead of time, frozen, and reheated. (Adapted from *Curye on Inglysch*, as found in *The Medieval Cookbook* and *Two Fifteenth-Century Cookery Books*, as translated in *To the King's Taste*)

TREDURE SOUP

9 c. chicken broth

7 eggs

1 1/2 c. bread crumbs

1/4 c. sugar

4 Tbsp lemon juice

1/2 tsp. coriander

1/2 tsp. cinnamon

1/2 tsp. cardamom

1/8 tsp. saffron

Heat the chicken broth over medium heat. While broth is heating, beat together the eggs, spices, and sugar in a medium-sized bowl. Lower the heat under the chicken stock to low and slowly stir in the egg mixture. Next, stir in the lemon juice, and finally stir in the bread crumbs. Continue stirring gently until the bread crumbs dissolve, thickening the soup. Serves 6 to 8. Can be made ahead of time, frozen, and reheated. (Adapted from *Forme of Cury* as reprinted in *Curye on Inglish*)

Second Remove

BOAR'S HEAD

Arrange with your butcher to get the head of a pig from the slaughterhouse. When the head arrives, trim any loose flesh from around the base of the head. Preheat the oven to 350° F. Pry open the mouth and wedge in a firm, red apple. Place the head in a large baking pan and roast it, uncovered, until it turns golden brown. For an added sheen, brush the head several times with a beaten egg during the last half hour it is in the oven. Place on a platter, garnish with greens, and serve to the high table. Can be made ahead and frozen until the day before it is needed. Allow at least 24 hours of thawing before serving. Since this is not intended to be eaten there is no reason to reheat the boar's head before serving.

COCKENTRICE

The medieval world was fascinated by the possibility of fantastic creatures. In addition to dragons, unicorns, and other fabulous creatures, there were also legends of the cockentrice, a mythical being with the front half of one animal (usually a bird) and the rear half of another. The following recipe creates two such wonderful beasts and, unlike the boar's head, it can actually be eaten.

1 suckling pig (appx. 7 pounds in weight)

1 large roasting chicken, capon or small turkey (appx. 6–7 pounds in weight) Note: it is best if you can get a bird with the head still attached—this will make a more convincing creature when finished.

6 egg yolks

1/2 c. all-purpose flour

1/4 c. white wine

1 Tbsp. fresh parsley leaves chopped fine

1 Tbsp. all-purpose flour

1/4 tsp. powdered saffron

Preheat oven to 375° F. Place the suckling pig and chicken (or other poultry) in separate baking pans. The pig will take about 3 hours to roast but the chicken only 1 1/2 to 2 hours, so put the pig in the oven at least an hour before the fowl.

When both chicken and pig are cooked, allow them to cool long enough that you can handle them. Cut both the pig and bird in half at about the midpoint so you are left with a front and rear half of each. Using butcher's thread or carpet thread and a heavy needle, sew the front half of the pig onto the rear half of the bird and vice-versa. You now have two wonderfully impossible looking creatures. If your bird still has its head attached, you

ROBERT WHITEHOUSE

may want to pin it in place atop the bird's back with roasting skewers so it does not flop loosely onto the plate.

Turn the oven to 400° F. While the oven heats, lightly beat the egg yolks. Mix in the saffron and enough of the 1/2 cup of flour to make a thick liquid about the consistency of paint. Paint this on the snout, beak, claws, and hooves of the animals. Return the animals to the oven long enough for the paint to set, about 20 to 30 minutes.

While the gilded creatures are in the oven, mix the parsley, white wine, and the remaining 1 Tbsp. flour until the liquid turns uniformly green. If the green does not seem bright enough add a little green food coloring to brighten it up. When the cockentrices have been removed from the oven and allowed to cool slightly, paint them with the green glaze prior to serving. Two cockentrices serve 10 to 12 people. If you plan on freezing the cockentrices, do so after they have been sewn together but before the color has been added. After thawing, warm the creatures thoroughly in a 300° F oven for about 40 minutes before applying the paint. While painting the creatures, increase the oven heat to 400° F and continue as described above. (Adapted from *Fabulous Feasts*)

FRUIT AND SALMON PIE

1 lb. cooked salmon cut into 1-inch pieces, or a similar amount of canned salmon, flaked

1/2 lemon

1 c. sweet red wine

1 c. figs, chopped

1/2 c. dates, pitted and quartered

1/4 c. raisins

1/4 c. currants

1 1/2 Tbsp. pine nuts

1/2 tsp. ground cinnamon

1/4 tsp. pepper

1/4 tsp. ground cloves

1/4 tsp. salt

1/8 tsp. mace

1/8 tsp. ground ginger

1 unbaked 9-inch pastry shell and top crust

Glaze

2 Tbsp. milk

1/4 tsp. pulverized almonds

1/8 tsp. saffron

Preheat oven to 375° F. Place the salmon in a bowl, squeeze on the lemon, and stir to distribute evenly on the fish; set aside. Simmer the figs in wine for 10 minutes, or until soft. Remove figs and place in a mixing bowl. In the same wine, simmer the dates for three minutes, then remove dates to a separate bowl. To the figs, add all of the spices except the pine nuts. Add the raisins and currants and mix well. Spread this mixture in the bottom of the pie shell, and sprinkle the pine nuts across the mixture. Alternate the salmon and dates on the surface of the pie. Close the pie with a top crust and crimp the edges. Pierce the lid with a fork, and make a small vent hole in the center. Combine the ingredients for the glaze, and brush on the surface of the pie. Bake 35 to 40 minutes or until well browned. Each pie serves 6 to 8. Not suitable for freezer storage. (Adapted from *Fabulous Feasts*)

CHICKEN WITH MILK AND HONEY

3 to 4 lb. chicken, cut into pieces

3 c. milk

1/2 c. flour mixed with 1/2 tsp. salt and 1/8 tsp. pepper

1/3 c. honey

1/3 c. pine nuts

3 Tbsp. oil

3 Tbsp. minced parsley

2 Tbsp. chopped mint

1 tsp. vinegar

1/8 tsp. dried sage

1/2 tsp. savory

1/2 tsp. saffron

1/2 tsp. salt

1/4 tsp. pepper

Dredge the chicken pieces in the flour. Brown the chicken in oil in a large skillet until golden. Mix milk, honey, herbs, salt, and pepper in a bowl. Pour the mixture over the browned chicken. Stir to combine the mixture with the natural juices of the chicken. Cover and simmer about 30 minutes, or until the chicken is tender. Stir in the pine nuts just before serving. Serves 6. (Adapted from *Two Fifteenth Century Cookery Books*, as translated in *To the King's Taste*)

HADDOCK WITH ROSES AND ALMONDS

2 to 3 lb. haddock or similar white fish cut into
  1- x 2-inch cubes

1$\frac{1}{2}$ c. whole milk

$\frac{1}{2}$ c. red rose hips or red rose petals. *Note:* if you use
  rose petals make sure they have not been sprayed
  with insecticide. You may also substitute 4 Tbsp.
  of rose-hip powder.

$\frac{1}{2}$ c. all-purpose flour

$\frac{1}{2}$ c. roasted almonds

$\frac{1}{4}$ c. all-purpose flour

$\frac{1}{4}$ c. butter or $\frac{1}{4}$ c. cooking oil

3 Tbsp. white sugar

1 Tbsp. brown sugar

$\frac{1}{4}$ tsp. salt

$\frac{1}{8}$ tsp. saffron

Spice Powder

$\frac{1}{2}$ tsp. brown sugar

$\frac{1}{4}$ tsp. cinnamon

$\frac{1}{4}$ tsp. nutmeg

(stir the above together and set aside)

Coarsely grind or finely chop the roasted almonds. Slowly simmer the almonds with the brown sugar and milk, stirring constantly. When well simmered, pour off $\frac{1}{2}$ c. of the almond milk and set aside.

Mix the white sugar, salt, and saffron with $\frac{1}{4}$ cup of flour.

In a mortar or blender crush the rose hips or rose petals. Mix the crushed rose with $\frac{1}{2}$ c. almond milk for a bright pink fluid. If the fluid is not pink enough add a few drops of red food coloring. Add the rose milk to the remaining almond milk and place over a low heat. Do not allow to boil. Slowly add the spice powder (above) and keep the liquid warm while you cook the fish.

Dredge the portions of fish in the $\frac{1}{2}$ c. of flour, coating each piece thoroughly. Fry the fish in oil or butter until tender—about 5 to 7 minutes. Drain the fried fish and arrange on a platter. Pour the rose milk liquid over the fish and serve while hot. Serves 4 to 6. (Adapted from *Fabulous Feasts*)

HERBS WITH VEGETABLES

4 c. fresh chopped parsley

1 c. chopped watercress

1 c. leeks, finely chopped

$\frac{1}{2}$ c. fresh chopped sage

$\frac{1}{2}$ c. chopped onion

3 cloves garlic, finely chopped

6 sprigs mint, finely chopped

$\frac{1}{4}$ c. olive oil

$\frac{1}{2}$ c. wine vinegar

salt to taste

Mix the ingredients together in a bowl, and toss them with the oil. Serve and sprinkle with vinegar and salt. Can be made several hours beforehand. Serves 6. (Adapted from *Two Fifteenth Century Cookery Books*, as translated in *To the King's Taste*)

COMPOST

$\frac{1}{4}$ head (about 1 lb.) cabbage, coarsely shredded

4 parsnips, peeled and cubed

4 carrots, peeled and cubed

3 turnips, peeled and cubed

2 hard pears, peeled, cored, and cubed

2 c. muscatel (sweet white wine)

2 c. white wine vinegar

$\frac{1}{4}$ c. currants or raisins

6 Tbsp. sugar

4 Tbsp. honey

4 Tbsp. salt

$\frac{1}{2}$ tsp. cinnamon

$\frac{1}{2}$ tsp. whole cloves

$\frac{1}{2}$ tsp each coarsely crushed aniseed and mustard seed

$\frac{1}{4}$ tsp. saffron

$\frac{1}{4}$ tsp. pepper

$\frac{1}{4}$ tsp. allspice

Add salt to 2 quarts water and bring to a boil in a 6-quart kettle. Add the vegetables and return the water to boiling. Reduce heat to simmer, cover, and cook for 5 to 7 minutes. Add the pears and cook an additional 10 minutes, until all ingredients are tender but still firm. Drain, place the vegetables and pears in a large mixing bowl, and set aside.

In a saucepan, combine wine, vinegar, sugar, and honey. Heat until bubbly. Add saffron and cinnamon, stirring until well blended. Pour the syrup over the vegetables, stirring until they are well coated. Place the remaining spices in a square of lightweight cloth, and tie it shut with a piece of string. Drop the pickling spices into the compost mixture. Add currants or raisins and stir the mixture well. Place the kettle in the refrigerator overnight. Remove the spice bag before serving. Can be served cold or warmed. Can be made well ahead and canned or stored in the refrigerator in an airtight container for up to two weeks prior to serving. Serves 12 to 14. (Adapted from *Curye on Inglysch*, as found in *The Medieval Cookbook* and *Two Fifteenth Century Cookery Books*, as translated in *To the King's Taste*)

ORANGE SALAD

The amount of orange included in this salad may seem small, considering it is an orange salad, but remember that unless you lived in Italy or Spain, oranges were rare and expensive items and even a tiny hint of orange was considered a rare treat.

4 heads of lettuce (use endive, romaine, leaf, or any other lettuce except iceberg)

2 cucumbers (sliced)

2 oranges (quartered)

1 lemon (quartered)

1 c. mint leaves

2/3 c. chopped walnuts

2/3 c. raisins or chopped dates

1/2 c. currants

red wine vinegar

sugar

Finely shred the lettuce by hand. Place a layer of lettuce in the bottom of a salad bowl. On top of the lettuce place a layer each of cucumber slices, mint leaves, nuts, raisins or dates, and currants. Squeeze an orange quarter and a lemon section over the salad and sprinkle with red wine vinegar and sugar. Repeat the process until the bowl is full. The top layer should display mint leaves, nuts, raisins or dates, and currants. Serves 4 to 6. (Adapted from *Sallets, Humbles and Shrewsbury Cakes*)

LEMON RICE WITH ALMONDS

2 lemons

4 c. water

2 c. uncooked white rice

2 c. dry white wine

2 c. fresh (or frozen) peas

1 1/3 c. currants

1 1/3 c. coarsely ground almonds

2/3 c. honey

2 Tbsp. butter or margarine

1 tsp. cinnamon

1 tsp. salt

Grate the zest from the lemons. Squeeze the lemons, reserving the juice and pulp. Discard the membranes and seeds. In a large saucepan, bring the water, rice, salt, cinnamon, butter, and lemon juice, pulp, and zest to a boil. Reduce to a simmer, cover, and cook until the water has been absorbed, about 15 minutes. Stir once during the simmering process. Add the peas to the rice for the last 7 minutes.

While the rice is cooking, simmer the almonds and currants in the wine for 7 or 8 minutes. When the rice is cooked, remove from the fire, and fluff with a fork, adding the wined almonds and currants as you stir. Dribble the honey on the surface of the dish just before serving. Serves 6. (Adapted from *Fabulous Feasts*)

CHESTNUT TORTE

1 c. coarsely ground or finely chopped chestnuts

2 eggs

2 bulb ends of scallions or spring onions, finely chopped

3/4 c. shredded mild cheese

1/2 c. heavy cream

2 Tbsp. melted butter

1/8 tsp. salt

Dash of white pepper

8-inch pie shell baked for 5 minutes at 400° F.

Preheat oven to 375° F. In a medium-sized bowl, lightly beat the eggs. Add the cream, scallions, and seasonings. In another bowl combine the chestnuts, cheese, and melted butter. Fold the chestnut/cheese mixture into the eggs and cream. Pour the mixture into the partially baked pie shell, place back in the oven, and bake for an additional 25 to 30 minutes or until the top of the pie and edges of the crust are golden brown. Serve warm or cold. Serves 6 to 8. If this is being served cold it can be baked, wrapped airtight in plastic wrap and stored in the refrigerator for up to two days before serving. Allow to come to room temperature for 3–4 hours before serving. (Adapted from *The Delectable Past*)

HERB FRITTERS

4 c. flour

3 c. lukewarm water

1 c. finely chopped fresh herbs, such as parsley, savory, sage, marjoram, chives, rosemary

2 pkgs. (1/2 oz.) dry yeast (active)

1 tsp. salt

frying oil

honey to garnish

Dissolve the yeast in 1 cup warm water. In a bowl, mix together the flour, herbs, and salt. Stir the yeast water into the mixture, and add enough water to make a smooth, thick batter. Stir until free of lumps. Cover the batter and let rise for 1 hour. Heat the frying oil. Drop the batter into the hot oil a large spoonful at a time. If you are not deep-frying the fritters, turn them once. Serve and garnish with honey. Makes 20 to 24 golf-ball-size fritters. (Adapted from *The Forme of Cury*, as found in *Pleyn Delit*)

PEARS IN COMPOST

6 large, ripe, sweet pears

3 c. malmsey (heavy, sweet red wine)

3/4 c. sliced dates

3 Tbsp. sugar

1 1/2 Tbsp. cinnamon

1/4 tsp. ginger

dash salt

Peel, pare, and quarter the pears. Parboil them until they begin to become tender; do not let them get soft. Drain. In a large saucepan, heat wine, cinnamon, ginger, and sugar. When the mixture is hot, add the dates, pears, and salt. Bring to a boil, lower heat to a simmer, and cook for 8 to 10 minutes. Allow to cool slightly before serving. Serves 6. Can be made a day ahead, covered with plastic wrap, and reheated. If you are reheating this dish, slightly undercook it so the pears do not become mushy when it is reheated. (Adapted from *Two Fifteenth-Century Cookery Books*, as found in *Recipes for Æthelmearc 12th Night*)

CANDIED VIOLETS

100–150 freshly cut violets with stems attached

1 large egg white

16 oz. superfine sugar

Note: If you do not have access to superfine sugar, granulated sugar can be broken down by placing it in a blender and blending on high speed until it is broken down into fine granules.

1/3 c. water

In a small bowl, combine the egg white and water and beat until the mixture begins to produce bubbles.

Pour a few ounces of the sugar into a shallow bowl or pie pan.

Dip one violet at a time into the egg mixture, gently shake off excess egg, and gently dip the violet into the sugar. To make sure the back of the violet is covered with sugar, spoon a small amount of sugar over the violet. Gently shake off excess sugar; holding the violet over a cookie sheet, gently snip off the stem. The candied violets can be dried at room temperature for several days or dried in an oven set at 150° F for 2 to 3 hours. To ensure the violets only dry and do not bake, leave the oven door ajar. Serves 8 to 10. When thoroughly dried the violets can be stored in an airtight container for 4 to 5 months. (Contributed by Brenda Rich)

CHERRY POTAGE

2 lbs. ripe red cherries

1¹/2 c. light, sweet red wine

3/4 c. sugar

4 Tbsp. unsalted butter

2¹/2 c. soft white bread crumbs

1/8 tsp. salt

Wash the cherries and remove the stems and pits. Puree with a mixer or in a blender, along with 10 tablespoons of the wine and half of the sugar. If necessary, add a little more wine. In a saucepan, melt the butter and add the fruit puree, bread crumbs, remaining wine, sugar, and salt. Simmer slowly, stirring constantly, until the mixture is very thick. Pour into a serving bowl, cover, and place in the refrigerator to cool. Just before serving, you may decorate the edge of the bowl with small, fresh flowers or spoonfuls of thick whipped cream. Serves 8. Can be made one or two days ahead, covered with plastic wrap, and stored in the refrigerator. Do not add the flowers or whipped cream while the dish is being stored. (Adapted from *Curye on Inglysch*, as found in *The Medieval Cookbook*)

Third Remove

PORK IN SPICY SYRUP

4-lb. pork roast with bone

2 c. malmsey or other heavy, sweet red wine

4 Tbsp. cooking oil or butter

1/2 c. currants

3/4 c. vinegar

3/4 c. sugar

2 onions, finely chopped

3/4 tsp. coarsely ground black pepper

1 tsp. ground caraway seeds

1 clove garlic, crushed (optional)

1 c. chicken stock or bouillon

Remove the skin from the pork roast, and prick the fat layer all over with a sharp knife or large serving fork. Sauté the onions and currants in the oil. When the onions have become transparent, remove from the heat and add the wine, vinegar, sugar, spices, garlic, stock, and seasonings. Place the pork roast in a covered stew pot and spoon the marinade over it. Cover the pot and place it in the refrigerator for 6 to 8 hours, turning the roast and spooning the marinade over it every 1¹/2 to 2 hours.

Preheat oven to 425° F. Cover the roast, place it in the oven, and bake it for 30 to 35 minutes per pound. During the last hour of cooking, remove the lid, spoon additional marinade over the roast, and return it to the oven uncovered to allow the roast to brown. Remove the roast to a serving platter and pour the remaining marinade into a pitcher to use as gravy. Serves 8. (Adapted from *Curye on Inglysch*, as found in *The Medieval Cookbook*)

PUMPES IN ALMOND SAUCE

2 lb. ground pork

3/4 c. currants, diced

3/4 tsp. salt

1/2 tsp. cloves

1/2 tsp. mace

Preheat oven to 375° F. Mix all ingredients until seasoning and currants are thoroughly mixed with the pork. Mold the meat into small meatballs about 1¹/2 to 2 inches in diameter. Place in a shallow baking dish and bake for 35 to 40 minutes or until cooked. Place the meatballs on a platter and gently pour the almond sauce (page 88) over top. Finish with a light sprinkling of sugar and mace.

ALMOND SAUCE

1^1/$_2$ c. whole milk

^{1}/$_2$ c. roasted almonds

1 Tbsp. brown sugar

4 Tbsp. all-purpose flour

^{1}/$_8$ tsp. salt

Coarsely grind or finely chop the roasted almonds. Slowly simmer the almonds with the brown sugar and milk, stirring constantly. Do not allow the milk to boil. When the milk has simmered for 6 or 7 minutes gently sift the flour and salt into the almond milk and stir the mixture until it thickens slightly to a gravy-like consistency. Serves 5 to 6. The pumpes may be made ahead of time and frozen in an airtight container. Allow to thaw for 24 hours before reheating. When reheating the pumpes, be sure to cover them with aluminum foil to prevent them from drying out. The almond sauce is not suitable for freezer or refrigerator storage. (Adapted from *Two Fifteenth-Century Cookery Books*)

GAME PIES

1 to 1^1/$_2$ lb. rabbit, jointed

1 to 1^1/$_2$ lb. chicken pieces

1 lb. bacon

4 ribs celery, finely chopped

4 onions, finely chopped

^{1}/$_4$ c. butter

8 egg yolks

2 egg whites, beaten until liquid

^{1}/$_2$ c. honey

^{1}/$_2$ c. applesauce

1 c. chicken stock or bouillon

2 Tbsp. chopped parsley

2 Tbsp. cornstarch

1 tsp. salt

^{1}/$_2$ tsp. pepper

^{1}/$_2$ tsp. grated nutmeg

^{1}/$_2$ tsp. cinnamon

2 9-inch pastry shells and top crusts

Parboil the chicken and rabbit for 15 minutes. Remove from water and allow to cool. Cut into 1-inch-square chunks, removing the skin from the chicken. Fry the bacon, and cut into ^{1}/$_2$-inch-long strips. Sauté the onions and celery in the bacon drippings until the onion is soft (add a little oil if necessary). Drain the onion and celery, and mix with the cubed meat.

Add the cornstarch to the chicken stock, seal tightly in a jar, and shake vigorously until well mixed. Place in a small saucepan and heat until slightly thickened, stirring constantly. Mix in the remaining ingredients, except the egg white; set aside.

Preheat oven to 425° F. Brush the inside of the pastry crust with some of the egg white. Place the meat, onion, and celery mixture into the crusts.

Pour the stock mixture over the meat and vegetables, crimp the lid securely into place, coat with remaining egg white, and pierce the lid with a knife in four or five places.

Bake for 15 to 20 minutes at 425°, then reduce the heat to 350° and bake for 40 to 45 minutes longer, until the crust is golden brown. May be served hot or cold. Makes 2 pies. Each pie serves 6 to 8. Can be made 1 or 2 days ahead, covered with plastic wrap, and stored in the refrigerator. If the game pies are to be reheated, cover them loosely with a tent of aluminum foil to keep the crust at the right consistency. (Adapted from *Two Fifteenth-Century Cookery Books*, as found in *The Medieval Cookbook*, and from *Warwickshire Country Recipes*)

CABBAGE WITH MARROW

8 marrow bones split lengthwise

5 c. beef broth or bouillon

1 medium head of cabbage

2 c. bread crumbs

2 tsp. salt

^{1}/$_2$ tsp. saffron

^{1}/$_2$ tsp. thyme

Boil marrow bones in beef broth until the marrow is soft, about 30 minutes. Skim the grease from the broth, remove the bones, and set the broth aside. Remove the marrow from the bones, coarsely chop the marrow, and set it aside. Wash the cabbage and chop coarsely. Add the cabbage to the broth, bring to a boil, and simmer for

10 minutes. Combine the spices with the bread crumbs and the marrow, and add to the cabbage. Stir together and simmer gently for 5 to 10 minutes. Serve in a large bowl with plenty of the broth. Serves 6 to 8. May be made 1 or 2 days ahead of time, covered with plastic wrap, and stored in the refrigerator. If this dish is to be stored and reheated, stir the ingredients together as stated above, but do not simmer for 5 to 10 minutes until immediately prior to serving to avoid the cabbage turning mushy. (Adapted from *Two Fifteenth-Century Cookery Books*, as translated in *Take a Thousand Eggs or More, Vol. I*, and *Fabulous Feasts*)

EMBER DAY TARTS

3 large or 4 medium onions, chopped

2 bunches parsley, chopped

4 eggs

1/2 c. cottage cheese

1/4 c. sage leaves, chopped

3 Tbsp. bread crumbs

3 Tbsp. currants

2 Tbsp. melted butter

1/2 tsp. salt

1/4 tsp. sugar

1/8 tsp. powdered cloves

1/8 tsp. powdered mace

1/8 tsp. saffron

1 9-inch pie shell (no top crust)

Preheat oven to 375° F. Parboil the onions and herbs, drain well, and add to melted butter. Blend the cottage cheese with the eggs. Add the cheese and egg mixture to the onions and herbs. Add remaining ingredients and pour into the pie shell. Bake for about 45 minutes, or until a toothpick inserted into the custard comes out clean and the crust is golden brown. Makes 2 tarts. Each tart serves 6 to 8. May be covered with plastic wrap and stored in the refrigerator for up to 2 days. Cover loosely with aluminum foil while reheating in a 325° F oven for 20 to 25 minutes. (Adapted from *Forme of Curye*, as found in *Pleyn Delit*)

TURNIPS BAKED WITH CHEESE

2 lb. white turnips

10 to 12 oz. Swiss cheese

1/4 lb. butter, melted

1/2 tsp. salt

1/4 tsp. allspice

1/4 tsp. nutmeg

1/4 tsp. pepper

Peel and boil the turnips until they are nearly tender. Remove from the water and allow them to cool. Mix the spices in a small dish and set aside. Shred or finely dice the cheese and then slice the turnips into thin slices. In a well greased or buttered casserole dish, alternate layers of turnips and cheese, ending with a final layer of cheese on the top. On top of each layer of turnips sprinkle a fine coating of the spice mixture before adding a layer of cheese. Bake in a 350° F oven long enough for the cheese to melt. Serves 6 to 8. (Adapted from *Pleyn Delit*)

FRUMENTY

2 c. No. 2 (medium–coarse) bulgur wheat or pearl barley

3 c. chicken broth

2 c. whole milk

3 egg yolks (lightly beaten)

1/4 tsp. saffron

In a large saucepan combine the broth and milk and bring the mixture to a boil, stirring constantly. Add the bulgur wheat or pearl barely to the liquid, along with the saffron; reduce heat to a simmer, cover the pan, and allow to cook for 30 to 50 minutes; barley will take longer than bulgur wheat to absorb the liquid. When the liquid is absorbed the grain is cooked. Stir in the beaten egg yolks and allow to simmer for a few minutes, stirring constantly. Serve hot. Serves 6 to 8. (Adapted from *Pleyn Delit*)

MUSHROOM TARTS

1 1/2 lb. button mushrooms, sliced thin

1/2 c. grated mild cheddar cheese

1/4 c. butter

2 Tbsp. olive oil

1/2 tsp. salt

1/2 tsp. ginger

1/4 tsp. pepper

1 9-inch pastry shell with top crust

Preheat oven to 375° F. Sauté the mushrooms in the butter; drain. Into the mushrooms, mix the oil, cheese, and spices. Pour the mixture into the pie shell, add the top crust, and crimp into place. Pierce with a knife in four or five places. Bake for 40 minutes, until pastry is golden brown. Makes 2 tarts. Each tart serves 6 to 8. (Adapted from *Le Menagier de Paris*, as found in *Recipes for Æthelmearc 12th Night*)

APPLESAUCE WITH PEARS

4 cooking apples

3 hard pears

1 Tbsp. cornstarch

1/2 c. sweet white wine

1/4 c. raisins

1/4 c. shredded almonds

1/4 c. dates, finely chopped

3 Tbsp. honey

2 Tbsp. sugar

1/4 tsp. cinnamon

1/8 tsp. ginger

Peel and core the apples, and parboil until they are soft. Remove from the stove and mash finely. Put the white wine and cornstarch in a jar with a tight-fitting lid and shake vigorously till blended. Add the wine mixture to the pulverized apples, add the remaining ingredients except the pears, and cook till the mixture begins to thicken. Remove from heat. Peel and core the pears, and parboil until they begin to soften. When they have cooled, cut into 1/2-inch squares. Mix the pears with the applesauce. May be reheated before serving or served chilled. Serves 6 to 8. Can be made several days ahead, covered with plastic wrap, and refrigerated before being served chilled or reheated. (Adapted from *Two Fifteenth-Century Cookery Books*, as found in *Take a Thousand Eggs or More, Vol. II*)

Fourth Remove

LIVE FROG PIE

Serves no one but is a lot of fun. This is a variation on the four-and-twenty-blackbird pie mentioned in the nursery rhyme—but in this version candy has been substituted for the family canary or, as was popular during the middle ages, a cluster of leaping amphibians.

DICK CLARK

top and bottom pie crusts to fit pan as described below
dried beans or peas, enough to fill the pie shell
2 egg yolks
1/2 tsp. cinnamon
3 to 4 lbs. brightly wrapped candy, cheap jewelry, and
  other "treasures" as necessary to fill the pie

Preheat oven to 425° F. Make a pie shell and lid to fit the largest baking dish you can find; even a turkey roasting pan isn't too big. When rolling out the dough, make it 50 percent thicker than normal. It's best to use a springform pan, so you can get the crust out of the pan without breaking it, or a cheap, disposable aluminum pan that you can cut through.

Lightly grease the pie pan and dust with flour. Press the bottom crust into the pan. Fill the pie shell with the dried beans, apply the top crust, and crimp the crusts together. Glaze with the egg yolk mixed with cinnamon. Bake 40 to 45 minutes, or until golden brown.

When the pie is cool, carefully remove it from the pan. Cut a hole in the bottom of the crust and allow the beans to spill out. With a disposable aluminum pan, the crust does not have to be removed from the pan; simply cut a hole right through the bottom of the pan. Carefully insert the candy and treasures into the pie shell. Slide the finished shell onto a large, decorative platter or silver tray.

Present the pie to the high table, without letting on that it's not a real pie, and allow a special guest to cut it. After the truth is revealed, pass the subtlety around for everyone to help themselves to the candy and treasures. May be covered with plastic wrap and kept in a cool place for 3 or 4 days or frozen and allowed to thaw for 24 hours prior to serving. If the pie is being frozen it is probably best to leave the beans inside and only extract them and insert the surprises after it has been thawed.

GINGERBREAD CASTLE

The gingerbread house, still popular at the holidays, can easily be converted into a medieval subtlety. We have redesigned the gingerbread house into a castle. Although there was a medieval gingerbread, our recipe is not authentic. Medieval gingerbread is too soft to be shaped without falling apart. Even this modern gingerbread recipe is a little crumbly, so be careful when assembling the castle.

2 c. molasses
1 1/2 c. shortening
12 Tbsp. packed brown sugar
7 1/2 c. whole wheat flour
3 tsp. salt
1 1/2 tsp. baking soda
1 1/2 tsp. ground cinnamon
1 1/2 tsp. ground ginger
1 1/2 tsp. ground cloves
1/2 tsp. ground nutmeg
1/2 tsp. ground allspice

Mix molasses, shortening, and brown sugar. Mix in remaining ingredients. Cover and refrigerate at least 4 hours.

Preheat oven to 375° F. Roll out dough on a floured board to about 3/8 inch thick. Cut 4 pieces 12 1/2 inches x 5 1/2 inches and 4 pieces 10 inches x 4 inches. Wrap the 12 1/2 x 5 1/2 pieces around four Quaker Oatmeal or Mother's Oats containers (or four 7-inch-long sections of mailing tube, 4 inches in diameter), covered with greaseproof, nonstick baking paper. The remaining pieces should be placed on cookie sheets. Bake until light brown, about 10 to 12 minutes.

Carefully remove the wall sections from their trays, and if possible pull the tubes out of the towers. Assemble the towers and walls on a large tray or piece of plywood covered with aluminum foil, carefully trimming the ends of the wall sections to fit snugly against the sides of the tower. The walls can be glued to the tower with cake frosting to form a square castle with four corner towers.

Let the frosting set for an hour or so. Then, around the outside of the castle walls, make a moat of blue frosting or aluminum foil, and provide access over it with a drawbridge made of Popsicle sticks or paper. Inside the castle and beyond the moat, use green icing sprinkled with shredded coconut dyed green or green sugar to create grass. Miniature plastic knights in armor, spraypainted silver, will add life to the scene. A plastic Tyrannosaurus rex dinosaur with paper wings glued to its back makes a suitable dragon. (Adapted from *Betty Crocker's Cookbook*, 1981.)

CHAPTER 12

Drinks and Thirst Slakers

Medieval people enjoyed a wide variety of beverages with and between meals, most of which were alcohol-based. Understandably, what people drank was largely dependent on their social and economic position. The rich drank wine. The middle class drank wine when they could afford it, but along with the poor, they subsisted largely on ale (beer without hops) and strong cider. But by and large, no matter what their position in society, everyone drank. We have included a few recipes for nonalcoholic drinks to add variety and sobriety to our largely alcoholic medieval cellar of thirst slakers.

Wines

In the medieval world, having the financial resources to buy, serve, and give wine as a gift was an immensely important symbol of social status. In Northern Europe, where wines had to be imported from warmer, southerly countries, a few casks of wine stashed in the cellar showed that you were rich and therefore important. Even in wine-rich countries like Spain and Italy, people

who made wine had to sell virtually their entire vintage just to make enough money to stay alive. Even as late as England's Tudor Age (1485–1603) wine was an important indicator of social status. In 1528, England's Henry VIII purchased a mixed shipment of 152 kegs of red, white, and claret wines from neighboring France. Considering the size of Henry's royal household, this was not an excessive amount, but the shipment cost the royal treasury a staggering 844 English pounds sterling. When we compare this with the average worker's annual wage of around 2 pounds, the cost of wine in the medieval marketplace becomes clear.

Medieval wines were generally heavier and much sweeter than most modern palates are accustomed to. The additional sugar content in medieval wines allowed them to last longer before turning to vinegar. Spoilage was always a problem with wines in an age before the invention of bottling. During the Middle Ages, French and German wines had a life expectancy of about one year. Consequently, most northern wines began to be consumed after being allowed to age for only three or four months. The stronger, darker wines of Spain and Italy lasted longer but were much more expensive in Northern Europe due to the additional distance they had to be transported to reach their intended market.

We have tried to select a representative variety of modern wines that come close to the qualities of medieval wine without having a great amount of dregs or being too heavy for the modern palate.

Malmsey is a very sweet, dark brown wine that is still readily available in any good wine shop at a reasonable price.

Muscatel is a very sweet white wine. The best muscatel today comes from Spain and is often labeled as Moscatel. Because it is no longer a major mover on the world market, muscatel is quite inexpensive.

The red wines from the Burgundy region of France were highly prized during the Middle Ages, and many are still highly regarded today. Many different kinds of burgundies are now being produced; many of them are made outside of France and are quite reasonably priced. Two of the more authentic are Pinot Noir and Gamay. Any domestic burgundy-type wine, as long as it is not dry, will be a reasonable facsimile of medieval burgundy.

During the Middle Ages, specialty wines were made from a staggering variety of fruits, flowers, berries, herbs, and vegetables. These included violet, lavender, sage, mint, strawberry, gooseberry, raisin, rhubarb, rose, currant, damson, birch, turnip, parsnip, blackberry, cherry, elderberry, wormwood, rose, apple, and balm. Some of these are still made by small wineries and can be found in specialty wine shops and through a wide variety of online wine merchants.

If your feast is being run on a tight budget, consider picking up a readily available Kosher wine such as Manechewitz. Because they are quite sweet, full-bodied, and come in a variety of grape and berry flavors, they are good substitutes for medieval wines. Whatever wines you choose to use at your medieval feast, be careful that they are not sparkling or bubbly wines, as these are a relatively recent development.

Beer and Ale

All medieval beer was actually ale; that is to say that it was made without hops, which gives modern beer its distinctive bitter aftertaste. During the Middle Ages beer and ale were far more than a refreshing drink. In a world where carbohydrates and calories were often lacking in the average diet, beer and ale provided both, along with a healthy dose of vitamin B and at least a small amount of vitamin C, both of which helped prevent bone-destroying diseases such as rickets. Three pints of ale a day were enough to provide a child between the ages of 10 and 13 with one-quarter of the necessary daily calories to keep them strong and healthy.

Ale was consumed by people of all ages and among all stations in medieval society. Medieval ale, and later beer, were both consumed in quantities as great as modern people consume water, although much of it was fairly low in alcohol content and was referred to as "small ale." Water, on the other hand, was avoided because, while the concept of bacteria did not yet exist, people knew that drinking water could make you ill. Considering that slaughterhouses, toilets, and tanneries all dumped their waste into the same rivers in which people washed and which, in turn, fed into public wells, the belief that water was dangerous was more than justified.

The importance of ale and beer to medieval life cannot be overstressed. Workmen's wages were partially paid in ale, and those whose jobs provided them with more than they and their families could consume sold the excess to their neighbors who did not have enough. As late as the Elizabethan Age, Good Queen Bess herself (reigned 1558–1603) regularly drank two gallons of strong ale every day, and she lived to the ripe old age of seventy.

Because medieval ale was poured directly from a wooden cask, it was also still, which means that it did not have the foamy head most of us are accustomed to seeing on a good beer. Like medieval wines, much of the ale of the time was heavy with sediment. All medieval ale had far more body than modern lagers and would therefore be more full-bodied than most American drinkers are used to. The closest that you are likely to come to medieval ale, without making it yourself, is modern English bitter or stout. Some of the brands most commonly found in the United States include McEwan's, Samuel Smith, Theakston, Speckled Hen, John Smith's, and Guinness. Alternatively, American brewers like Sam Adams make a few varieties of relatively bitter beer, and Pennsylvania's Yuengling Lager compares favorably with the best English bitter. There are also a wide variety of craft-brewery bitter beers that are occasionally available direct from the brewing company as well as in stores and online.

For a more medieval look and taste to your ale, try to purchase a small keg. Allow the keg to rest after transporting it, and serve it with a tap rather than a pump. To use a tap, the keg will have to be placed on its side rather than in the usual vertical position. This will allow the beer to be nearly still—that is, it will not have a head on it. We also recommend that it not be chilled before serving. All medieval ale was served at room temperature, because there was no way of keeping it cold, and even modern English bitter is designed to taste best if only slightly cool, not cold, the way American beer is usually served.

Ale was also used as the primary ingredient in a variety of drinks that were served both hot and cold. One of the most popular ale-based drinks was the rich, tasty winter drink known as Lambswool; this beverage was originally intended for the celebration of the Feast of the Epiphany, which took place on January 6, and was known during the middle ages as Twelfth Night. Twelfth Night celebrated the end of the Christmas holiday season and the arrival of the Wise Men who presented gifts to the infant Jesus. During the Middle Ages, gifts were exchanged on Twelfth Night rather than on Christmas Day.

Accompanying the gift-giving was general celebration and feasting. Toasts were exchanged over steaming mugs of Lambswool. The odd name of this drink was derived from the foamy head that floats on its surface.

LAMBSWOOL

8 apples, peeled, cored and coarsely chopped

2 quarts beer

1 c. sugar

1/4 c. butter

1 tsp. nutmeg

1 tsp. ginger

1 tsp. cinnamon

Combine all ingredients in a large kettle and bring to a simmer over low heat. Allow to simmer for 2 hours, stirring occasionally during the first half hour to make sure all of the sugar is dissolved. After 2 hours remove the apples, mash them into a fine pulp and return them to the kettle. Allow to cook for another 1/2 hour. Serve hot. Serves 6 to 8. (Adapted from *A Continual Feast*)

EUGENE SIREN

Mead

Often thought of as a Viking drink, mead was popular, although rare and therefore expensive, throughout the British Isles and Northern Europe during the Middle Ages. Mead is actually a type of wine brewed with honey, the only natural sweetener commonly available in the Middle Ages. Some specialty wine shops still have mead, or can get it, and it can be had from a variety of online wine stores. But mead may be too expensive, and too strong, for general consumption, especially among a company of hearty drinkers. We suggest serving it as an appetizer or an aperitif.

Cider

When Americans think of cider they envision the sweet, slightly pulpy juice of freshly pressed apples that appears in stores in autumn. In days gone by, Americans often turned sweet cider into an alcoholic drink, known as hard cider, by adding sugar to aid in fermentation and setting the cider keg in a cool place for several months until it had stopped working. It is this fermented drink that was known as cider during the Middle Ages; even today in England, Scotland, and Wales, the word cider implies a strong, alcoholic drink still available in most pubs. Fermented like wine, English cider is strongly alcoholic, and at 6 to 8 percent alcohol packs far more wallop than its mellow taste hints at.

The Normans supposedly introduced cider to England shortly after their conquest of 1066, and although it has remained popular there ever since, commercially manufactured hard cider has, until recently, been almost impossible to find in the United States. Now, however, there are several brands being exported to America, and a few domestic brands are coming onto the market. These should be available through a good beer distributor or in a wine store; a variety of ciders are also available online. Note that not all states have approved the sale of cider. When buying cider, choose a sweet, rather than a dry cider, to make it more authentically medieval.

Punches and Mixed Drinks

Since wines could not be aged during the Middle Ages, they started to turn sour over the course of eight to ten months. Consequently, people doctored old wine to make it more palatable. Some of these concoctions became very popular, particularly around the holiday season. The wassail drink that is sung about in the Christmas carol is most likely similar to the one described below. These recipes can be increased to make as much of the drink as desired.

HIPPOCRAS

8 oz. sugar (1 1/8 cups)

2 quarts red wine

1 Tbsp. ground cinnamon

3/4 Tbsp. ground ginger

1 tsp. ground cloves

1 tsp. grated nutmeg

1 tsp. coarsely ground black pepper

Mix spices together and set aside. Warm the wine until it begins to steam, add sugar, and stir until it is dissolved. Add the spices and allow to simmer for 10 minutes. Pour the mixture through a mesh cloth to remove the dregs of spice (an old piece of sheet or a pillowcase will do). Pour into a punch bowl and serve hot.

Wassail

Wassail was a traditional winter drink used for toasting during the holiday period. The drink is served hot, in a wooden bowl that is passed from person to person. As the bowl is passed, the person passing the bowl declares "wass hail" ("good health" in Anglo-Saxon). The recipient responds with "drink hail" ("drink to health"). Customarily, the passing of the bowl is accompanied by a kiss. The recipient takes a drink and passes the bowl to the next person, repeating the salute, and so on through the company. Our wassail recipe makes enough for about eight people.

WASSAIL

1$^1/_2$ quarts sweet hard cider (you may substitute half medium dry white wine and half American sweet cider if you can't find English cider)

1 cooking apple

$^1/_4$ c. butter

2 sticks cinnamon, broken into $^1/_2$-inch-long pieces

2 Tbsp. sugar

1 Tbsp. ground cinnamon

1 tsp. whole cloves

2 chopped nutmegs or $^1/_2$ tsp. ground nutmeg

Heat the cider in a saucepan till it simmers. Place the spices in a small square of cloth, and tie it shut to form a bag. Drop the spice bag into the simmering cider.

Slice the apple into $^1/_4$-inch-thick rings, removing the core but leaving the skin in place. Mix the sugar and ground cinnamon in a small bowl. Coat the apple rings with the sugar-and-cinnamon mixture. Melt the butter in a skillet; when it is hot, sauté the coated apple rings until they begin to soften. Remove the spice bag from the cider, and pour the cider into a wooden bowl. Pour the sautéed apples, along with the butter, into the hot cider and serve while steaming hot.

CAUDLE

6 egg yolks

3 quarts ale (if using modern beer, let it go flat before making the caudle)

8 Tbsp. sugar

$^1/_2$ tsp. saffron

$^1/_2$ tsp. salt

Beat the egg yolks until they begin to thicken. In a saucepan, warm the ale, sugar, saffron, and salt until lukewarm. Remove a cup or so of the ale, and stir it into the beaten egg yolks. Add the egg and ale mixture to the rest of the lukewarm ale. Raise the heat slightly, stirring the mixture continually until it begins to thicken. Do not allow the mixture to boil, or it will become lumpy. The finished caudle is best served immediately.

Berry Drinks and Cordials

All manner of berries were used to make fresh, tasty summertime drinks. Berry juice, water, and honey or sugar were combined to suit personal tastes. At other times, berry juice was added to white wines to make them lighter and fresher, and to add variety to an otherwise limited drink selection.

Sometime around the twelfth century, brandy (then known as brandiwine) became the first strong liquor and was produced by distilling wine. Cordials were invented as a way to make this strong drink more palatable to the delicate palate of ladies and refined gentlemen who were more accustomed to wine than hard liquor. Within two hundred years of their invention, cordials had gained nearly universal popularity among the noble classes and rich merchants who had the financial wherewithal to afford brandy.

CORDIAL

2 quarts of berry juice (see below) *Note:* This juice can be extracted from blackberries, raspberries, elderberries, strawberries, gooseberries, or any other variety of juicy berry.

2 pounds of sugar

1 pint brandy

$^1/_4$ oz. finely ground or rubbed cloves

$^1/_4$ oz. allspice

To extract the juice from the berries, place 8 quarts of fresh berries in a large kettle along with a few inches of water and boil over a medium heat until the berries become soft and pulpy. To assist in softening the berries, stir frequently and mash the berries with a wooden spoon or potato masher. Strain the juice from the berries by pouring the berry pulp through a cloth bag—an old pillowcase is ideal for this purpose. Suspend the bag over a large bowl or tub and slowly squeeze and twist the bag until all of the juice has been extracted. Eight quarts of berries should yield about 2 quarts of juice.

Return the juice to the original cooking pot, add the cloves and allspice, and reheat at medium heat. When the liquid begins to simmer, add the sugar and stir gently until the sugar is completely dissolved; allow to simmer gently for about 20 minutes, stirring occasionally. Remove from the heat and allow to cool slightly. Strain the liquid through a clean cloth and bottle while still warm and add the brandy immediately, mixing thoroughly by stirring briskly. The liquid may be bottled in wine bottles or in mason-type canning jars. Make sure the containers have been boiled and sterilized before filling with cordial. The cordial will keep indefinitely and mellows with age. If you prefer not to bottle the cordial, pour the cooled liquid into a pitcher or jar, cover, and place in the refrigerator. It will keep for up to three weeks. Makes about 3 quarts. (Adapted from a recipe in the *British Museum Cookbook*)

Brewing Your Own

If you are dedicated to putting on a truly authentic medieval feast and have some extra time on your hands, you might want to consider brewing your own ale, mead, cider, or wine. The most accessible and most authentically medieval recipe book for brewing is unquestionably *A Sip through Time*, by Cindy Renfrow. You should be able to order it through your local bookstore by giving them the ISBN number 0-9628598-3-4 or online via Amazon.com or a similar site by searching for title or author.

Nonalcoholic Drinks

There were a few nonalcoholic drinks popularly consumed during the Middle Ages. They were not overly common, because people depended on the natural sugars in wines, meads, and ales as an important part of their diet, but they did exist and it is important to include them here.

Milk
Milk, then as now, was served to children, but it was often cut with "small," or weak, ale. No medieval adult would have ever contemplated drinking milk.

Tea
Tea was made by immersing a two or three stalks of fresh mint in a mug of boiling water. If you want to make a batch of mint tea, use about two dozen 10- to 12-inch-long sprigs of mint to a gallon of water to make a properly tasty tea. The tea was often sweetened with honey, although sugar could just as easily be used. If you have access to a mint patch and want to preserve mint for use

in the winter, harvest the stalks when they reach 10 to 12 inches in length, place in the sun until thoroughly dry, and seal in ziplock plastic bags. The dried mint will last for two or three years.

Oxymel
A tasty and long-lasting alternative to plain mint tea is oxymel. Also known as Sekanjabin, this flavorful mint-vinegar drink was undoubtedly imported to Europe from the Middle East during the Crusades, when European knights and soldiers learned to appreciate the amazingly tasty, thirst-quenching qualities of this ancient recipe. Following the recipe below, you can make enough oxymel syrup to make 24 glasses of this novel and tasty drink.

OXYMEL

5 pounds sugar

2 1/2 qt. water

2 c. wine vinegar

25 to 30 sprigs of fresh mint 7 to 8 inches in length (*Note:* If the mint has begun to flower, remove the flowers)

Combine water and sugar in a large saucepan or kettle and heat until the liquid reaches a slow boil and the sugar is completely dissolved. Add mint, lower the heat to a simmer, cover, and continue to simmer for about 20 minutes. Dredge out the mint and add vinegar. Boil uncovered for an additional 15 minutes. Allow to cool. The oxymel may be poured into a pitcher or jar, covered, and stored in the refrigerator for up to three weeks. The liquid may be bottled in wine bottles or in Mason-type canning jars. Make sure the containers have been boiled and sterilized before filling. This recipe yields about one gallon of concentrated oxymel syrup.

To serve oxymel, mix about one part concentrate with three parts water and serve with a sprig of mint. You will probably want to add ice, but ice in the summer was unknown in the Middle Ages. (Adapted from *An Anonymous Andalusian Cookbook of the Thirteenth Century*)

CHAPTER 13

Games, Sports, and Pastimes

In the Middle Ages, diversions such as music, plays, or other skilled entertainments were only available when a troupe of professional players was performing them in your area. In a world where television, radio, Mp3 players, PlayStation, and Wii did not yet exist, and even literacy was a rarity, simple games had far greater appeal than they do today. If you can get the guests at your medieval celebration into the spirit of things, both you and they will be amazed at how much fun playing these games can be.

Most of the games are presented here in their original form; some of them will be familiar, some will be new, and some will even seem pretty strange by our standards. Others are adaptations of medieval sports that are simply not practical in the modern world; in some instances, the facilities for carrying them out do not exist in the venues available to most of us, and in others, we simply feel that the premium on life is higher than it was eight centuries ago and that the games are too dangerous to be played in their original forms, if at all.

Because some of these games must be played outdoors, and many of them require some preparation, the games you decide to offer at your event will depend on the time of year, the number of people in attendance, and the space and facilities available to you. If you plan to host a Christmas or New Year celebration it might be worth considering appointing a Lord of Misrule to help you plan and organize the day's games, activities and diversions (see chapters 4 and 5 on medieval Christmas and New Year celebrations). For other large events, consider appointing someone to be the Master or Mistress of Revels to help relieve you, the host, of some of the burden. It will fall to the Master of Revels to ensure everyone is kept busy and involved in the activities, and that all the games start at the appointed time and place. This will allow you, the host, to enjoy some of the party yourself and still have time to take care of the many unavoidable details and last-minute emergencies that will inevitably demand your attention. Whichever pastimes you select, we hope you'll be amazed at the appeal still present in these simple pleasures.

Indoor Games—Tabletop

Chess
Although the rules for chess are far too extensive to provide here, they can easily be found in modern game books or on the Internet in a very similar form to the rules used in the Middle Ages. Chess dates back at least to ancient Egypt. The game as we know it was played by the Vikings in the tenth century, and written rules for the game survive from the late thirteenth century. Cer-

tainly chess was one of the most popular board games of the Middle Ages.

Predominantly played by the noble classes, chess was used as a training ground for the strategy, tactics, and thought processes that were employed in besieging castles during times of war. The relative number of pieces accurately reflects the makeup of medieval armies and society at large. There are only one king and queen, supported by a small number of clergymen (bishops), mounted warriors (knights), and castles (rooks). The bulk of the army is then made up of conscripted peasant forces (pawns), who are thrown at the enemy before the elite troops are committed to battle.

Chess, in roughly its modern form, appeared in Southern Europe around the end of the fifteenth century and quickly became popular across the continent. The powers of certain pieces were increased and new rules were added such as castling, the two-square pawn advance, and en passant. The most important changes turned the fers into the most powerful piece of all, the queen, and the alfil into the far-ranging bishop by granting it the power of diagonal movement.

The history of the individual chess pieces is also a story worth telling. Until the mid-nineteenth century, pieces tended to come in one of two extremes. The rich would display very ornate, expensive decorative pieces with delicately crafted representations of kings, queens, and other figures, which were often top-heavy and impractical, while everyone else mostly used roughly hewn wooden lumps with only the height of the pieces to distinguish between them.

In the Middle Ages, chess was sometimes played by monarchs with living chessmen in a court paved to represent a chessboard. If you attempt this at your medieval event, an interesting variant on "living chess" has the participant "chessmen" or "pieces" engage in some sort of combat for conquest of a given square. This is to say that if a knight wants to move onto a square occupied by a bishop, the knight does not automatically gain possession of the square, but rather, the knight and the bishop must fight for it. Depending on the participants and attendees at your event, this combat can take many forms, from fully armored battles with sword and shield to simple rounds of rock-paper-scissors, a roll of dice, or cutting for the higher card from a deck. Whatever combat system is to be employed, the chess master (judge) should ensure that various chessmen have certain combat advantages suitable to their rank (a queen should be four times as powerful as a pawn, and so on). Remember to make the contest as safe as rea-

Chess was played by both sexes; among men it was considered the best learning tool for developing battle tactics. EUGENE SIREN

sonably possible; it is, after all, only a game being played for fun. If your combat is going to be of a physical nature, remember that an overused piece will grow tired as the game progresses. It might be worth having substitute champions to take on some of the burden of combat.

Bear in mind that live chess will also alter gameplay, as one player may actually lose his or her piece in an attempt to capture a square, rather than automatically acquiring the territory. If you attempt this type of live chess, we suggest that simple tabards be constructed indicating what pieces the different players represent so it is easier for spectators to understand the course of the game.

Draughts

Essentially identical to the modern game of checkers, draughts was common during the Middle Ages. The game, however, seems to have been far more popular on the continent than it was in England, where it did not take hold until the late sixteenth or early seventeenth century.

It is thought that the earliest form of checkers was a game discovered in an archeological dig at the ancient city of Ur in modern-day Iraq. Carbon dating indicates that this game was played around 3000 B.C. However,

Both chess and draughts (checkers) were enjoyed by men and women. Chess was reserved for the upper classes but draughts was played at all levels of society.

the game used a slightly different board and a different number of pieces, and no one is quite certain of the exact rules.

In ancient Egypt, 3,400 years ago, a similar game called alquerque, which had a five-by-five-inch board, was a common and highly popular game. It was a game of such popularity that it was played all over the western world for thousands of years.

Around 1100, a Frenchman got the idea of playing the game on a chessboard. This meant expanding the number of pieces to twelve on a side. It was then called "Fierges" or "Ferses." It was soon found that making jumps mandatory made the game more challenging. The French called this version *jeu force*. The older version was considered more of a social game for women and was called *le jeu plaisant de dames*.

Books were written on the game in Spain as early as the mid 1500s and in England a mathematician name William Payne wrote his own treatise on draughts in 1756. Once the rules for checkers as we know it were set, the game was exported to England and America. In Great Britain the game was called "draughts" and in America it became "checkers."

Fox and Geese

The medieval game of Fox and Geese is a descendant of the ancient game of tafl, which was played on a cross-shaped board. A fragment of a gaming board of 18 by 18 squares, found in Wimose, Denmark, and dated prior to A.D. 400 is the first evidence of tafl, which also regularly appears in the early Icelandic sagas. The first probable reference to an ancestor of the game is that of hala-tafl ("the fox game"), which is mentioned in the Icelandic saga *Grettis*, which is believed to have been written after A.D. 1300 by a priest living in the north of the country. Tafl apparently developed into hnefatafl (which lit-

erally translates as "king's table"), which was played by the Saxons as well as other Northern Europeans on the same size board and which is mentioned in Icelandic sagas from the beginning of the fourteenth century. The Vikings took the game with them on their forages, which helped it to spread far and wide.

A Latin text written during the reign of the British Anglo-Saxon King Athelstan (A.D. 925–40) describes the Saxon form of hnefatafl, which was played in England at the time. It was most popular in Northern Europe during the dark ages until chess started to take over during the eleventh century; the last references to it being played are in Wales in 1587 and in Lapland in 1723. It isn't known exactly how either tafl or hnefatafl were played, but rules for its descendant, called "fox and geese" or "fox and hounds," can readily be found online. A notable reference to the game can be found in the accounts of the royal household of Edward IV of England (A.D. 1461–83) for the purchase of two foxes and twenty-six hounds of silver over gilt.

Games in the tafl family are distinguished by the unequal size of the opposing forces. The objective is usually for the force of fewer numbers to take all the members of the larger forces, whose aim is generally to stop them doing so.

Evidence shows that the game of tablut, described by a traveler called Linnaeus during his trip to Finland in 1732, is likely to have been very similar to hnefatafl. It is played on a nine-by-nine-inch board with one player controlling a king who starts in the center and who is supported by eight blond Swedes, versus the other player who moves sixteen dark Muscovites (Russians). All pieces move in straight lines forward, backward, or sideways, like a rook in chess. One player's objective is to move the king to one of the corners, while the other's is to take the king.

Tables

Very much like the modern game of backgammon, tables was enjoyed by both sexes—anyone who could afford, or was skilled enough to make, a board and marker pieces could play. In fact, one did not even need an actual board to play tables, as the board could be scratched out in dirt or sand and played with small stones. A pair of dice could also be hastily carved or painted and then abandoned or stashed in a player's home or carried in a purse. The rules of tables are similar enough to those of backgammon that the use of a backgammon board at a recreated medieval feast would not be at all out of place.

We know that a variation of this game was popular in the Anglo-Saxon culture by the early seventh century and, during the Crusades, the game once again gained influence as an activity for soldiers and traders under the name "tables" or "tabula." The Church attempted on a few occasions to outlaw the playing of tables due to the gambling that frequently accompanied its play, but the prohibition was always unsuccessful. The last attempt to outlaw what we now know as backgammon came in the early part of the sixteenth century by Henry VIII's notorious Cardinal Woolsey. The cardinal ordered all boards burned and declared the game "the devil's folly," but English craftsmen quickly came up with the idea to fold the boards in half in a book-type arrangement to creatively disguise the board. This folded design is the standard way in which backgammon sets are still made to this day.

Known to medieval culture as "bac gamen" or "back game," the game eventually became known as "backgammon" in the mid 1600s, and the name remains unchanged to this day. The actual term "backgammon" is derived from the Welsh and translates as "wee battle." The famous writer and gamesman Edmund Hoyle published a work on backgammon in the mid 1700s in which he outlined the rules and documented the game's history. As backgammon found its way to America with

Like chess, the game of tables (backgammon) was a game of skill enjoyed by people of all social classes and both sexes.

the new settlers, it became a solid a fixture in early American homes alongside chess and other popular board games of the day.

Playing Cards and Card Games

Playing cards undoubtedly originated in China before A.D. 1200 and were subsequently introduced to Europe in the thirteenth century. It is generally accepted that in the late 1300s, the Mamelukes of Egypt introduced their particular style of playing cards to Europe. A pack of Mameluke cards consisted of four "suits" of thirteen cards each, just like modern playing cards. The suits were polo sticks (the forerunner of today's clubs), coins (diamonds), swords (spades), and cups (hearts), and each had ten numbered cards and three court cards—King, Vice-King, and Second Vice-King.

The earliest references to cards in Europe are mostly in France (the records of King Charles VI show that he bought three packs in 1392). These original cards featured four suits (cups, swords, coins, and batons) of fourteen cards each; there was an additional card in each suit—the "Cavalier" or "Mounted Valet," the lowest of the four court cards. The suits mentioned above are still favored in most Latin countries such as Spain and Italy. Additionally, there were also twenty-two extra "high cards" that did not belong in any suit and had designs that may have come from ancient Egyptian mysticism. Each card was individually painted, a unique work of art in its own right, and affordable only by the very rich. These were what we would think of as tarot cards although they were used for playing games as well as for divining the future.

The Europeans adopted a wide range of different suits and styles according to local tastes and the preference of the person drawing the cards. Sometimes decks had five suits instead of four. Playing cards with suits of spades, clubs, diamonds, and hearts first appeared in France in the late 1400s. The French have a story to account for this. These suits were supposedly invented by a famous knight, Etienne Vignoles, who went by the pseudonym of LaHaire. He designed his cards to accompany his newly invented card game of piquet. The individuality of the earlier cards and the cavalier card were eliminated in these packs of thirty-six cards. Piquet is supposed to be a game of knights and chivalry and so the suits were created accordingly: *coeurs* (hearts) denotes the Church; *carreaux* (diamonds) denotes the arrowheads that are symbolic of the peasant class from which archers were drawn; *trefles* (clubs) or clover signifies the farmers; and *piques* (spades or swords) denotes the sword and lance, symbols of the knightly class. As such, the suits in a standard deck of playing cards were a symbolic representation of medieval society—very much like the playing pieces on a chessboard. Another, not too different, theory claims that the four suits represent the four classes of person at the time—military, peasantry, clergy, and aristocracy.

The English adopted this system from France, and the first English reference to cards occurred in 1462, when they were banned by parliamentary decree. Presumably, if they were banned they must have already been widely popular for some time. Later on, the spread of the English and French empires resulted in this style of cards being disseminated all over the world, and made it the most popular design almost everywhere.

Cribbage

Cribbage is one of the most enduring classic card games. Cribbage is actually no more than an extension of the well-established Tudor game of noddy (also spelled noddie). Noddy means fool or dimwit, and in *The Compleat Gamester*, published by Charles Cotton in 1674, the upturned jack in "cribbidge" is referred to as "Knave Noddy." Cribbage is exactly like noddy in all respects, including the use of the special scoreboard, except that noddy does not use a crib.

Although there is some mystery as to the origin of the modern game, it is generally credited to Englishman Sir John Suckling (1609–42), who purportedly also changed its name from noddy to cribbage. Sir John—a poet, playwright, master bowler and gambler, and notorious womanizer—was only eighteen when his father passed away, leaving him a considerable estate. After receiving the inheritance, he spent most of his fortune traveling, carousing, and, of course, gambling.

At the age of twenty-one, Suckling was knighted by King Charles I, but the king quickly regretted the decision. Suckling left the court and became involved in a string of military adventures. In 1632, Suckling quickly came back into King Charles's good graces and after that he pretty much filled his time gambling and womanizing for the rest of the decade, during which time he is said to have invented cribbage. Sucking died in 1642, but cribbage remains one of the most popular card games in the English-speaking world.

Primiera

The sixteenth-century Italian card game of primiera is sometimes referred to as the "ancestor of poker." The game was very fashionable and had equivalents in other countries at the time, such as prime in France and primera in Spain. In England, a game called primero is known to have been played by Elizabeth I. Primiera is unlikely to have been a direct ancestor of poker but it was probably the first game that featured the idea of betting based on different combinations of cards ranked in particular orders. Primiera was played with a forty-card deck (a standard fifty-two-card deck without the eights, nines, and tens). Two cards were dealt, following by betting and then two more cards for a four-card hand. The different combinations, ranked from lowest to highest, are interesting and provide enough information for your guests to play the game:

1. Numerus: two or three cards of the same suit
2. Primiera (Prime): four cards, one of each suit
3. Supremus: the highest-value three-flush (ace, six, and seven)
4. Fluxus (Flush): four cards of the same suit
5. Chorus (Quartet): four cards of the same value

Poker as we play it today appeared in New Orleans at least as early as 1829.

Basset

The game of basset migrated from Italy to France in the fifteenth century. This game requires the services of a "house," or banker, and was played as follows. Each player is dealt thirteen cards face up, and after each round is dealt, players can place bets. The banker then alternately deals cards, face up, onto two piles of cards in front of him. To start, the banker deals a single card and wins the stakes placed on any cards of the same value. The banker then deals cards in pairs—for the first card of the pair dealt, the banker wins the stakes placed on any cards of the same value but for the second card of the pair, the player wins the value of the stake if the bets match. The dealer continues dealing pairs until all stakes are gone.

This is fairly simple stuff but the sting in the tail is that when a player wins a stake, he has the option of leaving the winnings on the table—if he wins a second time, the bank must pay seven times the value of the stake. This can be repeated with the winnings rising to fifteen, thirty, and sixty times the value of the initial stake.

To the greedy, the temptation to leave the stake there must have been pressing but, as is clear after a moment's thought, the chances of winning at those high odds diminish drastically—and therein lies the loss of many a fortune and the source of the appalling reputation that basset came to have. Richard Seymour, in his improved version of *The Compleat Gamester* in 1725, said "the dimmest eye may easily see, without a pair of spectacles, how much and considerable the design of this court game is in the favour of the Banker."

Basset eventually was replaced by its descendent faro, which was similar but added some new rules, such as the ability to bet for or against a particular rank appearing and half the stake going to the bank when the bank dealt a pair of cards of the same value. By the nineteenth century, faro was the world's most popular casino game but by 1900 it had been replaced by blackjack and baccarat.

Piquet

The game of piquet, or cent (the game's English name in the Middle Ages), has been played since at least the end of the fifteenth century. It is mentioned in literary and scholarly works as diverse as Rabelais's *Gargantua et Pantagruel* (1534) and Girolamo Cardano's *Liber de Ludo Aleae* (Book on Games of Chance, 1564), a treatise on probability theory. One of the earliest instruction manuals for a card game was *Le Royal Ieu du Piquet Plaisant et recreatif* (The Royal and Delightful Game of Piquet).

Piquet is a game for two players, using thirty-six cards (sixes through aces). The dealer is called the younger; the other player is called the elder. Each hand of piquet is divided into five parts: blanks and discards; ruffs; sequences; sets; and tricks.

The parts are played in that order. Scores are counted in each part of the hand; the first player to reach one hundred points is the winner. This may take several hands. We recommend using either a score sheet or a cribbage board to keep score.

The players cut for the deal of each hand, and the holder of the low card is the dealer. Each player is dealt twelve cards in increments of two to four cards. The remaining stock of twelve cards is placed between the players.

Blanks and discards: Each player may discard up to eight cards, and draw as many from the stock. The elder discards and draws first, followed by the younger. Both players must discard and draw at least one card. A hand with no face cards is called a blank. If the elder has a blank, he may declare the blank along with the number of cards he is going to discard. After declaring, he shows the hand to the other player. The younger discards and draws new cards if he does not have a blank. Then the elder discards, draws, and receives ten points for the blank. However, if the younger also has a blank, he declares and shows it. No points are awarded, and play continues as though neither had a blank. The younger may not declare a blank independently.

Ruffs: A ruff is the total number of points in a single suit. Aces are worth eleven points, face cards are worth ten, and number cards are worth their number. The elder declares the number of points in his largest ruff. If the younger has an equal or higher ruff, he declares these points, too. If the ruffs are equal, then neither player scores. If not, the owner of the high ruff receives points for all cards in the hand: one point is scored for each ten points in the hand. One to four points are rounded down, and five to nine points are rounded up. The loser may ask to see the winning ruff.

Sequences: A sequence is a group of three or more consecutive cards in a suit. The elder declares the number of cards in her longest sequence. If the younger has an equal or higher sequence, she declares it. If the sequence sizes are equal, both declare the largest card in the sequence. If both sequences are of equal length with the same high card, then neither player scores. Otherwise, the owner of either the longest sequence or the sequence containing the largest card receives points for all sequences in the hand. Sets of three and four score three and four points, respectively. Sets of five and up score ten points plus the number of cards in the sequence. The loser may ask to see the winning sequence.

Sets: A set is three or more tens, jacks, queens, kings, or aces. The elder declares the number of cards in her largest set. If the younger has an equal or higher set, she declares it. If the set sizes are equal, the set card is declared. The owner of the largest set, or, if both have sets of equal size, the set with the highest card receives points for all sets in the hand. Sets of three score thirteen points and sets of four score fourteen points. The loser may ask to see the winning set.

Tricks: Tricks are played like no-trump tricks in bridge. For the first trick, the elder leads a card, and the younger tries to play another, higher card in the same trick. The highest card in the "lead" suit wins the trick. The winner of the trick leads for the next trick, and so on until all cards are played. Tricks are scored both during and after play. Players receive one point for leading a ten or larger, one point for winning a trick, two points for winning the last trick with a ten or higher, and one point for winning the last trick with a nine or lower. After all tricks are played, the players count the number of tricks they have won. A player with seven through eleven tricks receives ten points; a player with all twelve tricks (known as a capet) receives sixty points.

Repique and Pique: Players may also score points for preventing the other player from scoring during a hand. A player gets a pique if he reaches thirty points during the tricks and the other player still has no points. A pique is worth thirty points. A player gets a repique if he reaches thirty points during the first four parts of the hand and the other player has no points. A repique is worth sixty points. Players must declare that they have a pique or repique, or else they do not receive any points for them.

Merrills

Also called nine man's morris, merrills is extremely old, with variations of it certainly dating to the early Middle Ages. The illustration below shows the layout of the board. Markers can be small stones, coins, or any other small movable object. Most surviving boards tend to be about eight inches square, but the size varies from four-and-a-half to ten inches square. (For instructions on how to reproduce an actual medieval merrills board, see *Medieval Furniture: Plans and Instructions for Authentic Reproductions,* by Daniel Diehl and Mark Donnelly, Stackpole Books, 1999.)

Rules for merrills, according to the Ryedale Folk Museum, North Yorkshire County, England, organizers of the annual World Championship Merrills Tournament:

The board has three concentric squares linked through the center point of each side. This provides twenty-four intersection points arranged in sixteen lines of three, on which the pieces are placed.

The play is divided into three stages but the object throughout is to get three pieces in a line; this is called a "mill." When a player forms a mill, one of the oppo-

nent's pieces is removed from the board. The game is won by the player who reduces an opponent's pieces to only two or blocks them from moving in the middle stage of the game.

The opening stage of the game begins with an empty board. Each player, in turn, places one piece on any vacant point on the board, until both players have played all nine pieces. If either player makes a mill, that player removes any one of the opponent's pieces, providing that piece is not itself part of a mill. Throughout the game, pieces forming a mill are safe from capture. Once a piece is removed from the board it takes no further part in the game.

Note: Moves and lines of three can only be made along the horizontal and vertical lines on the board, never across the diagonals, where no lines are marked.

The middle stage of the game commences when all the pieces are on the board except those lost in play. Play continues alternately; each player moves one piece to any empty adjacent point, again with the object of forming a mill and removing one of the opponent's pieces. Once a mill has been formed it can be "opened" by moving one piece from the line if there is an empty point next to it and "closed" by returning it in a subsequent move. Each time a mill is closed another of the opponent's pieces is removed. In a "running mill," opening one mill will close another, so that a piece is removed every turn. If a player is unable to move any pieces because there are no empty points next to any pieces, then that player has lost the game. Otherwise, play continues until one player is reduced to three pieces.

The final stage allows the player with only three pieces to move any one piece each turn to any empty point on the board, regardless of its position in relation to his men. The other player must continue to move to adjacent empty points, unless both players are reduced to three pieces. The game ends when one player is down to two pieces and so can no longer form a mill.

Shove-board

Now popular on cruise ships and at retirement communities in Florida, what we know as the outdoor game of shuffleboard began as the English indoor game of shove-board, which was later known as shovel-board. Popular in Tudor times, shovel-board was played by the English upper classes on enormous narrow tables as long as 30 feet (9 meters). Players shoved metal weights down the tables, attempting to get them as near as possible to the other end of the table without falling off. Presumably, the game is a formalized version of a pastime played on

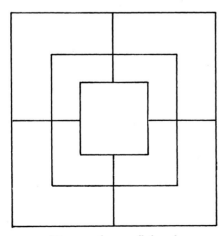

Diagram of a merrills board.

the long dining tables of the upper classes after dinner. One of the earliest references is from the English royal privy expenses of 1532, which show that Henry VIII lost £9 to Lord William at shovel-board. Meanwhile, the subjects of Fat Harry were banned from playing this and most other recreational games—an even earlier reference, purportedly from 1522, says "None of the society shall play at the game called Shoffe boorde or Slypgrote." Slightly earlier, during the fifteenth century, a scaled-down, indoor version of shovel-board called shove groat or slype groat (a groat being a coin worth four silver pennies) was played in English inns and taverns. A descendant of shove groat has been played in English pubs ever since, evolving into the game known today as shove ha'penny.

Port and King

At some point in the 1400s, people began to play a version of ground billiards indoors on a table. It's likely that the green cloth was supposed to represent the lawn from which the game had been stolen. Other outdoor sports have been adapted for the indoors from time to time in Northern Europe—games including quoits, old English skittles, and western skittles and bowls. Presumably players did not want to stop playing when the long nights, the incessant English rains, or the inclement weather of winter set in. The earliest evidence found for the existence of billiards played on a table was in 1470 in an inventory of items purchased by King Louis XI of France. Listed were "billiard balls and billiard table for pleasure and amusement." The earliest mentions of billiards in England were in 1588 when billiard tables were in the possession of the Duke of Norfolk and the Earl of Leicester, as well as Mary, Queen of Scots, who had a billiard table in her prison cell while she awaited execution.

Table billiards was apparently an extremely popular game throughout France by 1630 and in England it was described in various publications during the 1600s and 1700s, including the first description of the rules by Charles Cotton in *The Compleat Gamester*, published in 1674. Although variations in the rules probably existed and there were definitely variations in dimensions and type of equipment, the most popular version was a two-player game played on a table with six pockets. The pockets, called "hazards," were simply there as obstacles to be avoided—like bunkers in golf. The table featured a croquet-like hoop at one end called the "port" and an upright skittle at the other called the "king." Each player was allocated a single ball that was pushed,

rather than struck, with a "mace" (a stick with a special wooden end). The idea was to be the first through the port in the correct direction (if your ball went in the wrong direction, you were deemed a "fornicator") and then back to touch the king without knocking either port or king over. A point was scored for each time you did this, and the winner was the first to a number of points—typically five.

If this sounds simple, remember that the tables were rarely flat, the balls often not completely round, and the maces were hardly implements of precision. Additionally, like croquet, the game was as much about knocking the opponent's ball into penalties as about furthering one's own cause. Pushing the opponent's ball into a hazard, sending it the wrong way through the port, or causing it to knock over the king was as beneficial as passing through the port yourself.

It is also important for the modern player to bear in mind that the concept of a "break," something we take for granted, was completely unknown at this time. Players simply took turns striking their balls. This fundamental difference made older versions of the game entirely different from the game we know as billiards.

Bingo

The game of bingo originated in Italy in the sixteenth century. The game was derived from the Italian lottery known as Lo Giuoco del Lotto d'Italia. The Italian National Lottery was started in 1530 during the unification of Italy and is still operating to this very day. Today the lottery is an indispensable part of the Italian government's budget, contributing at least seventy-five million dollars a year. It quickly became very popular in France, where by 1789 it had morphed into the game of lotto. Although bingo has had many variations over the centuries, some of which did not even use a card with numbers, medieval bingo was similar enough in concept that the modern game can be played as an understandable and reasonable variation on the original game.

Dice Games

In the Middle Ages, dice came in a variety of interesting shapes, not just the cubes we are familiar with. The spots, or pips, however, were arranged in the same way they are today. In addition to the games described here, dice are a good tool for selecting the order of contestants in many other games, such as blindman's buff, climbing the greased pole, and selecting the rotation in archery competitions.

Playing dice in any form is almost universally associated with betting. Here, players using three dice bet for small plums—a sweet delicacy in the Middle Ages. DICK CLARK

Dice games in the Middle Ages, as now, seemed to somehow invite gambling. There are recorded instances of men losing their sheep, their clothing, and even their wives and children in a game of dice. We do not recommend such heavy wagering as a way to make your medieval banquet a success, but gambling with tokens or perhaps modern chocolate coins would help to add a suitably medieval risk factor to the gameplay.

Cent

The simplest dice game is for the players, numbering two or more, to add up their points toward a final score of one hundred. The order of play is decided by each player taking a preliminary roll, the highest number rolling first, next highest number rolling second, and so on. The players throw the dice in turn, marking down their scores on a piece of paper. The first player to reach one hundred points or more wins. A little bit of tension can be brought to the game by demanding that the winning score be exactly one hundred. If a player has, say, ninety-seven points, he must roll exactly three to win; any score above that does not count and the player loses a turn. If a player reaches a score of ninety-nine, he is eliminated because it is impossible to roll a one when throwing a pair of dice.

Raffles

Raffle requires three dice and is scored similarly to a game of poker. The object is to get all three, or at least two, of the dice to land with the same numbers showing. If the highest throws involve two or more players with the same pairs, then the winner is determined by the number on the third die. For example, a pair of fives and a six will beat a pair of fives and a three.

Passage

The first player rolls three dice until he gets a pair. If the total combined value of the pair is under ten, the player is out, and loses. If it is over ten, he wins. If the throw is exactly ten, then the dice are passed to the next player but the cash or other wager is not collected.

Other Indoor Games and Pastimes (non-tabletop)

Pass the Parcel

We don't know if this game is actually medieval in origin, but we have seen it played at a lot of living history events, and it is great fun. It can also be played right at the feast table and makes a wonderful diversion between removes.

The "parcel" is made up of a series of cloth squares wrapped one inside the other, each tied securely with a piece of ribbon. Tucked inside each of the layers is either a prize or a forfeit. The parcel starts at one end of the table and is passed from guest to guest while musicians play. Whoever is holding the parcel when the musicians abruptly stop must unwrap one layer to find his or her prize or forfeit. Then the musicians begin again and the parcel continues on its way.

The prizes are no more than a foil-covered chocolate made to look like a coin (not exactly medieval, but who doesn't like chocolates?), a cheap ring, a small piece of medieval-looking jewelry, or some other such token. The forfeits come in the form of demands to perform some slightly embarrassing act, such as singing a song, reciting a poem (which may or may not be included in the parcel), or juggling several pieces of fruit taken from the table. At the center of the parcel is a slightly better prize that will be the reward for the last person to receive the parcel. When you make up the parcel, be sure that there are enough layers to allow each guest to have several prizes or forfeits. If you are hosting a large banquet, you may wish to have more than one parcel made up. With slightly different prizes and forfeits, this can make a wonderful kids' game.

Queek

Using a large, checkered cloth spread on a hard, smooth surface, or a checker or chessboard, children take turns throwing a pebble onto the board, calling out in advance whether the pebble will land on a light or dark square. This game has also been used as an extremely simple gambling game for adults.

Hoodman's Blind (Blindman's Buff)

Blindman's buff has been around for at least two thousand years and probably longer. It is known to have been played in Greece about the time of the Roman conquest in 146 B.C. It has gone by various names. In Spain, it is known as *gallina ciega*, which means blind hen. In France it has a more martial name, *Colin-Maillard*, the name of a French lord who continued to fight in a battle, driving off those on all sides with his sword, even after he had been blinded.

Unlike the Victorian version of this game, the medieval version had a lot more physical contact and was slightly rougher. One person is chosen by lot to be "it"

During the Middle Ages, blindman's buff was played by adults as well as children.

and is blindfolded, either by having a bag pulled over the head or, in the truly medieval version, by having the hood of his lirapipe pulled down over his head. The player is then spun around several times and seeks to find his tormentors. Unlike later versions of the game, where the player simply wanders around in the dark while the rest of the players try to avoid him, in the medieval version the other players actively torment him by pulling at his clothes, shoving him, and striking at him with willow whips. In all-male versions of the game, the tormenting may have become fairly rough. It is this shoving, or buffeting (hence the word "buff"), of the blind man that gives the game its name. When he successfully captures another player, the blind man is released from darkness, and the captured person becomes "it." There is no logical conclusion to the game.

A Children's Variation

Like most children's party games, blindman's buff is a simple game that does not require too much in the way of equipment, merely a blindfold and an ample playing field. The blind man is spun around three times while the other players find a place to stand in the room or, if the game is played outside, within a reasonable distance from the blind man. Once positioned, these players are not allowed to move their feet. However, they may contort their bodies to avoid being touched. The blind man moves about until he touches a person. Having touched a person, the blind man, by feeling his or her features (in a modest way), must then guess who the person is. If the blind man guesses correctly, the tagged player then becomes the blind man.

Another Children's Variation

Instead of the blind man moving, he stands in the middle of the room while the other players walk in a circle around him in an orderly fashion. When the blindman orders "stop," all the players stop moving. The blindman then points and asks, "Who is there?" The person thus pointed to then must pronounce the words, "It is me." The player may disguise his or her voice. The blind man must then guess the identity of the player. If he guesses correctly, the selected player now becomes the blind man.

Other Children's Games

Surprisingly, most medieval children's games are still enjoyed by youngsters today. Hide and seek, seesaw, tag, and walking on stilts were all popular among medieval children.

Outdoor Games

Archery

Archery was one of the most common competition sports of the working man in medieval Europe and was particularly popular in England and Wales, where skilled longbowmen became the terror of the medieval battlefield. To ensure that their subjects were well practiced with the longbow, a succession of English kings outlawed all other forms of sport and decreed that every able-bodied man was to practice with the bow for at least two hours every Sunday after church.

To stage an archery competition, you need nothing more than a few bales of straw, a simple bull's-eye target to attach to a straw bale, two good longbows, and a dozen or so arrows. The target should be painted white and inscribed with three concentric circles, the largest of them about thirty inches in diameter. The smallest circle, at the center of the target, should be about five inches in diameter and colored red.

Depending on their level of skill, contestants should stand anywhere from forty to two hundred feet from the target. It requires a fairly skilled archer to hit the target, let alone the bull's-eye, at two hundred feet, but the longbow has an effective range of up to four hundred yards.

Contestants loose, or shoot, in rotation, one arrow per round. In traditional medieval archery competitions, a total of three rounds were taken. The contestant coming closest to the bull's-eye was declared the winner of the match. A complete archery contest consists of a series of elimination matches, with subsequent rounds made up of winners from previous matches.

An alternative to the bull's-eye target shoot is to "shoot a wand." In this variation, a stick, or wand, is planted vertically in front of the bale of straw, instead of a target of concentric circles. To make the wand as visible as possible the bale can be covered with white paper or cloth or the wand can be painted white. The object is to get as close to the wand as possible. If your arrow is touching the wand, you are unlikely to lose. If you actually manage to split the wand, think about going professional.

Another truly medieval variation of an archery competition involved laying out a large target several feet in diameter flat on the ground. Archers were then positioned one hundred yards (or more) away and would loose their arrows high into the air in an attempt to calculate the right trajectory to land their arrow within the target circle. If you plan this type of competition make sure there are no buildings, cars, or people for a very long distance from the target. (For more information on the history of archery and different methods of shooting, please refer to chapter six of *Siege: Castles at War*, by Mark P. Donnelly and Daniel Diehl, Taylor Publishing.)

Tennis (Jeu de Palme)

Most historians credit the origins of what we now know as tennis to eleventh- or twelfth-century French monks, who began playing a crude version of handball against their monastery walls or over a rope strung across a courtyard. The game took on the name *jeu de palme*, which means "game of the hand." Many who dispute more ancient origins argue that the name tennis derived from the French *tenez*, which meant something to the effect of "take this," said as one player would serve to the other.

Field archery can be enjoyed by men, women, and older children, making it an ideal family-oriented activity. EUGENE SIREN

As the game became more popular, courtyard playing areas began to be modified into indoor courts, where the ball was still played off the walls. After bare hands were found too uncomfortable, players began using a glove, then either a glove with webbing between the fingers or a solid paddle, and finally webbing attached to a handle—essentially an early tennis racquet. Rubber balls were still centuries away, so the ball was a wad of hair, wool, or cork wrapped in string and cloth or leather, then in later years, hand-stitched in felt to look something like a modern baseball.

The nobility learned the game from the monks, and some accounts report as many as 1,800 tennis courts in France by the thirteenth century. The game became such an all-consuming popular diversion that both the pope and Louis IV tried unsuccessfully to ban it. It soon spread to England, where both Henry VII and Henry VIII were avid players who promoted the building of more courts, at least for the nobility—commoners were forbidden to play.

By the year 1500, a wooden-framed racquet strung with sheep gut was in common use, as was a cork-cored ball weighing around three ounces. The early tennis courts were quite different from the modern "lawn tennis" court most of us are familiar with. The early game matured into what is now called "real tennis," and the tennis court built in 1625 at Hampton Court Palace is still used today. Only a handful of such courts remain. It's a narrow, indoor court where the ball is played off of walls, which include a number of openings and oddly angled surfaces toward which the players aim for various strategic purposes, much like the bank shots employed in pool or billiards. The net is five feet high on the ends, but three feet in the middle, creating a pronounced droop.

Assuming you do not have access to one of these rare "real tennis" courts and do not have time to build one, a modern game of lawn tennis is a perfectly suitable substitution, particularly if you raise the net to five feet in height and allow it to droop significantly in the middle.

Croquet

There seems to be some controversy about the precise origin of croquet. It might be French, or it might be Swiss. It certainly evolved into other games over time (billiards, golf, and others, apparently). The Fédération Française de Croquet says, as quoted on the Oxford Croquet website, that "Croquet is a very old game, widely known and practiced in France since the eleventh cen-

tury under the name of 'jeu de mail'. Borrowed by the British around 1300, it was modified over the centuries."

Croquet itself has been traced back to France of the 1300s, where it was called *paille-maille*, which translates roughly to "ball-mallet," and it is thought that it may have been an indoor version of lawn bowling designed to be played in times of inclement weather. The players enjoyed it enough to take it back outside for the summer months.

During this period in history the French and Scottish were loyal allies, and as a result there were certain cultural norms that crossed the channel. One of these was the game of paille-maille. In 1604 the crowns of Scotland and England were united under James VI of Scotland, soon to be known as James I of England. When he moved into the palace in London, he brought with him a paille-maille set as well as a set of golf clubs.

James's grandson, Charles II, enjoyed the game mightily and played it often in St. James Park. A nearby road was named "Pall Mall" after the game. This boulevard was much frequented by strollers and soon any road conducive to pleasant walks in the city became known as a mall. Modern retailers adopted the name and now call any conglomeration of stores with a covered walkway a "mall."

Meanwhile, a French doctor changed the rules of paille-maille slightly and recommended it for his patients. He called the new game "croquet," after the crooked stick used to hit the balls through the wickets. It then migrated to Ireland where it was called "crooky." From there it came back to England, where it supplanted pall-mall.

Croquet became popular throughout the British Empire. It gained such tremendous popularity that an association was formed at Wimbledon and formal rules were laid down in 1868. Many fields were dedicated to croquet. But this popularity was to be short-lived. The game of tennis hit England in general and Wimbledon in particular and most of the old croquet fields were turned into tennis courts. But since we are concerned only with the Middle Ages, and we are uncertain what the exact rules of medieval paille-maille were, feel free to play modern croquet as an acceptable substitute.

Camping

Camping was the precursor of football, soccer, rugby, and most other games in which two teams vie for control of a ball. The camping ball, usually made from a pig's bladder filled with dried peas, was kicked or thrown to score points against the opposing team. In this primitive version of football, natural landmarks such as trees, boulders, and stone walls were used as goal points, and streams and fences were used as obstacles that the teams had to overcome in pursuit of scoring a point. The field of play might be no larger than the village green, or the goals might be miles apart, as was the case when two villages played against each other. When the game was between two neighboring villages, it was not unusual to find the goalpost of one team in their village and the goalpost of the other team in theirs. Players would then have to carry the ball from one village to the other, with the opposing team in hot pursuit.

No official rules for the game seem to have been established, and each town and village had its own variations. Considering the period, it is not surprising that brute force was at least as important as following any set rules, and there were no fixed numbers of players who could be on a team. Sometimes it might be only four or five players, and other times it might be a hundred or more. There are records of games made up of bachelors against married men, married women against spinsters, and trade guilds against one another. In general, players seem to have been allowed to throw, carry, pass, and kick the ball while opponents tried to tackle them, or used whatever other means they could come up with to take the ball away and turn it in the opposite direction. Your own version of medieval camping can be as wild and wooly as you chose and cover as much ground as your site allows. The best ball is probably a modern soccer or basketball, but unless you can find a way to fill it with dried peas it will weigh considerably less than its medieval ancestor.

Calcio Fiorentino

Calcio Fiorentino was an early form of football that originated in sixteenth-century Italy. The Piazza Santa Croce of Florence is the cradle of this sport, which became known as *giuoco del calcio fiorentino* ("Florentine kick game") or simply *calcio* ("kick").

The official rules of calcio were published for the first time in 1580 by Giovanni de' Bardi, a Florentine count. It was played by teams of twenty-seven, using both feet and hands. Goals could be scored by throwing the ball over a designated spot (such as a fence or wall) on the perimeter of the field. The playing field is a giant sand pit with a goal running the width of each end. There is a main referee, six linesmen, and a field master. Each game is played out for fifty minutes, with the winner being the team with the most points, or *cacce*.

Originally, calcio was reserved for rich aristocrats, who played every night between Epiphany and Lent. In the Vatican, even popes, such as Clement VII, Leo XI, and Urban VIII, were known to play.

Bat-and-Ball Games

Sticks were used in games vaguely similar to baseball, in which a thrown ball was batted with the stick. Unfortunately, no known rules for these games survive, but as with so many medieval games, it is likely that the rules varied by region or were made up on the spot, so feel free to make up your own game to suit the size and skill level of your teams.

Bowls

Similar to modern bocce, a modern version of bowls is still played in England and many former British colonies. The playing field is a bowling green, a smooth lawn where contestants roll balls for points. The object is to roll grapefruit-size balls toward a target ball that is slightly smaller than a tennis ball. Points are gained for how close players can place their balls to the target ball without actually striking it. Players also use their balls to knock their opponents' balls away from the target ball.

Bowls historians believe that the game developed with the Egyptians. Artifacts found in tombs dating from around 5,000 B.C. show that an Egyptian pastime was to play skittles with round stones. The sport spread across the world and took on a variety of forms, and names: *bocce* (Italian), *bolla* (Saxon), *bolle* (Danish), *boules* (French) and *ula miaka* (Polynesian). The oldest bowls green still played on is in Southampton, England, where records show that the green has been in constant operation since A.D. 1299. There are other claims of greens being in use before that time, but these are, as yet, unsubstantiated.

Certainly the most famous story in lawn bowls involves Sir Frances Drake and the Spanish Armada. On July 18, 1588, Drake was in the middle of a bowls game

Different forms of lawn bowling, such as English bowles and the Italian bocce, have remained popular since the Middle Ages.

at Plymouth Hoe when he was notified that the Spanish Armada was approaching. His immortalized response was, "We still have time to finish the game and to thrash the Spaniards, too." He then proceeded to finish the match (which he lost) before embarking for the fight with the Armada—which, as we all know, he won. Whether this famous story really took place has been heavily debated.

A generation before Drake, King Henry VIII was also an avid lawn bowler. However, he banned the game for those who were not wealthy or "well-to-do" because "Bowyers, Fletchers, Stringers and Arrowhead makers" were spending more time at recreational events such as bowls than practicing their trades. Henry VIII requested that anybody who wished to keep a green pay a fee of one hundred pounds. However, the green could only be used for private play and he forbade anyone to "play at any bowle or bowles in open space out of his own garden or orchard."

King James I issued a publication called *The Book of Sports* and, although he condemned football (soccer) and golf, he encouraged the play of bowles. Likewise, we encourage you to try your hand at bowles. If you do not have access to a regulation set of bowls balls, bocce balls will substitute nicely.

Ground Billiards

Ground billiards was played on a small outdoor court with a hoop at one end and an upright stick at the other. This croquet-esque pastime required people to strike balls around the court with maces. No rules are known for the game at this time but it seems likely that they would have been pretty similar to the rules for port and king (see page 105).

Clive Everton, in his *History of Billiards*, states that ground billiards crystallized into existence in the 1340s and carried on into the 1600s. It was apparently played throughout much of Europe—in Italy it was known as *biglia*; in France, *bilhard*; in Spain, *virlota*; and some texts say that in England it was known as *ball-yard*. The game appears to be critical to game history since it apparently led to the families of both billiards and croquet games. There is no evidence of an ancestor of billiards prior to ground billiards, unless you lower your criteria to count all the other games played with bats, balls, and skittles.

Tournament Jousting

Medieval warfare produced entertainments in the form of ritualized battles, known as tournaments or tourneys. Tournaments seem to have been invented in the eleventh century by Geofroyde de Preuilly. They were particularly a feature of French courtly life, and were far less popular in England except in the time of Edward III.

A tournament was a battle in which prisoners were taken and, although deaths could occur, these battles were chiefly symbolic reenactments of the type of events that were taking place in reality. As time went on, the tournaments became increasingly entertainments rather than practice wars, with music, dancing, and betting.

The joust, more popular in England, was a small-scale tournament that was increasingly popular from the fourteenth century on. It was a one-to-one combat with any of a variety of weapons, carried out on horseback or on foot. Jousts were also used to open a tournament.

While specifics varied from country to country and century to century, the basics of jousting remained the same: two mounted knights charged at each other with blunted lances eighteen to twenty feet in length. In most instances, the contestants were protected by heavier-than-normal padding and armor, so the danger of injury was kept at a minimum. The challengers faced each other at a distance of several hundred yards, a distance gauged to allow their horses a chance to reach top speed. Separating the combatants was a fence four to five feet high. This fence kept the horses from colliding and ensured that the only thing that reached a knight was the opponent's lance. On a given signal, the armored knights would charge toward each other, each carefully aiming his lance. A winner was declared when one of the knights was struck squarely enough by his opponent's lance to throw him from his horse.

The joust—also known as the "tilt"—was immensely popular among the nobility, who used it as a display of, and training ground for, mounted warfare. It could also be lucrative for the contestants. On winning a tilt, a knight had the right to claim the armor, and sometimes the horse, of his defeated opponent.

An interesting variation of jousting—"river jousting"—takes place in Coulanges-sur-Yonne, France, every August 15. Coulanges's annual bout of river jousting has its origins in the region's history as France's main timber-producing area. Contestants in rowboats "joust" each other with long poles, attempting to throw their opponent into the water. The fights are accompanied by the merriment of the Coulanges fête with music, dancing, and plenty of wine. This seemingly bizarre event actually has a sound historical basis. The forests of Morvan have, since the Middle Ages, been a rich source of timber, and logs were floated downstream to the major urban centers. Hence, while in most parts of the country disputes between chevaliers were resolved by jousts on horseback, in this part of the country jousting took to the water, where the knights had at each other with lances while standing in boats being rowed furiously by their squires.

A Modern Variation of the Joust for your Medieval Event

While we do not suggest holding an actual joust—and perhaps not even a river joust—we have come up with an alternative that can be challenging, enjoyable, and exciting. The "knights" face each other on a "jousting horse," a log or pole eighteen to twenty feet in length and eight to ten inches in diameter. A discarded telephone pole will serve the purpose, but to avoid the possibility of injury, it must be free from all nails and splinters. The length provides the combatants room to move, and the diameter is necessary to support their combined weight and allow them something to grasp with their thighs.

This pole should be supported on two tripods four feet high, set about eighteen inches from each end of the pole. The tripods should be made from nothing less than four-by-four posts, to ensure good support. Two legs of the tripod should cross in such a way that they form a saddle for the pole to sit in. The third leg simply ensures that the structure does not collapse from the movement of the jousters. The structure should be bolted together, as shown in the construction diagram, with quarter-inch-diameter lag bolts. The tripods must be staked firmly into the ground to ensure that they do not collapse under the jostling that will take place on the pole. See the accompanying illustration for full construction details. We recommend that you enlist the help of someone familiar with construction techniques when building the structure.

With the aid of a jousting horse, even the commonfolk can feel like a mounted knight.

To hold the tournament, two challengers straddle the pole, one at each end. Each "knight" is armed with a bag of tightly packed straw the size of a pillowcase. The knights shinny toward each other on the pole. When they get within reach, they swing at each other with the bags of straw in an attempt to "unhorse" their opponent. Swinging too fast or too early can unbalance a knight, giving the opponent an early advantage. You will be surprised just how exciting this can get. Whether the winner is awarded a prize or the loser is required to surrender his armor and horse to his opponent is up to you.

Palio Race

In medieval Italy, the sporting event of the year was undoubtedly the palio race. The palio was a wild, free-for-all horse race through the streets of the city, each horse being backed by a local company, merchants' guild, nobleman, or neighborhood. Beginning in 1275, several Italian city-states held palio races, the most prominent being Siena, which still holds the race every year. The object was to back the horse that crossed the finish line first. As this was medieval Italy, there were no set rules. Unhorsing an opponent, or even killing him, was all part of the game. The winning horse did not have to have its rider on its back when it crossed the finish line, and even if the rider was there, he did not have to be alive. There was no second place. The palio itself was a bolt of expensive cloth that was presented to the owner or sponsor of the winning horse.

While we do not expect you to stage an actual horse race, nor do we recommend killing any of your contestants, we have devised an amusing alternative to this breathtaking event. The course in our version of the race may be either a straight line (usually no more than one hundred yards) or a circle around a building. If you have space to plot out a more interesting course, all the better, but it is not necessary. Any number of two-person teams may enter the race. One member of the team will serve as the rider, the other as the horse. Riders (preferably small women or teenagers) mount their trusty steeds (men eager to display their athletic prowess) by sitting on their shoulders and locking their legs under the men's armpits.

Gather your teams at the starting line, and tell the riders to mount up. When everyone is mounted (this alone can be a source of great fun for the spectators), they should line up evenly along the starting line. At a predetermined signal, the race begins. There are no other rules. Pushing, shoving, and spitting mouthfuls of water at opponents is encouraged, and the rider need not

JOUSTING HORSE CONSTRUCTION

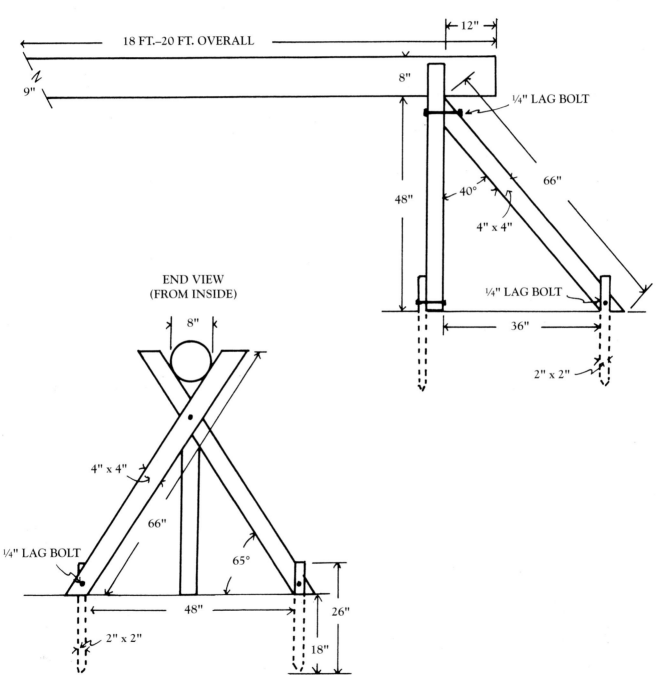

SIDE VIEW

18 FT.–20 FT. OVERALL

12"

9"

8"

¼" LAG BOLT

48"

40°

66"

4" x 4"

¼" LAG BOLT

36"

2" x 2"

END VIEW
(FROM INSIDE)

8"

4" x 4"

66"

65°

¼" LAG BOLT

48"

26"

2" x 2"

18"

A modernized version of the medieval palio race has contestants ridding piggyback in a mad scramble towards the finish line.

be on the winning horse when it crosses the finish line. Cheers, jeers, and shouts of encouragement from the sidelines are essential to keeping up the tension and competitive spirit. Presentation of five or six yards of fine fabric to the winning rider is both historically correct and a real crowd-pleaser, and a box of oatmeal presented to the winning horse is the perfect ending to this absurd bit of medieval-esque horseplay.

Wrestling

Wrestling is the oldest and purest of personal combat sports. Men have been trying their strength and unarmed skill since the beginning of time. Egyptian murals on the tombs of Beni Hasan, dating back to 3000 B.C., show wrestlers in combat, and we know that this sort of competition was part of the early Olympic games. In fact, it is said to have been introduced at the eighteenth Olympic games, in about 704 B.C.

Wrestling has for a long time been part of the English sporting pattern; for instance, during the Middle Ages it was customary in London to hold wrestling matches on Lammas Day. Wrestling was universally popular among male members of the working and peasant classes during the Middle Ages. No equipment was necessary, and the rules seem to have varied widely—assuming, of course, there were any rules. Traditionally the challenge took the form of the challenger throwing a cap into the air; whoever wanted to fight him would pick it up. The most common objective of the wrestling match was to throw one's opponent so that he landed with both hips and one shoulder, or two shoulders and one hip, squarely on the ground. Alternately, combatants could either fight to a throw, until one of them successfully pinned the other to the ground (at the shoulders, hips, or any combination thereof), or until one of the men upset the balance of the other and forced him outside the boundary of a "ring," a circle four to six feet in diameter that had been drawn in the dust.

One unusual variation on wrestling took place when the contestants sat on the shoulders of two other men and carried out their competition in the air. The object here was to send one's opponent tumbling to the ground. This variation can still sometimes be seen being played by pairs of children in waist-deep water.

Tug of War

This familiar game is perfectly medieval and still a lot of fun today. All that is required are two teams and a length of stout rope. We recommend using a one-inch-diameter hemp rope if possible. The diameter gives the contestants something to grip, and hemp is less likely to stretch than plastic or nylon. To make the game more authentically medieval, the teams should assemble on either side of a hazard. This could be a low wall, a hedge, a mud puddle, or a stream. On a signal, each team tries to pull the other off balance and across, or into, the hazard. The game ends when one side encounters the hazard or gives up from sheer exhaustion.

Stone Throwing

This game is not very sophisticated-sounding but it is a good test of skill or strength, depending on the size of the stones being thrown. Small stones that could be held in the palm of the hand were generally thrown for distance and accuracy, frequently at some predetermined target. Larger stones, sometimes weighing up to fifty or sixty pounds, were thrown for distance. Remnants of this variation still exist in Scottish and Swiss games and were the precursor to the Olympic sport of shot putting.

Climbing a Greased Pole

The object of this game is for contestants to climb to the top of a greased pole and claim a prize. The prize, traditionally a haunch of meat, was sometimes tethered to the top of the pole and had to be pulled loose; at other times its place was taken by a ribbon, which also had to be pulled from the pole. In some instances, the winner was simply the first person to climb high enough to lay the flat of his hand on top of the pole.

The pole you use should be eight to twelve inches in diameter and fifteen to sixteen feet long. The diameter allows the contestants to gain some kind of hold on the pole, no matter how slight, and the length allows for five feet of the pole to be buried firmly in the ground and still leave ten or more feet exposed for climbing. The pole must be completely smooth. Any splinters can cause injuries, and rough spots or knots can give a climber an unfair advantage. The portion of the pole to be buried in the ground must be firmly enough anchored that the pole will not tilt to one side as it is repeatedly assaulted by contestants attempting to reach the top. When the pole is firmly fixed in the ground, it should be covered with a solid lubricant that will not run off, such as lard or shortening.

Contestants determine the order of play by drawing lots or rolling dice. The first contestant who successfully reaches the top of the pole, or pulls down the prize, wins. The biggest problem is the mess that the competition makes of contestants' clothes. Considering the lack of practice most of us have in climbing poles these days, the game will probably work just as well if the pole is not greased, and everyone will come away a lot cleaner.

Catching a Greased Pig

In the modern world, few of us have access to a piglet. If you do, pick one that is small enough to be caught but big enough to run away from its pursuers—two to three months of age should do nicely. The game will need to take place in a well-fenced area so neither the pig nor the contestants can escape. Greasing the animal with lard or shortening will ensure a good, slippery pig.

Traditionally, the contestants surrounded the fenced area. The referee entered the ring, carrying the pig in a feed bag. When he reached the center of the ring, the pig was released and the insanity began. The person who successfully captured the little fellow got to take him home and either raise him or have him for dinner.

Practically speaking, there are few of us who have access to, or use for, a two-month-old pig. Fewer still would have the heart to kill and eat it. A fairly reasonable facsimile of the game can be played, however, by greasing a soccer ball or basketball. It may not run and squeal, but its round shape makes it very hard to keep hold of when six or eight people are all fighting for possession at the same time.

A summertime variant of this game takes place in the water, where a greased watermelon may be substituted for the pig. Swimmers must catch hold of the "pig" and move it safely to one of two designated spots. This is not as easy as it may sound, especially since everyone is trying for the same "pig."

Blood Sports

The hardships and brutal realities of the medieval world placed a fairly low value on human life. It is not surprising, then, that an even lower value was placed on the lives of helpless animals. We include a brief description of these "sports" only as an insight into the medieval mind, certainly not as a recommendation that any of these activities be recreated in any form whatsoever.

In bull and bear baiting, a captured bear or a bull was tethered to a pole in the center of a large pit. A pack of specially trained hunting dogs was then turned loose on the restrained animal. As with most such games, betting

Blood sports such as bear baiting, bull baiting, dogfighting, and cockfighting exposed the most barbaric and despicable aspects of life in the Middle Ages.

on the outcome was an integral part of the play. A winner was declared when the bull or the bear had killed all of the dogs, or the dogs had torn the frenzied animal to pieces.

In dog and cockfights, a pair of dogs or roosters that had been trained to attack their own kind would be released into a ring, or pit, and tear at each other until one of them was dead. Amazing as it seems today, cockfighting was considered a perfectly acceptable sport for boys over ten or twelve years of age. Similarly, "cock throwing" was a game that involved boys chasing down a rooster while pelting it with stones. A good, stunning blow disabled the bird, thereby allowing its capture.

Even worse, in Italy and France, teenage boys would impress their girlfriends by nailing a live cat to a tree and proceeding to batter the tortured animal to death with their heads. Yes, really—with their heads.

Hunting was a special and rarified form of medieval entertainment, much appreciated by the nobility of the day. In the Middle Ages, hunting became an art as well as a science with strict rules. Hunting with hounds was known by the French name of the "chase," as early French authors established a set of rules for it, organizing it into a heavily codified system. Of course, the chase, like so many medieval sports, was restricted to the nobility. Should any peasant be caught hunting—particularly on land owned by a member of the nobility (and almost all land was owned by the nobility)—he would be lucky if his only punishment was to have his ears, nose, or bowfingers cut off, and a second offense was likely to bring execution or, at the very least, having at least one hand hacked off.

Falconry, the first traces of which are lost in obscure antiquity, was the delight of the nobles, and noblemen and ladies who prided themselves on their skill at the sport seldom appeared in public without a hawk on the wrist as a mark of dignity. Although falcons are still kept and trained, their possession is severely restricted by law and only licensed falconers are allowed to keep these magnificent, endangered birds.

Mummers' Plays

During the Middle Ages the only things approaching mass entertainment were the plays performed by churches and small groups of traveling players. Church-related performances were invariably religious in nature and were generally of the genre known as "mystery" plays (because they explored the mysteries of God, Christ's resurrection, and salvation). Most of these mystery plays involved dozens of short plays performed over a number of days, or weeks, and each segment enacted one story from the Bible; a complete cycle of mystery plays could encompass the entire span of biblical writ from the creation to Armageddon. The few full-length plays that existed during this period were also based on religious themes or were intended to present a clear interpretation of the struggle between good and evil. The concept of the fully developed stage presentation as we know it—comedy, drama, tragedy, and so on—did not come into existence in medieval Europe until the middle of the sixteenth century with the rise of such playwrights as Ben Johnson, Christopher Marlowe, and William Shakespeare.

Plays performed by troupes of medieval traveling players, or occasionally by a few daring townsfolk, were known as mummers' plays, and those who performed them were alternately known as mummers or mimmers. Most of these were merely pantomime shows, where unskilled volunteers silently improvised action to go with the words read by a narrator. Vestiges of the names for these silent plays and their players survive today in the white-faced mimes who still annoy people with their street corner performances in large cities, and in the phrase "mum's the word," used to ensure silence. In the more complex mummers' plays—usually the ones performed by professional players—the actors actually spoke their lines like modern actors.

The characters represented in these plays tended to be limited in number and the same stock characters appeared in many different plays. While this may seem boring and repetitious, remember that plays were only performed in any one location on a very few occasions during the year, and when they only lasted a few minutes it was easier for the audience to identify with the characters if they were already familiar. Much the same can be said for characters in today's television series. Like today's soap operas or "sitcoms," characters in medieval mummers' plays were easily identified archetypes representing good or evil, cleverness or stupidity, making it easier for the audience to follow the action and predict the outcome: good always won out over evil.

Among the most popular "good guy" characters in these plays was St. George (who was later sometimes transformed into Robin Hood, or Robyn Hode, as he is called in one of our plays). Another popular hero was known as the Bold Slasher, the Bold Soldier or the Bold Roamer, who represented a brave but unnamed knight. Because these plays were part of an oral tradition and seldom written down, the names often became corrupted over time. In some versions Bold Roamer is amusingly referred to as the Ball Roomer.

The evil character was frequently known as the Turkish Knight, a reference to the Saracen enemy during the Crusades. Again, the Turkish Knight's name was frequently corrupted over decades of telling and retelling until he became known as the Churlish Knight (as he is in one of the plays below) or, inexplicably, the Turkey Snipe.

Other stock characters included the pathetic character of Little Johnny Jack, a poor peasant whose many children were represented by small rag dolls suspended around his neck, and the Doctor or the Physician, whose magical powers always rescue the hero from certain death just before the close of the play.

The text of these early plays was frequently not written down until the eighteenth or nineteenth century, so there is little original text available, but since there were unlimited variations to the stories, there were never any "correct" versions. Nor were there ever any written stage directions to accompany the script; the actors simply pantomimed the action dictated by the lines they were speaking, or that were being read by the narrator.

It is always best if the actors have a chance to rehearse the play ahead of time and learn their lines by heart, but in medieval times, members of the audience sometimes volunteered to serve as impromptu members of the cast, reading their lines when their turns came (assuming they could read). It is perfectly acceptable, even expected, for the audience to cheer the hero, hiss and boo at the villain, and applaud and laugh as they feel appropriate.

The first of our plays deals with the ever-popular Robin Hood and is ideal for use at May Day festivities, which was known as Robin Hood's Day in late medieval England. Curiously, in this play, the Saracen, who is usually a bad guy, plays the part of the hero Doctor while the villain is the nefarious Sir Guy of Guisborne, the villain of so many Robin Hood stories.

Robyn Hode

Cast
Friar Tuck: a fat monk
Sir Guy of Guisbourne: a nobleman, the villain of the play
Robyn Hode: the hero
Saracen: a Turkish alchemist with magical powers

The Play

FRIAR TUCK. In come I, good Friar Tuck, welcome or welcome not.
I hope that Friar Tuck will not be forgot.
Although we've come, we've but a short time to stay,
But we'll bring you sport and pastime before we go away.
Room, room, gentles I pray,
For I now bring Sir Guy of Guisbourne this way.

SIR GUY. In come I, Guy of Guisbourne, lately come from France,
And with the Sheriff of Nottingham's men
I'll make that wolf's head dance.
And if Robyn Hode were here, I wonder what would appear?
I'd cut him up as small as flour dust (*draws sword*)
And send him to old Friar Tuck to make a pie crust.

ROBYN HODE. In come I, Robyn Hode, from Sherwood did I spring,
And with my bow and merry men, I'll give Guisbourne a nasty sting.
I'll take from the rich and give to the poor
And guard Old England for Richard our King.
I'll fight Guisbourne with courage bold;
If his blood's hot, I'll make it cold.

EUGENE SIREN

SIR GUY. Down under thee I'll never bow nor bend;
I never took thee to be my friend.

ROBYN. For why, for why, sir, did I ever do you any harm?

SIR GUY. You saucy man, you ought to be stabbed!

ROBYN. Stab for stab, that is my fear.
Appoint me the place, and I'll meet you there.

SIR GUY. My place is pointing on the ground,
Where I mean to lay your body down!

ROBYN. Pull out your sword and fight!
Pull out your purse and pay!
For once, satisfaction I will have
Before I go away.

SIR GUY. No money will I pull out nor pay,
But you and I must fight this battle most manfully.
Bold and Slasher is my name;
With sword in hand, I aim to win this game.
My head is made of iron, my body lined with steel,
And brass unto my knuckle bones, I'll fight you in
    this field.

ROBYN. Stand off, stand off, Sir Guy, or by my sword
    soon you'll die.
I'll cut your doublet through and through
And make thy buttons fly.
I've traveled o'er England, France, and Spain
And many a dog I have slain.
For what our king shall have is right,
This nasty man I'll now fight.

(ROBYN and SIR GUY fight. SIR GUY slays ROBYN.)

SIR GUY. Behold, behold, what I have done.
I cut him down like the evening sun.
And ten more of such men I'll fight,
For what the sheriff shall have is right.

FRIAR TUCK. Alas, alas, poor Robyn's slain,
Between two arms his body's lain.
For what some doctor must come and see
Where this man lies bleeding at my feet.
Oh, is there a doctor to be found,
To raise this poor man from the ground?
I would pay a full five pounds
If there were a doctor to be found.

(Enter a SARACEN.)

SARACEN. In come I, Achmed the Good,
With my hand I can stop the blood.
I can stop the blood and heal the wound
and raise this man from the ground.

FRIAR TUCK. What can you cure?

SARACEN. I can cure the hipsy, pipsy, palsey, or gout,
Strain within or strain without.
If a man's neck be broke, I'll set it again,
or else I won't have a penny for my fee.

FRIAR TUCK. What's your fee?

SARACEN. Ten pounds.

FRIAR TUCK. Ten pounds?!
I can't pay as much as that.

SARACEN. Saddle my horse and I'll be gone.

FRIAR TUCK. Stop, stop, oh wondrous one.
What is your lowest fee?

SARACEN. Nine pounds, nineteen shillings, and eleven
    pence,
And that's a penny under price, because you're a poor
    friar.

FRIAR TUCK. Then do please try thy skill.

SARACEN. I have here a potion, brought from the east.
It is called the golden elixir, and with one drop,
I will revive Robyn Hode with these magic words:
"Sim Salabim."
Rise up young man
And see how your body can walk and sing.

ROBYN. I now waken from my sleep, but friends,
    I cannot stay.
I must continue on the fight
To curb the sheriff's evil ways.
Before I go, however, a boon I ask, I pray.
Dig deep in your purses for the doctor's bill to pay.

[This is a perfect time to collect for a local charity.]

The next play is a Christmas play, but it can be performed at any time during the Christmas holidays, from just prior to St Nicholas' Day (December 6) through Twelfth Night (January 5).

St. Nicholas and the Schoolboys

Cast

First Schoolboy: a victim and hero
Second Schoolboy: a victim and hero
Third Schoolboy: a victim and hero
An Old Innkeeper: a villain
An Old Woman (the innkeeper's wife): a villain
St Nicholas: the hero

SCENE I

(*Enter three* SCHOOLBOYS *and the* INNKEEPER.)

FIRST SCHOOLBOY. Led by a noble ambition,
    here we stand;
We've come to study in this foreign land.
But while the sinking sun still gives us light,
We'd better find lodging for the night.

SECOND SCHOOLBOY. Apollo's coursers now
    approach the brink
Of ocean, and beneath it soon will sink.
To us this country is entirely strange,
And so our lodging we had best arrange.

THIRD SCHOOLBOY. What have we here?
    Though fast it's growing dark,
These lights reveal an aged patriarch.
Let's ask him and perhaps if we're polite,
He'll be our host and take us in tonight.

SCHOOLBOYS (*together say to the* INNKEEPER).
    Good host, behold three schoolboys far from home,
In eager quest of knowledge thus we roam.
It's getting late, and would you be so kind,
Sir, as to take us in, if you don't mind?

INNKEEPER. God, who created all men, shelter you.
But as for me, I've other things to do.
I don't see where there's any profit in it.
You've come to me at a very awkward minute.

(*Enter the* OLD WOMAN)

SCHOOLBOYS (*to* OLD WOMAN). Dear lady, though
    it may be as you say,
That you'll gain nothing, won't you let us stay?
Perhaps God will observe the kindness done,
And send you as reward a baby son.

OLD WOMAN (*to* INNKEEPER). Dear husband,
    in the name of charity,
Let us take in these boys, who seem to be
Respectable and studious as any.
We won't get rich, but we won't lose a penny.

INNKEEPER. I'll take them in, my love, just as you say.
(*To the boys*) just as a favor, boys, come right this way.

SCENE II

INNKEEPER (*to* OLD WOMAN, *while* SCHOOLBOYS *are asleep*):
    Look at those purses, how they bulge!
I swear there must be quite a pile of treasure there.
Think, all that money could belong to us!
No one would know, no one would make a fuss.

OLD WOMAN. Long as we've lived—too long it seems
    to me!
We've had to bear the load of poverty.
Now here's a chance, if we are not too queasy,
To take the rest of life a bit more easy. Where is
    your sword?
Go, kill them where they lie;
And so from this time on shall you and I
Live like old King Midas. Do the job up right,
And God won't know what's happened here tonight.

(INNKEEPER *and* OLD WOMAN *slay* SCHOOLBOYS.)

SCENE III

(*Enter* ST. NICHOLAS.)

ST. NICHOLAS. I am a pilgrim, and the road is hard.
I cannot drag my feet another yard.
Therefore, as you do hope your souls' salvation,
Grant me I pray a night's accommodation.

INNKEEPER (*to* OLD WOMAN). Now what do you
    advise, beloved spouse?
Shall I admit the old man to the house?

OLD WOMAN. He looks a most respectable old party;
And so look sharp, and give him welcome hearty.

INNKEEPER. Come in, come in, good pilgrim, come inside.
For men like you we always can provide.
If there is any nice dish you prefer,
I'll do my best to get it for you, sir.

ST. NICHOLAS, *seating himself at table.* None of these
  things before me can I eat.
Only one thing I want, and that's fresh meat.

INNKEEPER. I'll cook you up a steak tender and hot;
It isn't fresh, sir, but it's all I've got.

ST. NICHOLAS. That is a lie, old man, come straight
  from hell.
You have here in this house, I know right well,
Meat that has just been slaughtered. Foul the deed,
And foul the vice that led you to it—Greed!

INNKEEPER and OLD WOMAN, *falling on their knees.*
  Have mercy on us, mercy, we implore you!
O saint of God, see, we fall down before you.
Our sin is black as Satan's hide, but still
It can be pardoned wholly if God will.

ST. NICHOLAS. Bring here the bodies in their sad
  condition,
And let your hearts be smitten with contrition.
By God's grace shall these boys arise.
Go, mortify yourselves with tears and sighs.

(SCHOOLBOYS *are carried or led before St. Nicholas.*)

ST. NICHOLAS (*prays*): God, to whom sky and air
  and sea and land
Are only playthings in Thy powerful hand,
Those who now cry to Thee do Thou forgive,
And grant that these young scholars rise and live.

(SCHOOLBOYS *come back to life.*)

Our third play is intended for New Year's presentation
(either March 25 or January 1) but can be performed at
any time by simply changing the last two words in the
script. Note how portions of this play are similar to our
Robin Hood play, indicating the repetition of theme
found throughout these simple medieval plays. Note too,
how the one-size-fits-all villain, the Turkish Knight, is
referred to here as the Churlish Knight.

Johnny Jack's New Year

Cast
Little Johnny Jack: a pathetic hero with many rag dolls
  around his neck
Old Father Time: a representation of human mortality
A Noble King: a hero
Churlish Knight: the villain
A Doctor: a hero

EUGENE SIREN

(*Enter* JOHNNY JACK.)

JOHNNY JACK. In comes I, Little Johnny Jack,
With my family climbing on my back.
The burden's not light though they be small,
I can scarce find bread to feed them all.
So for a fare we will dance and sing,
Some money in my purse is a capital thing.
Ladies and gentlemen give what you please,
And all of that we'll welcomely receive.

(*Enter* OLD FATHER TIME.)

OLD FATHER TIME. In comes I, Old Father Time,
welcome perhaps or welcome not,
Sometimes cold and sometimes hot,
I hope I'll never be forgot.
Though I've come far, I've but short time to stay,
We'll show you sport and pastime before we go away.
Room, room Ladies & Gentlemen, room I pray,
I am the man that leads the Noble King this way.

(*Enter the* NOBLE KING.)

NOBLE KING. In comes I, the Noble King,
just lately come from foreign lands,
With my sword there and jolly men
I made the Churlish Knight to dance.
And if I had him close by here,
I wonder what would soon appear?
I'd cut him up as small as dust,
and send him to the baker to make a pie crust!

(*Enter* CHURLISH KNIGHT.)

CHURLISH KNIGHT. In comes I, that Churlish Knight,
Just come from the distant land to fight;
I'll battle this King and all his crew
Aye, country-folk and warriors too.
I'll cross this King with courage bold,
His blood runs hot, but I'll make it cold.

NOBLE KING. Down under thee I'll never bow nor bend,
No good man ever mistook thee to be a friend.

CHURLISH KNIGHT. For why, for why, sir, did I ever do you
  any harm?

NOBLE KING. You saucy man, wherever you go they sound
  alarm.

CHURLISH KNIGHT. So stab for stab, I have no fear,
appoint me the place, and I'll meet you there.

NOBLE KING. That place is here, this patch of ground,
Where I mean to lay your fair body down!

CHURLISH KNIGHT. Thus said pull out your sword and
  fight!
Or pull out your purse and pay,
For one satisfaction I will have,
Before I go away.

NOBLE KING. No money will I pull out nor pay,
But you and I will fight until one's done away.
Stand off, stand off, you Churlish Knight,
or by my sword you shall soon die,
I'll cut off your driblets through and through,
I'll make your buttons fly.

(*A fight ensues until the* NOBLE KING *falls.*)

CHURLISH KNIGHT. Behold, behold, what I have done.
I cut him down like the evening sun;
And ten more such men I'll fight,
For that I shall claim what is my right.

(JOHNNY JACK *rushes to the fallen* KING *and lifts his head.*)

JOHNNY JACK. Indeed, indeed, the King is slain,
Between these two arms his body's lain,
For what some Doctor must come and see,
Where this man lies bleeding at his feet.

OLD FATHER TIME. Oh, is there a doctor to be found
nearby to here this Christmas night?
Come heal this good man's bloody wound
and make him stand up right.

(*Enter the* DOCTOR.)

DOCTOR. In comes I, Doctor Too Good,
With just my hand I can stop the blood.
I can stop the blood and heal the wound,
And raise this dead man from the ground.

OLD FATHER TIME. What can you cure, Doctor?

DOCTOR. I can cure the itch, the pox, the palsy or gout,
Pain within or strain without,
I have plaster and potions, poisons and pills,
Some to cure and others to kill.
If his neck be broke, I'll set it right,
Or else won't accept my fee this night.

JOHNNY JACK. O Doctor, Doctor what is thy fee,
  this champion for to rise?
The sight of him doth trouble me to see how dead
  he lies.

DOCTOR. Full fifty guineas is my fee and money to
  have down
But since 'tis for his majesty I will do it for ten pound.

OLD FATHER TIME. Better try your skill then, Doctor.

DOCTOR. Now, you see, ladies and gentlemen,
I've got a bottle in my pocket filled with drops golden,
I puts a drop on his temple and a drop in his mouth,
I puts a drop on his heart, and he'll move about.

(*The* NOBLE KING *stirs, the* CHURLISH KNIGHT *slinks off stage.*)

OLD FATHER TIME. So he did, Doctor. So he did!

DOCTOR. You see ladies and gentlemen, I told no lies.
But I can raise the dead before your eyes,
And so you all shall see. Rise up good King,
And see how boldly you once more can walk and sing.

(*The* NOBLE KING *rises.*)

NOBLE KING. Good morning to you, maids and
  gentlemen,
Good sleep I have had, and now I am awakened
With this Good Doctor here I rise to fight another day,
I pray Good Doctor, take here this purse your bill to pay.

(*The* NOBLE KING *pulls out his purse and gives it to the*
  DOCTOR *who smiles, counts the money and gives*
  some to JOHNNY JACK.)

ALL: Our tale is done, and we must be gone;
We can tarry no longer here.
So God bless you all, both great and small,
And send you a happy New Year.

[This is a good time to collect money for a local charity.]

CHAPTER 15

Songs, Ballads, and Carols

Music has always been, and continues to be, an integral part of festivities, both public and private. Today we rely on radio, CDs, and both local and internationally famous live bands to keep our toes tapping and feet dancing at large gatherings. But during the Middle Ages there was no convenient way for a host to provide music for their guests' enjoyment. With luck, the host was wealthy enough to keep court musicians, or at least hire a few traveling minstrels to provide background music and lead the company in singing their favorite songs, as well as introduce them to a few new ones. For those in less affluent communities and households it was largely up to the participants to make their own music and so they tended to rely on old, familiar tunes that everyone knew and felt comfortable singing. Because of their original longevity, many of these songs have captured a strong enough place in our shared history that they remain familiar nearly half a millennium after they were first written down.

Certainly, many of the songs in this chapter will be new to you and your guests, but you may be surprised at how many of them you already know, especially among the Christmas carols.

The main problem you will face in bringing these songs to life will be providing background music to accompany the singing and to provide musical background during the feast. A partial solution can be provided by the wide selection of medieval music available on CD and Mp3. This will at least keep your guests from becoming restless during the meal, and should help establish an appropriately medieval atmosphere for your feast.

When the time comes to raise the group's collective voice in song, there are several possible options. If you live near a college or university, there may be a medieval recreationist group that counts among its number a few musicians who might be enticed, or hired, to play for a few hours. You would be amazed at how eager these individuals are to share their talent and knowledge of medieval music with members of the public.

In the absence of other options, if you know someone who plays a mandolin it will make a suitable alternative to the most popular of medieval instruments, the lute. Lacking more historically appropriate instruments, a piano, portable organ, or acoustic guitar may have to suffice for musical accompaniment. If you or your event is associated with a church, you might also be able to convince at least some members of the choir to lead the audience in song.

Alternatively, the local college music department likely has a few students or faculty members familiar with medieval music, and they may even have medieval-type instruments that will provide a realistic sound for your event. While these professional or semiprofessional musicians may not come as inexpensively as medieval reenactors, the possibility of proper period instruments will make it well worth the extra cost.

If your guest list is going to number into the hundreds, it might be wise to arrange for much of the music to be performed concert-style, with the guests invited to join in on a few selected numbers. Whatever the case, have the songs photocopied and available to guests. It is probably best to pass out the song sheets just prior to the time they will be used; otherwise, they will tend to get lost over the course of the day.

Before you launch yourself into song, it is good to understand just how medieval songs differed from their modern counterparts. Following are some brief notes on a number of medieval song types.

Ballads

Ballads were the pop music of the medieval world. Usually taking the form of a narrative story, ballads told about love, adventure, bravery, and great sadness—the same elements that are still central to today's popular music. The difference between music in the Middle Ages and modern music is that seven hundred years ago, ballads were also a primary source of news. When a great battle had been fought, a king had died, or a rich lord had married off his idiot son or doltish daughter, the event was immediately put into a song that served as both entertainment and a source of news. These timely tunes were then carried from place to place by minstrels or troubadours who studied long and hard, training themselves to remember the complete text of the ballads, which sometimes ran five or six thousand words in length. It has been said that a truly skilled troubadour could memorize and flawlessly repeat two thousand lines after a single hearing. A good memory was essential in a world where literacy was a rarity, and the hunger for entertaining stories and news of any kind was voracious.

Many popular ballads were specific to particular times of the year, and we have arranged the songs in this section accordingly, beginning with spring and ending with winter.

EUGENE SIREN

SPRING HAS COME

(G. S.)

Piae Cantiones, 1582.   Ibid., Tr. Steuart Wilson.

Now the spring has come again, joy and warmth will follow;
Cold and wet are quite forgot, northward flies the swallow;
Over sea and land and air spring's soft touch is everywhere
    And the World looks cleaner;
All our sinews feel new strung, hearts are light that once were wrung,
    Youthful zests are keener.

2. All the woods are new in leaf, all the fruit is budding,
Bees are humming round the hive, done with winter's brooding;
Seas are calm and blue again, clouds no more foretell the rain,
    Winds are soft and tender;
High above, the kingly sun laughs once more his course to run,
    Shines in all his splendor.

3. God is in the midst of her, God commands her duty;
Earth does but reflect his light, mirrors back his beauty;
God's the fount whence all things flow, great and small, above, below,
    God's their only maker;
We but poorest patterns are of that Mind beyond compare,
    God our great Creator.

SUMMER IS A COMING IN

THE AIR FROM A MANUSCRIPT SIX HUNDRED YEARS OLD.

Words modernized

Sum-mer is a coming in, Loudly sing, Cuck-oo! Meadows green a-round are seen Be-

-spangled o'er with dew, Sing, Cuck-oo! Young Alein, the shepherd swain, Is gath'ring vio-lets

blue;　　　He will car-ry wreaths to Ma-ry, Glad as thou, Cuckoo,　Cuck-oo,　Cuck-oo, We

welcome thee, Cuck-oo, That wak'st the world a-new.

Prophet of the merry throat, Loudly sing, Cuckoo!　　For thou bring'st, whene'er thou sing'st, Good

(continued on page 128)

(continued from page 127)

tidings, aye and true: Sing, Cuck-oo!   Mary's love may fickle prove, False hopes the swain may

cres.   **pp**

rue: May's returning, falsehood spurning, Singest thou, Cuckoo! Cuckoo! Cuck-oo! Hail,

cres.   *f*   **pp**

bird of truth! Cuck-oo! That wak'st the world a-new.

f   *dim.*   *p*

THANKSGIVING CAROL

GEOFFREY SHAW.

Eleanor Farjeon.

Fields of corn, give up your ears,
Now your ears are heavy,
Wheat and oats and barley-spears,
  All your harvest-levy.
Where your sheaves of plenty lean,
Men once more the grain shall glean
  Of the Ever-Living,
God the Lord will bless the field,
Bringing in its Autumn yield
  Gladly to Thanksgiving.

2. Vines, send in your bunch of grapes,
  Now the bunch is clustered,
Be your gold and purple shapes
  Round the altar mustered,
Where the hanging bunches shine
Men once more shall taste the wine
  Of the Ever-Living,
God the Lord will bless the root,
Bringing in its Autumn fruit
  Gladly to Thanksgiving.

3. Garden, give your gayest flowers,
  Hedge, your wildest bring in,
Turn the churches into bowers
  Little birds shall sing in.
Where the children sing their glee
Men once more the Flower shall see
  Of the Ever-Living,
God the Lord will bless the throng,
Lifting up its Autumn song
  Gladly in Thanksgiving.

129

BRING US GOOD ALE

Chorus

Bring us in good ale, good ale, And bring us in good ale For our bless - ed La - dy's sake, Bring us in good ale. Bring us in no brown bread, for that is made of bran, Nor bring us in no white bread, for there in is no gain. But bring us in good ale, good ale, And bring us in good ale, For our bless - ed La - dy's sake, bring us in good ale.

2. Bring us in no beef, for there is many bones,
   But bring us in good ale, for that go'th down at once:

3. Bring us in no bacon, for that is passing fat,
   But bring us in good ale, and give us enough of that:

4. Bring us in no mutton, for that is passing lean,
   Nor bring us in no tripes, for they be seldom clean:

5. Bring us in no eggs, for there are many shells,
   But bring us in good ale, and give us nothing else:

6. Bring us in no butter, for therein are many hairs,
   Nor bring us in no pig's flesh, for that will make us bears:

7. Bring us in no puddings, for therein is all God's good,
   Nor bring us in no venison, that is not for our blood:

8. Bring us in no capon's flesh, for that is often dear,
   Nor bring us in no duck's flesh, for the slobber in the mere (mire):

THE HUNT IS UP!

Old English
Arr. by GEOFFREY SHAW

2. The East is bright with morning light,
   And darkness it is fled;
   The merry horn wakes up the morn
   To leave his idle bed.

3. The sun is glad to see us clad
   All in our lusty green,
   And smiles in the sky, as he riseth high
   To see and to be seen.

4. Awake, all men, I say again,
   Be merry as you may,
   For Harry, our King, is gone hunting
   To bring his deer to bay.

BARLEY MOW

from collection of National English Airs
pub. Chappell Publishers, London 1840

Moderately fast and in a Jovial style   *Bass by Warren*

And we'll drink out of the nipperkin boys, good health to the Bar - ley Mow . . . . . . And

we'll drink out of the   pipperkin   boys, good health to the Bar - ley Mow . . . . . . The nipperkin pipperkin

Slower   *Chorus in the first time*

and the brown bowl, good health to the Bar - ley mow my boys, good health to the Bar - ley Mow . . . .

2. And we'll drink out of the well boys,
   Good health to the barley-mow.
   And we'll drink out of the well boys,
   Good health to the barley-mow.

   The nipperkin, pipperkin, etc.

3. And we'll drink out of the lake boys,
   Good health to the barley-mow.
   And we'll drink out of the lake boys,
   Good health to the barley-mow.

   The nipperkin, pipperkin, etc.

132

DOWN IN YON FOREST

2. In that hall there stands a bed:
   It's covered all over with scarlet so red:

3. At the bedside there lies a stone:
   Which the sweet Virgin Mary knelt upon:

4. Under that bed there runs a flood:
   The one half runs water, the other runs blood:

5. At the bed's foot there grows a thorn:
   Which ever blows blossom since he was born:

6. Over that bed the moon shines bright:
   denoting our Saviour was born this night:

Christmas Carols

The singing of songs in celebration of Christmas dates from the very early Middle Ages. There are two distinctly different types of Christmas music: songs with a strictly religious content, which were intended for more pious performance, and songs that were as much secular as sacred. We have included examples of both types of Christmas songs in this section. The more religious songs have a distinctly different feel than the secularly oriented songs, and during the Middle Ages secular Christmas songs were considered slightly inappropriate for such a sacred season. Unlike today, when wandering groups of carolers are one of the more charmingly old-fashioned aspects of the season, in the Middle Ages, bands of carolers usually collected money from passersby, and were therefore considered beggars—an undesirable social element. The public singing of secular carols was once outlawed by both church and civil authorities—but these prohibitions obviously failed. Thanks to the failure of this legislation, we can still enjoy these wonderful songs.

One of the most popular secular Christmas songs today is "The Twelve Days of Christmas." But the familiar refrains of "five golden rings, four calling birds, three French hens, two turtledoves, and a partridge in a pear tree" were only standardized in the nineteenth century. Originally this was a free-form song, in which the first singer would invent his own "gift." When another singer took up the second verse, he would add his own "gift" and repeat the first singer's verse. The verses might just as easily have been "five barking dogs, four casks of ale, three thrusting daggers, two velvet gowns, and a necklace of tiny white pearls." The song was more a memory game to entertain dinner guests than a familiar song to be sung by rote. Try performing it in this manner; it may be a real challenge, but the results are likely to be amusing if not totally hilarious. Because the song involves the Twelve Days of Christmas, it is especially appropriate on Twelfth Night (January 5), the traditional date on which the three Wise Men visited the infant Jesus, and the official end of the Christmas season. The carols presented here include some familiar selections and some that will probably be unfamiliar. We hope some of these will find their way to becoming a part of your personal list of favorite Christmas carols. All these songs date from the fourteenth and fifteenth centuries.

IN EXCELSIS GLORIA

(NATIVITY)
First Tune
A. H. Brown

When Christ was born of Ma - ry free, In Beth - lem in that fair ci - ty,

Angels sung e'er with mirth and glee, In ex - cel - sis glo - ri - a,

(continued on page 136)

135

(continued from page 135)

Christo paremus cantica,
In excelsis gloria.

2. Herdmen beheld these angels bright—
   To them appeared with great light.
   And said, 'God's son is born this night':

3. This king is come to save his kind,
   In the scripture as we find;
   Therefore this song have we in mind:

4. Then, dear Lord, for thy great grace,
   Grant us the bliss to see thy face,
   Where we may sing to thy solace:

NOWELL, NOWELL: IN BETHLEM

(continued on page 138)

137

(continued from page 137)

mai-den and wife; he is both God and .... man, . . . take shrift; no - well.

mai-den and wife; he is both God and man, . . . take shrift; no - well.

This Prince of peace shall cease all strife, and wone with us .... per - pe - tu - al.

[This] Prince of peace shall cease all strife, and wone with us per - pe - tu - al.

2. This child shall buy us with his blood
And be nailëd on a rood;
His ransom passeth all earthly good,
Nowell!
Alas what wight dare be so wood
To slay so gentle a jewel?

3. By his powst this child shall rise;
Fro hell he shall take his emprise
And save mankind in this wise;
Nowell!
Thus telleth us the prophecies,
Herebeforn as they did tell.

SOMERSET WASSAIL

(CHRISTMAS AND NEW YEAR, SECULAR)
Traditional
Oxford University Press, 1923

In Quick Time. Voices in Unison (Semi-Chorus) (M. S.)

Was - sail, and was - sail, all o - o - ver the town the

cu - p it is white and the a - ale it is brown the cu - up it is

made of the go - od ash - en tree A - nd so - o is the malt of the

Chorus

best b - ar - ley *for it's your was - ail, and it's our was -*

(continued on page 140)

(continued from page 139)

-sail and it's joy   be to   you and a   jol - ly   was - sail

2. O master and missus, are you all within?
   Pray open the door and let us come in;
   O master and missus a-sitting by the fire,
   Pray think upon poor travellers, a-travelling
        in the mire:

Chorus

3. O where is the maid, with the silver-headed pin,
   To open the door, and let us come in?
   O master and missus, it is our desire
   A good loaf and cheese, and a toast by the fire:

Chorus

4. There was an old man, and he had an old cow,
   And how for to keep her he didn't know how,
   He built up a barn for to keep his cow warm,
   And a drop or two of cider will do us no harm:

   No harm, boys, harm; no harm, boys, harm;
   And a drop or two of cider will do us no harm.

5. The girt dog of Langport he burnt his long tail,
   And this is the night we go singing wassail:
   O master and missus, now we must be gone:
   God bless all in this house till we do come again.

   For it's your wassail, and it's our wassail!
   And it's joy be to you, and a jolly wassail!

MAKE US MERRY

R, ff.12v.-13

in die circumcisionis

(continued on page 142)

(continued from page 141)

Ga - bri - el,... brighter ...... than ...... the ...... sun, gra - cious-ly .... greet - ë ...

Ga - bri - el,... brighter ..... than .... the ...... sun, gra - cious - ly .. greet - ë ...

that .... mai - den .. free; tho - rough her meekness Christ .... have we ... found;

that .... mai - den free; tho - rough her meek - ness Christ .. have we ...... found;

Ec - ce, an - cilla Domi - ni ....

Ec - ce, an - cil - la Do - mi - ni ....

2. Ave Maria, virgin bright;
   We joyeth of the benignity;
   The Holy Ghost is in thee light;
   Thou hast conceivëd thy Son so free.

3. Now is that maidë great with child,
   Herself alone also credibly;
   Fro the fiend she shall us shield,
   so sayeth bookës in their story.

YEOMAN'S CAROL

(CHRISTMAS)
Church-gallery book

(M. S.)

Let Christ - ians all with joy - ful mirth, Both young and old, both great and small, now think up - on our sav - ior's birth who brought sal - va - tion to us all.

(continued on page 144)

(continued from page 143)

Chorus

This day did Christ man's soul from dea - th re - move,

with glor - ious saints to dwell in Heaven a - bove.

2. No palace, but an ox's stall,
   The place of his nativity;
   This truly should instruct us all
   To learn of him humility:

Chorus

3. Then Joseph and the Virgin came
   Unto the town of Bethlehem,
   But sought in vain within the same
   For lodging to be granted them:

Chorus

4. A stable harboured them, where they
   Continued till this blessed morn.
   Let us rejoice and keep the day,
   Wherein the Lord of life was born:

Chorus

5. He that descended from above,
   Who for your sins has meekly died,
   Make him the pattern of your love;
   So will your joys be sanctified:

Chorus

Mother's Day Carols

Most of us think of Mother's Day as a fairly modern invention; in the United States, it was only institutionalized during the 1930s by order of President Franklin Roosevelt. But in fact, Mother's Day (or Mothering Sunday, as it is called in Great Britain) dates to the late fourteenth or early fifteenth century. The honoring of mothers everywhere was always celebrated during the Lenten season. The rare Mothering Sunday carol included here dates from about 1450.

MOTHERING SUNDAY

(MID-LENT)

'He who goes a-mothering finds violets in the lane.'

German, 14th century
George Hare Leonard

Sopranos sing words, other parts hum accompaniment

(M. S.)

It is the day of all the year, of all the year the one day

When I shall see my mo-ther dear and bring her cheer a-mothering on Sun-day

Faux Bourdon Version for choice of verses
Tenors sign words, other parts hum accompaniment

(continued on page 146)

(continued from page 145)

For Last Verse all sing words

It is the day of all the year, of all the year the one day

and here come I my mother dear to bring you cheer a-mo-the-ring on Sun-day

2. So I'll put on my Sunday coat,
   And in my hat a feather,
   And get the lines I writ by rote,
   With many a note,
   That I've a-strung together.

3. And now to fetch my wheaten cake,
   To fetch it from the baker,
   He promised me, for Mother's sake,
   The best he'd bake
   For me to fetch and take her.

4. Well have I known, as I went
      by
   One hollow lane, that none day
   I'd fail to find—for all they're
      shy—
   Where violets lie,
   As I went home on Sunday.

5. My sister Jane is waiting-maid
   Along with Squire's lady;
   And year by year her part she's
   And home she stayed,   [played,
   To get the dinner ready.

6. For Mother'll come to Church
      you'll see—
   Of all the year it's the day—
   'The one,' she'll say, 'that's made
   And so it be: [for me.'
   It's every Mother's free day.

7. The boys will all come home from
      town,
   Not one will miss that one day;
   And every maid will bustle down
   To show her gown,
   A-Mothering on Sunday.

8. It is the day of all the year,
   Of all the year the one day;
   And here come I, my Mother dear,
   To bring you cheer,
   A-Mothering on Sunday.

FURRY DAY CAROL

(MAY)
Traditional
Oxford University Press, 1923

(M. S.)

Re - e - mem - ber us poor Ma - yers all And thus we do

Be - gin - a to lead our lives in right - eous - ness

or else we die in - sin - a With Ho - lan - to

Ho - lan - to, Ho - lan - to, sing mer - - ry,

2. We have been rambling half the night,
   And almost all the day-a,
   And now, returnèd back again,
   We've brought you a branch of many-a:

Chorus

3. O, we were up as soon as day,
   To fetch the summer home-a;
   The summer is a coming-on,
   And winter is agone-a:

Chorus

4. Then let us all most merry be,
   And sing with cheerful voice-a;
   For we have good occasion now
   This time for to rejoice-a:

Chorus

5. Saint George he next shall be our song:
   Saint George, he was a knight-a;
   Of all the men in Christendom
   Saint George he was the right-a:

Chorus

6. God bless our land with power and might,
   God send us peace in England;
   Pray send us peace in England;
   For ever in merry England:

   Chorus

Easter Carols

Although they have now disappeared entirely, Easter carols were once as common as Christmas carols. We hope you will find the Easter carol included here as delightful and interesting as we do.

EASTER CAROL

French tune
N. S. T.
Oxford University Press, 1923

(M. S.)

Cheer up, friends and neigh - bours, now it's East - er tide

Stop from end - less la - bours wor - ries put a - side

Men should rise from sad - ness e - vil fol - ly strife

When God's mi - ghty glad - ness brings the earth to life.

2. Out from snowdrifts chilly,
   Roused from drowsy hours,
   Bluebell wakes, and lily;
   God calls up the flowers!
   Into life he raises
   All the sleeping buds;
   Meadows weave his praises,
   And the spangled woods.

3. All his truth and beauty,
   All his righteousness,
   Are our joy and duty,
   Bearing his impress:
   Look! the earth waits breathless
   After Winter's strift:
   Easter shows man deathless,
   Spring leads death to life.

4. Ours the more and less is;
   But, changeless all the days,
   God revives and blesses,
   Like the sunlight rays.
   'All mankind is risen,'
   The Easter bells do ring,
   While from out their prison
   Creep the flowers of Spring!

CHAPTER 16

Dances

Dance has always been an integral part of human celebration and social gatherings at all levels of society. Ever since people first learned to drum a simple beat on a hollow log, they have been tapping their toes and moving their feet in time with the rhythm. This chapter will provide you with all of the information you need to learn and teach two types of simple medieval dances. The first style of dance covered includes formal dances of the type we would now think of as ballroom dances; the second type are maypole dances.

If you would like to introduce the dance at your medieval celebration, there are a few things you should take into consideration. If your event is relatively small—say, under fifty or sixty people—it should be no problem for one or two couples to learn the steps ahead of time and teach them to any interested guests. If, on the other hand, you are expecting several hundred people, it might be wiser to find four or five couples who would be willing to learn the dances and perform them during or after the feast as a form of entertainment. Trying to teach two hundred people how to dance, particularly if they have had a few drinks, might cause more confusion than you want to deal with. If you don't know anyone who is adept at dancing, try to make contact with a local medieval recreationist group through a local college or university; they undoubtedly have people who can execute medieval dances with grace, style, and in the appropriate costume, and they are usually glad to put on a dance performance for a small fee.

Many of these same considerations should be taken into account for the maypole dances. The greatest num-

ber of people who can take part in dancing around one maypole is twenty-four and, considering that the maypole dance is a very visual experience, you might want to pick your maypole dancers ahead of time, teach them the dances as described below, and have them execute the dances for the enjoyment of the rest of the guests.

Formal Dances

Unfortunately, there are virtually no documented dance steps surviving from earlier than 1400. There is earlier surviving dance music, but we do not know which steps were danced to it, and we are not even sure of the speed at which the music should be played, so we will concentrate on dances of the fifteenth century. Fifteenth-century dance fell into two basic styles: the Burgundian style and the Italian style. Burgundian refers to those dances generally found in high-court circles. They were very fancy, with lots of elegant patterns and athletic leaping in the air. The people who practiced these dances considered dance an essential part of a courtly education; they spent a lot of time at it and often got quite good. Italian-style dancing, on the other hand, was far simpler. These were the dances of the middle classes, used on those occasions when hard-working merchants held or attended a feast, wedding, or other celebration. Though this style is called Italian, it was common in England and was probably the basic style of dance found in most western European countries. The three dances in this chapter are well-documented fifteenth-century French dances in the Italian style.

Our dances come from a book entitled *Orchéso-graphie*. Written by a French ecclesiastic named Jean Tabourot, *Orchésographie* was first published in 1588 and supplies a wealth of information on dancing. Unlike many other period sources, it includes details of steps, dances, and music, along with timings, drum rhythms, and useful social nuances ("spit and blow your nose sparingly"). Tabourot says that some of the dances in his book are old ("Our predecessors danced pavans, basse dances, branles and corantos."), and we know that the dances below date to at least the 1400s. In all, the book describes the Basse dance, the Pavan, Pavane d'Espagne, Courante, Allemande, Volte, Canary, Morisque, a sword dance called Les Bouffons, fifteen Galliard variations, and twenty-five Branles. The entire book is written in the form of a dialogue between a dancing master called Arbeau and his student Capriol. To give you a feel for the original book, we have retained bits of the conversation between the two characters throughout the instructions.

Capriol: I much enjoyed fencing and tennis and this placed me on friendly terms with young men. However, without a knowledge of dancing, I could not please the damsels, upon whom, it seems to me, the entire reputation of an eligible young man depends.

Arbeau: Kings and princes are wont to command performances of dancing and masquerades to salute, entertain and give joyous greetings to foreign nobles. We take part in such rejoicing to celebrate wedding days and in the rites of our religious festivals.

There are some general observations that can be applied to all medieval dances, and it is good to keep them in mind when you are learning the steps. During the Middle Ages, most dances, whether they were executed in the court of a great king or stomped out on the village green by a bunch of plowmen and their wives, would look to us like folk dances. They were danced in a line, two or more lines, a circle, or a series of circles. It is only the complexity of the steps that separated upper-class dance from peasant dance. If you don't get them the first time around, don't feel bad. As Arbeau says to his student, "Every dancer acquits himself to the best of his ability, each according to his years and degree of skill."

Assuming that most people at your medieval event will not know these dances, it might be best if you have one couple, or at least one individual, who can act as dance master, leading everyone through the individual steps, and through at least one dance, before the actual dancing begins.

The Basic Steps

When you have committed these seven basic steps to memory, you will be able to perform all three dances below, hopefully like a pro, in no time.

Révérence

To perform the révérence, you will keep the left foot firmly upon the ground and bending the right knee take the point of the toe behind the left foot, removing your bonnet or hat the while and bowing to your damsel and the company.

The révérence was the opening movement of most dances; it was no more than a way to pay honor to the lady with whom a man was dancing. Reverencing in the correct fashion was considered very important; some dancing manuals devoted whole chapters to it.

Pieds Joints

Pieds joints . . . is considered to be the correct position when the feet are placed side by side, the toes in a straight line and the dancer's weight equally distributed on both feet.

Pieds joints is no more than standing up straight with your feet together. If you can't figure this one out, you may want to consider leaving the dance floor.

Simples

You will perform a simple by making a pied largi with the right foot and to conclude a pied joint with the left foot.

A simple left is a step sideways onto the left foot, then a step to bring the right foot to the left. A simple right is a step sideways onto the right foot, then a step to bring the left foot to the right.

Doubles

A double consists of three steps and a pieds joints. To perform these sideways you will assume a proper bearing after the révérence of salutation, and, while keeping the right foot firmly in position, throw your left foot out to the side which makes a pieds largis for the first bar. Then for the second bar, keep the left foot firmly in position, bringing the right foot near the left which will make a pieds largis that is almost a pieds joints. For the third bar keep the right foot firm and throw the left foot out to the side which will make a pieds largis, and for the fourth bar keep the left foot firm and bring the right foot close to it which will make a pieds joints.

A double left is a step sideways onto the left foot, a step to bring the right foot almost to the left, a step sideways onto the left foot, then a step to bring the right foot next to the left. A double right is a step sideways onto the right foot, a step to bring the left foot almost to the right, a step sideways onto the right foot, then a step to bring the left foot next to the right. This is the basic, or common, version of the step; however, Arbeau gives a number of variations.

Sauts

There is a movement called saut which takes place when both feet are raised in the air and is livelier still. And you should understand that there are two kinds of saut, to whit, saut majeur and petit saut.

The saut, Arbeau says, is a leap. A saut majeur is a big leap in the air, landing with the feet together. A petit saut is a little jump or bounce on the move.

Capriole

While executing the saut majeur they move their feet in the air and such capering is called Capriole.

A capriole consists of a jump in the air while moving the feet backward and forward quickly, followed by a graceful landing (the hard part).

Grève and Pied en l'Air

The dancer throws his weight upon one foot to support his body and raises the other into the air in front of him as if he were about to kick someone. This movement is done in two ways, with the right foot when it is called grève droite and with the left foot when it is called grève gauche. Sometimes the foot is only raised slightly off the ground and moved a little, if at all, forward and this is called pied en l'air droit if the right foot is lifted. . . . The said movement must be performed barely off the ground and gently as a damsel might do it.

This description can be a little confusing, as the other step names generally tell you the direction of travel as well as the foot to start on. For a grève or pied en l'air, the name tells you which foot to finish the movement with (you will start by moving slightly in the opposite direction, onto the opposite foot). For a pied en l'air right, spring onto the left foot, holding the right foot forward, raised a little above the ground. For a grève, kick higher. For a pied en l'air or grève left, spring onto the right foot and kick with the left.

The Dances

The Pavan

The pavan . . . is usually danced before the basse dance. The said pavan has not become obsolete or gone out of fashion, nor do I believe it ever will although in truth it is less popular than it was in the past. Our musicians play it when a maiden of good family is taken to Holy Church to be married or when they lead a procession of the chaplains, masters and brethren of some notable confraternity. On solemn feast days the pavan is employed by kings, princes and great noblemen to display themselves in their fine mantles and ceremonial robes. And it is the pavans . . . that announce the grand ball and are arranged to last until the dancers have circled the hall two or three times, unless they prefer to dance it by advancing and retreating.

The pavan is basically a processional dance. As Arbeau says, it can be danced as a processional for the entry of a bride. It could equally well be used as a grand entrance into the hall for the diners at a feast.

Arbeau: The pavan is easy to dance as it is mearly [sic] two simples and one double forward and two simples and one double backwards. It is played in double time, you will note that the two simples and the double forward are begun with the left foot and the two simples and the double backwards are begun with the right foot.

Capriol: Then the tabor and other instruments play eight bars while the dancers advance and eight bars while they move backwards.

Arbeau: That is so, and if one does not wish to move backwards one may continue to advance all the time.

EUGENE SIREN

Capriol: I find these pavans and basse dances charming and dignified, and well suited to honourable persons, particularly ladies and maidens.

The pavan is danced as a long line of couples, with a very simple pattern of stepping, repeating until the music stops:

Simple left, simple right, double left.
Simple right, simple left, double right.

If you wish to make the dance last longer, you can use backward steps; the entire line of dancers can also make turns. As Arbeau says, "Upon approaching the end of the hall you continue to guide the damsel forward while you yourself move backwards as she advances until you are facing the opposite direction from which you started."

Branles

Branles, or brawles, as they were known in England, belonged to the middle rung of society, not the court. Some were written for masquerades; others had their origins in the round dances of earlier times or the dances of the French peasantry. Whatever the source, their nature is fairly raucous and their humor earthy, especially in branles performed as mime.

Capriol: I have noticed that in good society they usually begin the dancing with a branle. Tell me how these should be danced.

Arbeau: You should understand that the branle is danced by moving sideways and not forward.

Capriol: I like branles because a number of persons can enjoy them together.

Arbeau: When you commence a branle several others will join you, as many young men as do damsels, and sometimes the damsel who is the last to arrive will take your left hand and it will thus become a round dance.

Arbeau's descriptions indicate that branles can be danced in a variety of formations, such as lines or circles, and the structure of the dances is fairly loose; the participants can join in at will and turn a line into a circle midway through a dance. This is still true of modern French folk dances, where the band starts playing and people join in when they feel like it, nip off for a glass of wine, and return at will.

Branle Des Pois

Among the branles with mimic gestures is the Pease branle, otherwise known as the Margueritotte, which is danced in light duple time either like the common branle or the Haut Barrois, as one prefers. Any equal number of men and women take part and they dance it in the manner you will see described in the tabulation which follows.

The Branle Des Pois, or Pease Brawl (meaning peas), is a dance for any number of couples in a circle.

Steps

Everyone joins hands in a ring, then:
Double left, double right, double left, double right; drop hands.
Men only: Saut majeur (women watch amazed).
Women only: Saut majeur (men eye them up).
Men only: Step left, then three petit sauts to left.
Women only: Saut majeur.
Men only: Saut majeur.
Women only: Step left, then three petit sauts to left.
Repeat until the dancers or musicians get tired.

Branle de l'Official

The men take the women by the waist and assist them to leap into the air and alight upon the said cadence. Meanwhile the men remain firmly upon both feet to support their partners and are much hindered in these circumstances if they perforce must lift a damsel who will make no effort herself.

"Official" in the title of this branle either refers to the "office"—that is, the household servants—or to an "official," meaning an ecclesiastical judge, a post which the author, Jean Tabourot, held at one point in his career.

Like the Branle Des Pois, this dance is for any number of couples in a circle.

Steps

Double left, double right, double left, double right.
Simple left six times.
Pied en l'air right, pied en l'air left, then women jump in the air assisted by the men.

A nice variation is for the women to jump across the men into the next position in the ring. Repeat until the exhausted dancers return to their original partners.

Maypole Dances

As we explained in the chapter on May Day celebrations, the maypole dance probably dates from before recorded history. Even during the Middle Ages the dance steps were passed on orally rather than being written down. All of the surviving instructions for maypole dancing come from nineteenth-century sources, but we can reasonably assume that the various dances and basic steps remained much the same in the nineteenth century as they were five or six centuries earlier.

All of these dances should be done with a skipping step set to moderately quick-paced music. Any catchy tune with a 4/4 beat should do and will help the dancers keep their steps in time with the music and with each other's movements. The dancers may want to sing along with the tune to help keep their steps in pace with the music.

The Gypsy Tent

For this dance you need an equal number of men and women.

1. The men stand in a circle around the maypole, equally spaced from one another, facing outward so their backs are toward the pole. They should stand about 6 to 8 feet away from the pole.
2. The women stand in front of the men, facing one-quarter turn to the right, so their left shoulders are pointing toward the men's chests.
3. All dancers hold a ribbon in their right hands. The men should hold their ribbons level with the tops of their heads and the women should hold their ribbon as high above their heads as they can reach.
4. While the men stand still, the women move forward, walking behind the first man they pass (between the man and the maypole), in front of the next man, and so on, weaving in and out around the men.
5. The women continue around the circle, moving in and out among the men.
6. As the women move around the circle their ribbons will build a tent-like canopy around the men's ribbons.
7. When the women have no more ribbon, they can reverse directions and unwrap the tent.

Dancing around the maypole was an essential part of almost every spring festival during the Middle Ages. SCARBOROUGH RENAISSANCE FESTIVAL, WAXAHACHIE, TX

157

The Grand Chain

1. Position an equal number of men and women in a circle around the maypole. They should all stand an equal distance apart. The men should hold their ribbons in their left hands and the women should hold their ribbons in their right hands.

2. The men turn one quarter turn to their right, so their left arms are facing the pole.

3. The women turn one quarter turn to their left, so their right arms are facing the pole.

4. All of the dancers move forward in the direction they are facing.

5. As the couples approach one another, the men hold their ribbon high in the air, and the women bend down slightly so they can pass under the ribbon of the man they are approaching.

6. Immediately after passing under the men's ribbons, the women should raise their right arms (holding the ribbon) high into the air and the men should lower their left arms.

7. As the dancers approach the next individual, the men should duck under the women's raised arms.

8. Continue alternating the steps with the women passing under the men's raised arms and the men then passing under the women's raised arms until the ribbons are wrapped completely around the pole and the dancers are too close to the pole to duck under each other's arms.

9. The dancers may either tie the ribbons to the pole and end the dance or reverse their steps and unwrap the ribbons and end the dance when they return to their original places.

Note: Wrapping the pole will take some practice but getting it unwrapped will take even more. Don't be surprised if the ribbons become tangled and the dancers break down into uncontrollable laughter.

The Three-Strand Dance

For this dance you will need a number of participants that is divisible by both two and three—six, twelve, eighteen, twenty-four, or thirty-six.

1. The dancers stand facing the pole, about 8 feet away from the pole, each holding a ribbon in their right hand.

2. The dancers should arrange themselves in groups of three. Each member of each group should be no more than one foot from their nearest partner, but there should be as much space in between the different groups as possible.

3. Each group of three should assign themselves numbers; the dancer furthest to the left is number 1, the dancer in the middle is number 2, and the dancer on the right is number 3. Each group will now braid their three strands together by executing the following steps.

4. Dancer number 2 will hold their ribbon high in the air while dancer number 3 passes in front of them and under the ribbon. Dancer number 3 now raises their ribbon high into the air and passes behind dancer number 1, who bends down to allow number 3 to pass.

5. Dancer number 2 now ducks down and passes in front of and beneath dancer number 1's ribbon. Dancer number 2 then raises their ribbon high into the air and passes behind and over dancer number 3.

6. While dancer number 3 raises their arm into the air, dancer number 1 ducks and passes in front of them and under their ribbon. Dancer number 1 next raises their arm and crosses behind dancer number 2, who ducks to allow number 1 to pass.

7. Repeat these steps, beginning with step 4, and continue repeating the steps until each group of three dancers has a completely braided strand of ribbons.

8. The dancers may now unbraid their ribbons by reversing the steps above, or dancers numbers 1 and 3 may step away, leaving the end of the braided ribbons with dancer number 2.

9. If the dancers elect to pass the braided ribbons to number 2, the remaining group of dancers may now execute the Grand Chain dance as described above.

10. If the dancers have elected to unbraid their braided ribbons by reversing steps 4 through 7, all of the dancers may now choose to continue the dance by executing the Grand Chain dance as described above.

Three-strand maypole dance, position 1

Three-strand maypole dance, position 7

BRANLE DES POIS

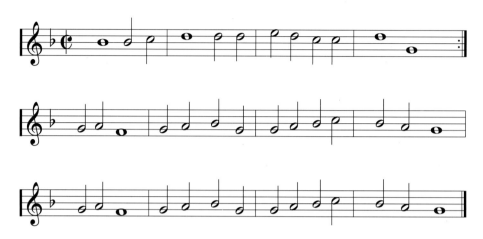

BRANLE DE L'OFFICIAL

BELLE QUI TIENS MA VIE

1. Fair one, who holds my heart
   Captive within thine eyes,
   Whose gracious smiles impart
   Secrets of Paradise
   Give me hope to cherish
   For without I perish

2. Fly not, I entreat thee,
   For in thy presence fair
   I am lost completely
   To myself and care.
   Thy divine perfection
   claims my whole affection.

3. Such grace of form and face
   Kindles a sweet desire,
   My icy heart yields place
   To a heart all afire,
   Fanned by ardent yearning
   Passionately burning.

4. I wandered fancy free,
   Nor glance nor sigh I gave
   Till love imprisoned me,
   And I became his slave,
   Ready to die for him,
   Sworn to his slightest whim.

5. Draw near, O mistress mine,
   Come closer to me still.
   Since I am wholly thine
   Soften thy rebel will,
   Mend my heart with the bliss
   of one sweet healing kiss.

6. Angel, my life's eclipse,
   In thine embrace I die.
   The honey of thy lips
   Sweetens my parting sigh,
   And my soul soars above
   Borne on the wings of love.

7. Oceans shall surge no more
   And heaven's eye wax cold
   Full many a moon before
   My love for thee grows old,
   Or wanes a single jot
   If thou forsake me not.

CHAPTER 17

Costumes and Clothing

No single element will add more to the authenticity of your medieval event than attractive costumes. Somehow, putting on the costume of a far-removed time and place alters not only our perception of ourselves and each other but also, unless we actually fight against it, our behavior. Simply put, if you look medieval, you are a whole lot more likely to feel and act medieval.

That's the easy part. The hard part is getting all of your guests appropriately dressed. So before we discuss costume styles and patterns, here are a few facts about costumes you need to consider. First, if your medieval feast is a private function, you have every right to insist that anyone who attends wear a costume. However, unless your friends and guests are all very enlightened, or are really good sports, there are dangers in demanding that everyone wear a costume. Some will only dress up grudgingly, although they may get into the mood when they see everyone else is in costume. Others will simply refuse to come in costume because they don't want to "dress funny."

If, on the other hand, your feast is a public or semi-public affair, be it a church-sponsored Twelfth Night feast or a wedding, there is absolutely no way you are going to persuade everyone to come in costume. It won't happen, and there is nothing you can do about it, so don't make yourself crazy worrying about it. If you examine the wedding photos in this book, you will almost

inevitably see people in modern clothes. Encourage everyone as much as possible, but understand it will have limited effect. If, however, the event is repeated annually, you will find that those who come back a second and third time will slowly come around to wearing costumes. It is a real thrill to see someone who previously insisted on wearing a polo shirt and blue jeans to finally appear dressed like they stepped out of the fourteenth century. Whatever the case, for the medieval experience to be completely effective, it is important that there be as many proper costumes as possible. Dancing the pavan or enjoying a sumptuous feast in T-shirt and jeans or a business suit simply doesn't have the same effect.

With these limitations in mind, let us move on to our discussion of medieval dress. Having decided that everyone really ought to attend in costume, the big question is how to find the right look. The easy answer is to rent the clothes from a costume shop. There is, however, a downside to rented costumes. Unless you are in a major metropolitan area where there are companies that rent costumes to professional theaters and movie companies, the selection of medieval clothing is likely to be severely limited and pretty tacky. Besides, a lot of the other guests will want to rent their costumes, and if there are none left to rent, they might give up. This leaves you with the choice of ordering premade costumes, having them custom made, or making them yourself.

Above: *Children love dressing up and medieval events are more fun for the whole family when mom and dad join in.* EUGENE SIREN Right: *Here, the authors host an event dressed as historical characters Leonardo da Vinci (left) and Pope Julius II.*

For those who decide to buy premade costumes, an online search for "medieval costumes for sale," "medieval costumes for men," "medieval costumes for women" or "medieval costumes for children" will provide you with a vast selection of costumes in all conceivable price ranges and styles. But if you decide to make your own costume, or possibly even make a few simple costumes to make available to those who have a last-minute change of heart after they arrive at your event, there remains the question of style and patterns.

Medieval fashion changed almost as rapidly as modern styles. With every generation, an entirely new look became popular. Naturally, the ability to keep up with the latest fashion trend depended on where you lived and how much disposable income you had. Since the period of our feast is roughly the mid-fourteenth century (around 1350), and most of our food, music, and customs have come from England and France, we will concentrate on clothing styles from that place and time. While we will offer patterns for very simple, easy-to-make,

EUGENE SIREN

man-on-the-street–type clothes, we will also provide patterns and instructions for clothes suitable to the upper and middle ranks of society.

Some of you are skilled enough, especially considering the simple techniques used during the Middle Ages, to make costumes based solely on the photos and illustrations scattered throughout this book or by doing an online search for "medieval costume patterns." Still others will need both patterns and step-by-step guidance. To those of you who fall into this latter category, we dedicate the remainder of this chapter.

To make medieval clothing construction easy to digest, we will break the general categories of clothing into bite-size pieces. First, understand that medieval clothing did share one thing with modern clothes: many of the same items were worn by both men and women. Today it is T-shirt and jeans; then it was tunics, kirtles, and surcoats. We will start by identifying the types of material you should be looking for, and then take the basic garments one by one, beginning with the simplest styles and working our way through the more complex ones.

Fabric

Fabric made seven hundred years ago was considerably heavier than that used in today's clothing. For many more ornate pieces of clothing in this chapter it is better to use upholstery fabric than clothing fabric; not only is it more authentic, but the heavier-weight fabrics will allow the clothes to hang correctly.

Medieval fabric colors tended to be rich and vibrant; pastels were unknown. Deep red, deep blue, emerald green, ocher, bright yellow, and chocolate brown were worn by both sexes. Ladies might wear deep pink, soft blue, or light green, but that was about as far from the primary color scheme as fabrics varied. Colors were mixed freely. An emerald-green gown might be lined with bright gold and worn over deep-blue hose. The most elaborate and expensive material was reserved for the cotehardie, the main outer-garment. Here, fine velvets, brocades, and damasks were common. Stripes, dots, and small patterns were virtually unknown, and although diamond patterns did exist, they were on a very large scale, the diamonds usually being four to five inches in height.

Buttons

The fourteenth century saw the introduction of buttons. Unlike today's flat buttons, fourteenth-century buttons were generally tiny balls of cloth stuffed with wool. To achieve a similar effect, use small, round, pea-size buttons. Since buttons were only used on more expensive clothes during this period, you will only need to worry about buttons and buttonholes for the most complex of our patterns.

Tunic

The medieval tunic was nothing more than a large, loose-fitting T-shirt–type affair, and was the most common upper-body garment worn by both men and women of the peasant and artisan classes. Men's tunics ended anywhere from just below the crotch to mid-thigh, although older men might wear their tunics mid-calf length. Women's tunics generally ranged from mid-thigh to knee-length but, as was true among males, older women might wear their tunics longer. Men augmented their tunics with loose, baggy trousers while women added a full-flowing, ankle-length skirt. Both sexes belted the tunic at the waist. Belts are discussed later in this chapter.

To make a tunic, select a piece of fabric in a weight appropriate to the season: heavier for late autumn and winter, lighter for spring and summer. Choose a bright,

primary color; yellow, green, red and blue are all good choices. Avoid cloth with a pattern; the tunic is a simple garment and the cloth from which it is made should be all one color.

Most modern upholstery fabrics, both lightweight and heavyweight, standardly come in 54-inch widths and we will assume that you will be working with something of about this width. Cut your fabric twice as long as you want your finished tunic to be; for an average-height man, 64 to 72 inches is a good length. As women tend to be shorter than men, a piece of fabric of the same length will make a slightly longer tunic of a suitable length for a lady. If you prefer a more scientific approach, measure the distance from the top of the shoulder to the point where you want the tunic to end, add two inches, and double the measurement. This is the length to cut your cloth.

Fold the cut fabric in half lengthwise, so you have a double thickness of cloth 54 inches wide and half its original length. If your fabric has a "finished" surface, or "right side," that you want visible on the outside of the finished garment, fold the cloth so this surface is on the inside. Now fold the cloth again, widthwise this time, and lay it out on your work surface so the open edges (the edges without folds) are on the right and the bottom edges of the cloth. Folded edges should be on the left and top edges of the folded fabric. Make sure all of the exposed edges are straight and even.

Next, take a very loose-fitting T-shirt and fold it in half so you can only see half of the body and one sleeve. Position the folded T-shirt along the folded edges of the fabric (the top and left edges) as shown in illustration 1.

Using a pencil or chalk, mark the sleeves of the tunic as shown on illustration 2. The sleeves of a man's tunic are normally cut straight but women may prefer a more flowing, bat-wing style, shown as a dotted line on the illustration. Make sure your sleeves are at least 3 inches wider than the sleeves of the T-shirt. Extend the line of the sleeve to the outer edge of the fabric. Now mark out the body of the tunic. Make sure the body joins the sleeve 3 inches out from, and 3 inches below, the point where the sleeve of the T-shirt meets the body. The body of the tunic should flare outward to within 3 or 4 inches of the outer edge of the fabric. For the neatest hemline, mark the bottom edge of the tunic in a slight arc as shown on the illustration.

Remove the T-shirt from the fabric and pin the fabric together 1 inch inside of the chalk outlines to make sure the fabric doesn't shift when you cut it. Now, cut along the outline. Remove the pins and unfold the fab-

TUNIC

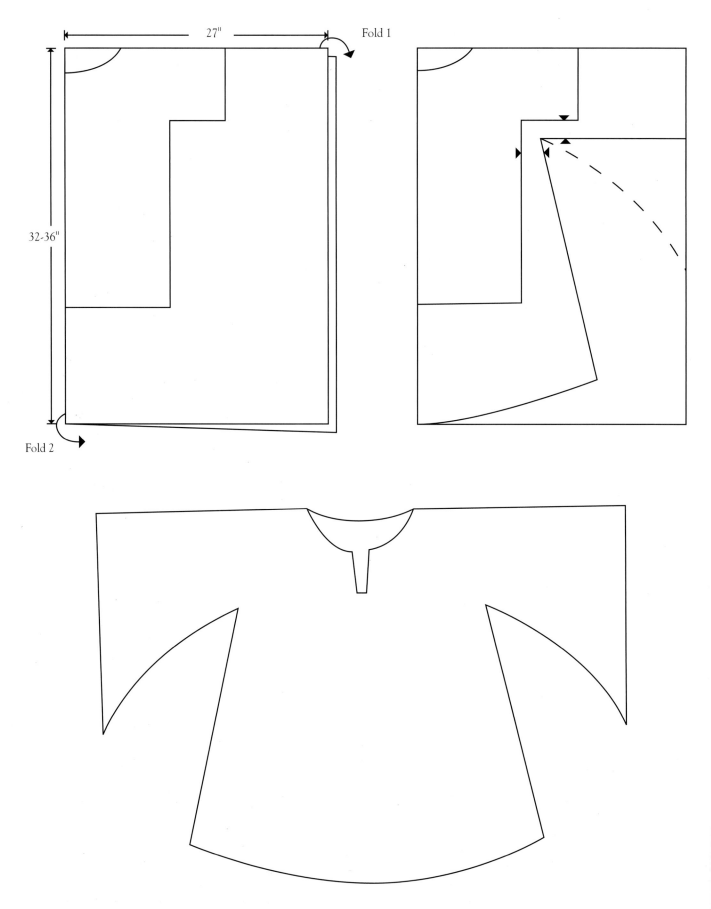

27"

Fold 1

32-36"

Fold 2

ric from right to left so you can see the full outline of the tunic as shown in illustration 3. Pin the seams of the tunic back together so the pins are 3/4 inch to 1 inch inside the edges of sleeves and sides of the body.

To mark out the neck opening, draw a half-circle where the front of your neck will be and a much shallower arc to fit against the back of your neck as shown in illustration 3. At the center of the front of the neck, cut a straight line that extends downward about 4 inches.

Leaving the tunic inside-out and pinned together, try it on to make sure you can get into it with no problem. The sleeves will probably end somewhere about mid-forearm length, but if you are a short person, and the sleeves are too long, fold the fabric back to mark the final length of the sleeves and pin them in place. Fold the bottom edge to form a rolled hem and pin the hem in place. Sew the side seams and the bottom of the arms and hem around the bottom, the ends of the sleeves and the neck. The bottom of the neck lacks any material to form a hem, so we suggest cutting two triangular-shaped pieces of cloth, about one inch to the side, hemming them, and sewing one triangle over the front and back points of the neck opening. Remove the pins and turn the tunic right-side-out. It is ready to wear.

For an added bit of embellishment you can sew decorative trim around the neck opening, one inch in from the ends of the sleeves, and one inch above the bottom hem.

Kirtle

Normally made of lightweight material, the kirtle was the basic medieval undergarment and is only slightly more complicated to make than the tunic. The kirtle was worn by both sexes. Women's were universally long, while men's were a variety of lengths, depending on what the man was wearing over it.

If you want to attend your medieval event in something a little more fashionable than a tunic, but are not up to making a complete ensemble, consider wearing just a kirtle made out of a slightly heavier cloth; the weight of the cloth will be determined by the season of the year. Even if you are wearing it as an outergarment, a pair of heavy dance tights will make your kirtle look very fashionable. Add a pair of shoes and a belt and the kirtle will give you a perfectly acceptable medieval look.

If the kirtle is going to be entirely covered by an overgarment, it can be made of nothing more exotic than lightweight linen or cotton; even though cotton

was unknown in medieval Europe it is an acceptable substitute for linen. If, on the other hand, the overgarment has a low-cut collar or open sleeves that allow part of the kirtle to show, then the kirtle should be made of a better-quality material, either heavy linen or upholstery-weight silk or satin. Virtually all kirtles were a single color. Men's were frequently white, but women's might be any color at all. Because little of the kirtle is seen, its construction can be extremely simple.

Our pattern shows a kirtle twenty-two inches wide. This should serve for most slim to medium-size people; for the more ample figure, the pattern will have to be adjusted for a comfortable fit.

Fold the material across the shoulders so both front and back can be cut from the same piece of fabric. The length will be determined by the sex of the wearer. Men's kirtles generally stop four to five inches below the waist, unless they will be wearing very short cotehardies, in which case the kirtles should be adjusted accordingly. Older men, who preferred a long cotehardie, might wear their kirtles longer. If you are wearing your kirtle as an outergarment you may want to it to fall to mid-calf length or longer. Women's kirtles, on the other hand, should always hang to the ankle. Cut the neck opening, making sure it falls slightly lower in the front than in the back. Next, cut two gores as shown in the illustration. (A gore is a wedge-shaped piece of cloth inserted into the seam of a garment to provide extra room to move.) For slim males, the insertion of a gore may not be necessary, but even the slimmest ladies will need the gore to allow free movement of the legs.

Sew the sides of the kirtle from the bottom of the arm opening to the top of the gore, and sew the gores in place. Turn the kirtle inside-out so the seams are on the inside. Have the wearer try on the body of the kirtle to make sure the arm openings are large enough, and set the hemline. Hem the bottom and neck hole. In one surviving medieval kirtle, the neckline is overlaid with a simple bias tape to provide an attractive finished edge.

Check the arm length of the wearer against the suggested arm length in the illustration. Fold the arm fabric along the top line of the arm so both the front and back of the arms can be cut from one piece of cloth. Cut the arms and sew the bottom seam, stopping about three inches above the wrist. Hem both sides of the three-inch opening to form a vent, similar to those found on modern dress shirts.

Turn both the kirtle and sleeves inside out, and sew the sleeves into the sleeve openings. Have the wearer put on the kirtle to check the length of the sleeves. They

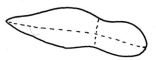

CHAUSES

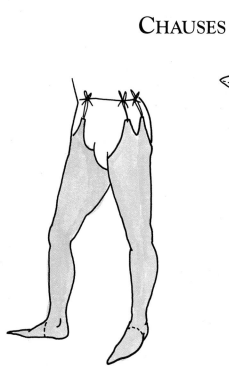

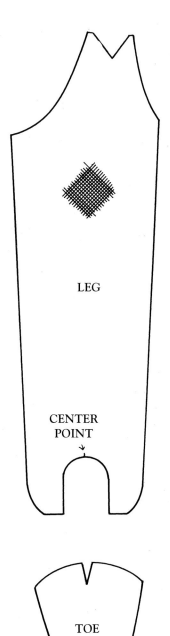

BOTTOM VIEW
SHOWING SEAMS

LEG

CENTER
POINT

TOE

KIRTLE

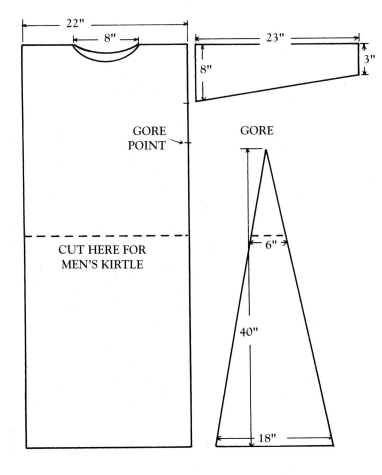

22"

8"

GORE
POINT

23"

8"

3"

GORE

GORE

6"

40"

18"

CUT HERE FOR
MEN'S KIRTLE

should be about one inch longer than the sleeves on a modern shirt. Adjust the length as necessary. The cuff may be closed either with one or two small buttons, similar to a modern shirt, or by sewing a small casing (tube) into the cuff hem through which a drawstring can be run. The drawstring can then simply be pulled snug and tied in a bow.

Chauses

Chauses were leggings—not really tights in the way we think of them today, but more like heavy socks that went up to the crotch. We have provided a pattern for a pair of chauses, but it is far simpler just to buy a pair of heavyweight dance tights. If you want to look really fashionable, buy two pairs and cut them in half along the crotch seam, reassembling them so that the left and right legs are different colors.

Ladies' hose were no more than a short version of men's chauses, secured at the knee with a pair of garters. Again, it is just as easy to use a pair of dance tights, or even knee-length hose or socks in a bright, plain color.

If you decide you want to make your own chauses, they will have to be custom-fit to each individual pair of legs, because they are made from non-stretch fabric. Following the pattern for the main leg section, cut a rough template from soft cloth, such as an old sheet. Wrap the template around the leg, making sure the tie points fall two to three inches below the waist. Next, fit the template around the leg, pinning it in position at the center back of the leg. Trim off the excess fabric, allowing a quarter-inch overlap. Leave enough material that the sides can be tucked under the foot far enough to overlap at least half an inch. Cut out the horseshoe-shaped area to fit comfortably across the top of the foot.

When the pattern fits comfortably, transfer it to the final cloth, making sure the weave of the fabric is on the bias—that is, the weave should run at a forty-five-degree angle to the pattern (see the small area in the illustration showing how the weave should lie). It is historically correct to make the legs different colors, and it makes an appropriately splashy fashion statement.

Turn the legging inside out, sew up the rear seam, and hem around the top, after making sure the tie points fall so that one is on the side of the body and the other in front of the hip. Put the legging back on the person who will be wearing it. Tuck the ends under the foot, and trim them so they overlap about a quarter inch and

fit neatly around the heel. Turn the legging inside out once again, and sew the two sides of the heel together and around the back of the heel.

Shape the toe piece around the foot and trim it so the bottom seam overlaps a quarter inch and the back end of the toe piece fits comfortably under the opening in the leg piece. Mark around the front edge of the legging where it rests on the toe. Trim any excess material from the toe as necessary, sew the two sides of the toe together, and attach the toe to the legging. The seam where the toe joins the legging can be seen in the main illustration, and the seams on the bottom of the foot are shown in the small illustration of the bottom of the foot. Be sure that any seams beneath the foot lie flat so they do not make the wearer uncomfortable when walking.

Since there is no crotch in the chauses, the wearer will still have to wear underpants. We suggest a pair of bicycle shorts, because they are sturdy enough to allow the tie points to be pinned fast without tearing the shorts or pulling them down when the wearer sits. Alternatively, a soft cloth belt can be tied around the waist and attached to the chauses by means of string or ribbon ties as shown in the main illustration.

Ladies' chauses are made essentially the same as men's, except that they only go up to the knee, where they are held in place with a ribbon or garter.

Cotehardie

As the primary outergarment, the cotehardie was made from the most sumptuous material the wearer could afford. The best material to use for your cotehardie is either a damask or velvet upholstery-weight fabric. A large, diamond-shaped pattern (a harlequin print) is appropriately medieval but will prove very hard to find. Upholstery fabric with a small pattern can be used but is not as authentically medieval as a larger pattern. The cotehardie was always lined, usually in a plain color, often in silk if the wearer could afford it.

Women's cotehardies were universally floor-length, sometimes with a train that might extend one to four feet behind the gown—lovely to look at, but a little clumsy if you are not used to them. Men's cotehardies varied tremendously. Some were extremely form-fitting affairs that ended at the crotch (most popular among young men with good legs and a firm rump); others were full-cut, floor-length versions (more popular among mature or slightly overweight guys). There were also knee-length and mid-calf-length versions.

Sleeve styles and lengths varied as much as the hemline. Some cotehardies had very tight sleeves; others had long, flowing sleeves that hung below the knee. If the sleeves were full, the tighter-fitting sleeves of the kirtle beneath would show. The front edges of these large sleeves were often ornamented in some way—possibly trimmed with fur or cut into decorative dags, examples of which are given below. If a man was wearing a knee-length or mid-calf-length cotehardie, the hem might be cut in dags to match the sleeves.

There are three basic styles shown in the illustrations: the men's short cotehardie, the men's long cotehardie (later called a houppelande), and a women's cotehardie. Any of the four sleeve styles is appropriate with any of the bodies. Similarly, the men's short cotehardie is shown with a high collar, which can also be used with the longer version. With the variety of patterns provided, you can mix and match an almost endless variety of styles, depending on your personal taste.

Men's Short Cotehardie

This most form-fitting of medieval garments is made from four identical sections, each making up one-quarter of the coat: front left, front right, back left, and back right. The only difference between the front and back panels is that the neck opening drops slightly lower in the front. The cotehardie in the illustration is sized for a man about five foot, ten inches tall, with a forty-inch chest and thirty-two-inch waist. Since the wearer may differ from this, we advise making cloth templates and fitting them first. Make the pattern in four sections and pin the back sections together, allowing one extra inch where they will be sewn together. Pin the back panels together and the front panels to the back, but do not pin the front seam together until the wearer has gotten into the pattern.

When the pattern is on the wearer, adjust the side and back seams to be relatively form-fitting. Allow the front sections to overlap sufficiently to install buttonholes and buttons. Do not make the cotehardie fit too tightly; it should fit slightly tighter than a suit coat, but no tighter than a loose vest or waistcoat. It can be more form-fitting on slim men than on stouter ones. To allow the body of the garment to fit across the hips, you will probably have to add a small gore between the side panels. The gore and its proper location are shown in the illustration. If the wearer has very small hips, the gore may not be necessary, but he has to be able to sit down without tearing the side seams. If you prefer not to use a gore, a vent on either side will allow the same ease of movement.

After marking the final seam locations, disassemble the pattern and cut the segments of the garment from the final fabric. To add interest to the cotehardie, consider making the front left and rear right panels one color and the front right and rear left another.

Before assembling the four sections of the body, install inner facings along both sides of the front closure. This will provide support for the buttons and buttonholes. Pin the sections together so the garment is inside out and sew them together. Stop the side seams three inches below the arm opening. When the arm is attached, you will need to insert a gusset at this point. When the cotehardie has been assembled, fit it on the wearer to make final adjustments to the fit and find the proper hem length. This can vary according to taste from just below the crotch to mid-calf, depending on how much leg you want to show. If you want to decorate the hem with dags, there are a variety of styles illustrated later in this chapter.

The sleeves can be made from one or two pieces of cloth. To make them from a single piece, fold the fabric in two along the top line of the arm before cutting around the outline of the sleeve. When the sleeves are set into the body of the cotehardie, make sure they taper into the armhole. To ensure ease of movement, insert a gusset into the underside of the sleeve. The long end of the gusset (four inches) is set into the seam on the bottom of the sleeve, and the short end (three inches) into the side seam of the body. A detail of this gusset, and its positioning on the garment, is shown in the illustration.

Though we have shown the collar fashionably high, the exact height of your collar depends on the taste and neck length of the wearer. The collar is simple to make. Just cut two identical pieces as shown and a third from a stiff lining material to give the collar rigidity. Lay the outside faces of the collar material together, place the lining material on top, sew around the edges, and turn it inside out. Then, attach the collar around the neck of the surcoat. The collar need not meet in front. Ideally, to make the garment hang right, it should be fully lined, but this is left to your discretion.

Mantle

The mantle was a shoulder-length cloak worn as much for decorative effect as for warmth and was most often seen in combination with the short cotehardie. The mantle in the illustration of the young man in a short cotehardie shows a garment that is no more than a variation on the hood and liripipe (see page 181). In this instance, the mantle has been used to its best decorative

Men's Short Cotehardie

MANTLE

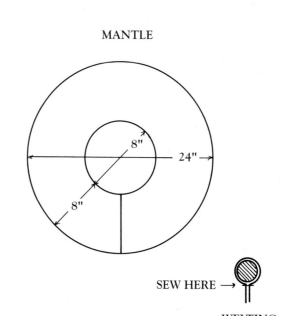

8"

24"

8"

SEW HERE →

WELTING
(CROSS SECTION)

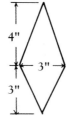

COLLAR

15"

2"

3"

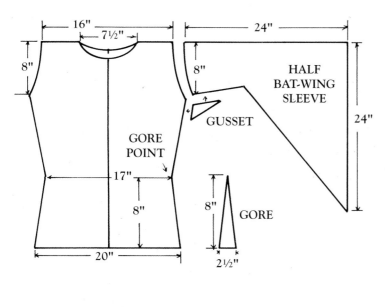

16"

7½"

8"

24"

8"

HALF
BAT-WING
SLEEVE

24"

GUSSET

GORE
POINT

17"

8"

8"

GORE

2½"

20"

23"

2"

3"

8"

BAG
SLEEVE

20"

GUSSET

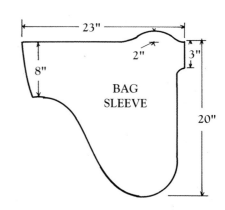

4"

3"

3"

effect by ornamenting the edges with dags that match those on the sleeves.

The mantle is simply a circle of cloth two feet in diameter, with an eight-inch-diameter hole in the center and a front opening so it can be tied around the neck rather than pulled on over the head. To give the mantle enough body to hang properly, it should be lined. The lining may be of any matching, contrasting, or coordinating fabric, but if it is designed to be worn with a specific cotehardie, we suggest reversing the color scheme of the cotehardie in the mantle. For example, if the cotehardie is blue velvet lined with gold satin, the mantle should be of gold velvet lined with blue satin.

An additional air of sophistication can be added to the mantle by finishing the collar with a thick welting. Similar to the welting used around the edges of sofa cushions, tailor's welting is nothing more than a layer of cloth sewn around a length of soft rope. Cut a length of three-eighths- or half-inch soft cotton rope to the length of the circumference of the neck opening—in this case, about twenty-five inches. Cut a strip of the same cloth as the outer surface of the mantle. The strip should be two inches longer than the rope, an inch and three-quarters wide, and cut on the bias. Wrap the cloth around the rope and sew it in place as shown in the welting cross-section illustration. The ends of the rope are covered by tucking the ends of the cloth around the ends of the rope and sewing them in place. When you are assembling the collar, insert the welting between the outer fabric and the lining, and sew it in place.

Men's Full-length Cotehardie (Houppelande)

The men's full-length cotehardie is a longer, fuller version of the short one. The body is made from two pieces of fabric, rather than four, and is cut fuller across the chest to allow it to flow better. Two variations of the body are shown in the illustrations. Variation 1 is for use with a patternless cloth, such as velvet. If you are constructing this version of the garment, you have a choice of two methods of adding fullness to the gown and providing ease of movement. The main illustration shows the gown with gores inset in the front and rear, and the side seams left open from mid-hip to the floor. (This version is designed for the man who may no longer be young, but is still proud enough of his legs that he doesn't mind showing them off.) A variant of this design is achieved by installing gores into the sides as well as the front and rear of the garment. If four gores are used, the individual gores are narrower than if only two gores are used.

Variation 2 provides a pattern for a cotehardie made with a damask-type material. Because it is impossible to inset a gore and keep the pattern consistent, the only way to provide the necessary fullness is to make the front and rear sections of the garment wider at the bottom. In this instance, you still have the option of leaving the side seams open, as shown in the main illustration, or sewing them closed. If the wearer has a stocky build, you have the option of setting a gore in the back of the gown. Although the pattern will not match where the gore is set in, the natural folds and pleats that form in the back of the cotehardie when it is belted will nearly hide the irregularities.

Whichever variation of the full-length cotehardie you choose, the bottom of the skirt should be cut in a semicircular shape. This allows the garment to hang properly and provides you with enough material to adjust the hem with no danger of the gown being too short in the front or rear. Properly, the full-length cotehardie should drag slightly on the ground, as shown in the main illustration. Walking in a gown of this length may take some practice. If you wish, make the hem slightly shorter so there is no danger of the wearer tripping.

The arms shown with this version of the cotehardie are constructed and set in place in the same manner as on the short-skirted version described above. Because the gown itself is fuller, the short end of the gusset can be made slightly smaller than in the short cotehardie. Any sleeve style is appropriate, and a collar is optional.

Women's Cotehardie

The women's cotehardie is very similar to the men's full-length version. The main differences lie in the neckline and the fullness of the body. The neck is wider than on the men's cotehardie, being open enough that it just rests on the edges of the shoulder. As in all cases, the front of the neckline should be cut slightly lower than the back. When cutting the neck, take care not to make it too large; the weight of the gown can easily cause the dress to pull off one or both shoulders. The skirt begins to widen immediately beneath the arms to give more room to the bust and make the entire garment more graceful and flowing. The rear panel is cut slightly longer than the front to provide some natural train, which can be accentuated by insetting an extended gore. Even if no additional train is desired, a rear gore the same length as the rest of the gown will make the cotehardie more full and attractive. For the fuller-figured woman, or for those who simply want a more flowing look, gores can also be added at the side seams. Note in

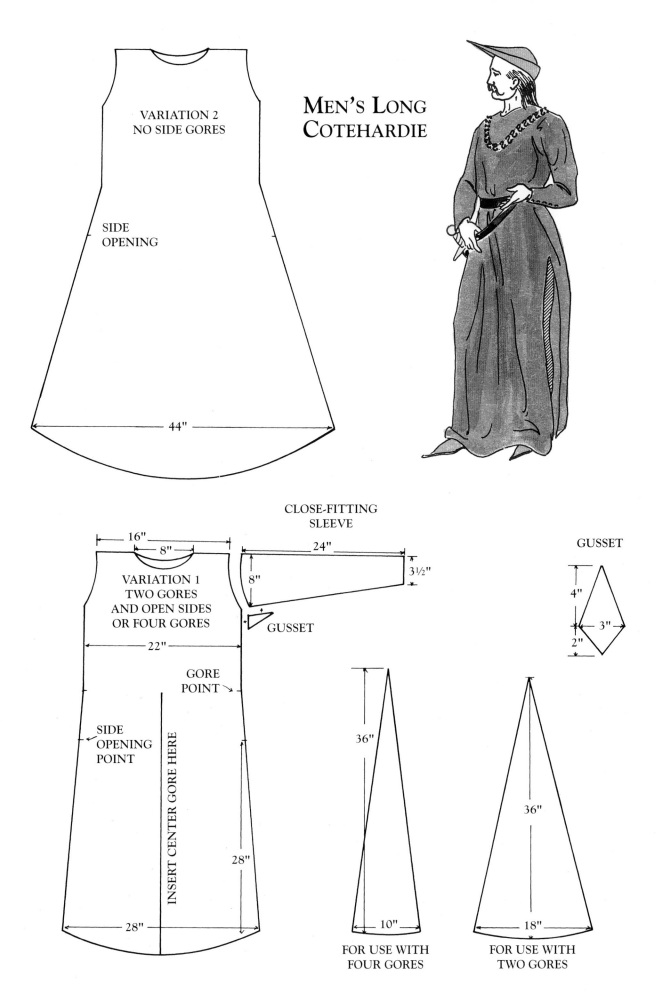

VARIATION 2
NO SIDE GORES

SIDE
OPENING

44"

MEN'S LONG
COTEHARDIE

CLOSE-FITTING
SLEEVE

16"

8"

VARIATION 1
TWO GORES
AND OPEN SIDES
OR FOUR GORES

22"

24"

8"

3½"

GUSSET

GUSSET

4"

3"

2"

GORE
POINT

SIDE
OPENING
POINT

INSERT CENTER GORE HERE

28"

36"

28"

10"

FOR USE WITH
FOUR GORES

36"

18"

FOR USE WITH
TWO GORES

173

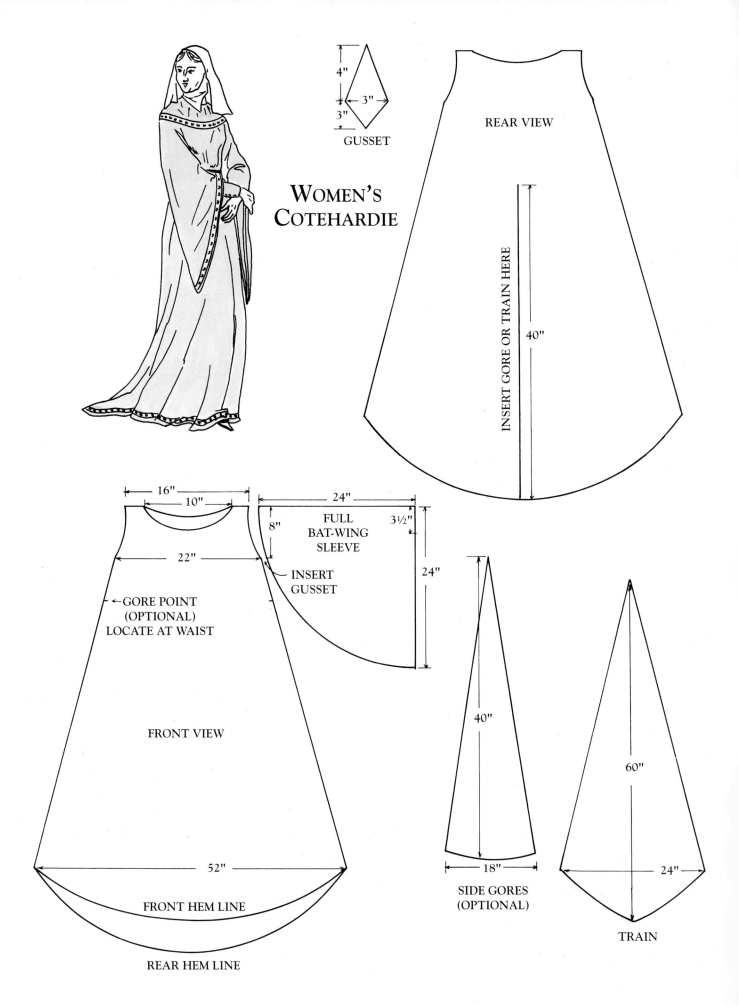

GUSSET

4"

3"

3"

WOMEN'S
COTEHARDIE

REAR VIEW

INSERT GORE OR TRAIN HERE

40"

16"

10"

22"

24"

8"

3½"

FULL
BAT-WING
SLEEVE

24"

INSERT
GUSSET

← GORE POINT
(OPTIONAL)
LOCATE AT WAIST

FRONT VIEW

52"

FRONT HEM LINE

REAR HEM LINE

40"

18"

SIDE GORES
(OPTIONAL)

60"

24"

TRAIN

the illustration that the side gores are only inserted from the waistline.

Again, the sleeves in the women's cotehardie can be adapted from any of the four styles shown. If you elect to use the bat-wing sleeve shown in the illustration, be sure to insert the gusset. Even though the sleeve itself is very full, the arm opening is only eight inches in diameter and will require a gusset if the arm is to move freely. The sleeves can be ornamented with decorative trim, as shown in the main illustration, or cut into decorative dags.

Surcoat, or Cyclas

The surcoat, or cyclas, was an extra layer of clothes worn over the cotehardie. Men's surcoats were generally no more than coats without sleeves; as with mod-

SCARBOROUGH RENAISSANCE FESTIVAL, WAXAHACHIE, TX

ern coats, some were made of fabric, some of leather. In either case, the lines were relatively simple. Women's surcoats tended to be longer and generally had vastly larger arm openings than those worn by men, allowing glimpses of the female form, wrapped in a close-fitting cotehardie (or occasionally just a fine silk kirtle) inside the surcoat. Generally, though not always, the surcoat was made from plain fabric, the more elaborate fabric of the cotehardie being exposed at the arms and along the bottom hem. To add luxury to the otherwise relatively plain surcoat, the hem, armholes, and neck were sometimes trimmed with fur, and sometimes the body of the surcoat was painted or embroidered with the family coat of arms.

Women's Surcoat

The women's surcoat is extremely simple in construction, but must be fitted to the individual wearer in order to hang right and still keep its shape. Because the surcoat was often considered a winter garment, it should be made of fairly heavy material. A lining will help it move properly but is entirely optional.

The body of the surcoat is made from identical front and back pieces, as shown in the illustration. The only points where the front is attached to the back are at the shoulders and for the few inches between the side opening at the hip line and the openings where the side gores are inset. It's best to make a pattern out of soft cloth, such as an old sheet, and tailor the neck and side openings to fit the wearer. Measurements such as the width across the hips will vary considerably, depending on the individual. The surcoat should not fit tightly but should move easily over the garments underneath. Be sure the side openings fall to the hips, as shown on the figure in the main illustration. The outer edge of the shoulder should rest just at the the wearer's shoulder. The depth of the neckline depends on the bustline of the wearer.

When you are satisfied that the pattern fits the wearer, cut the front and back sections of the surcoat, slit the panels to receive the front and rear gores, and sew the two panels together at shoulder and hips. Next, insert the gores at the front, back, and sides. Then hem around the neck and arm openings. The surcoat can vary in length, from dragging on the floor to allowing five to six inches of the cotehardie to show beneath the hem; this is entirely up to your taste. Additional interest can be added by sewing decorative trim or fur around the neck and side openings, as shown in the main illustration.

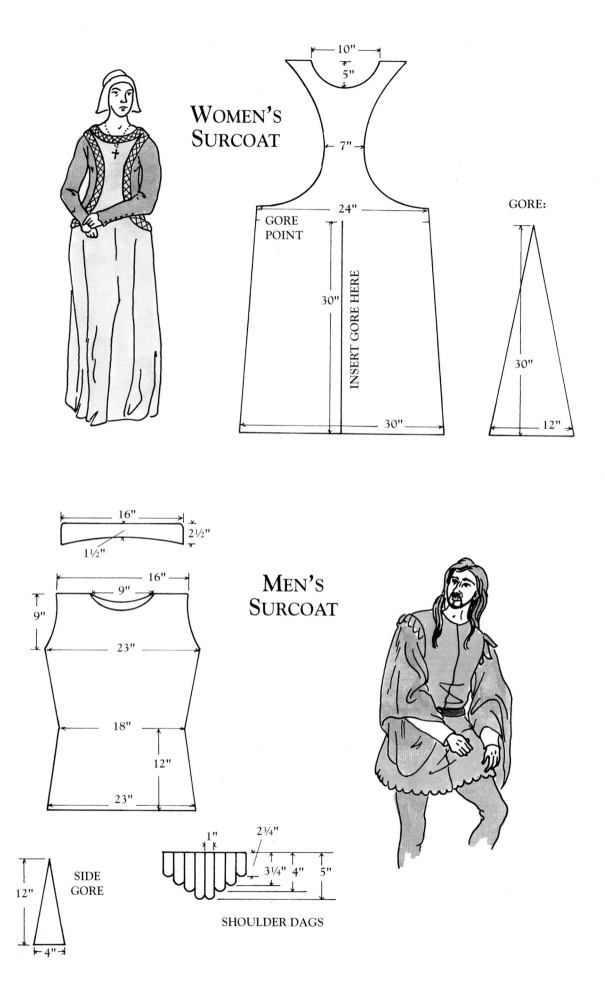

WOMEN'S SURCOAT

10"
5"
7"
24"
GORE POINT
30"
INSERT GORE HERE
30"

GORE:
30"
12"

16"
2½"
1½"

MEN'S SURCOAT

16"
9"
9"
23"
18"
12"
23"

SIDE GORE
12"
4"

SHOULDER DAGS
1"
2¾"
3¼" 4" 5"

Men's Surcoat

The men's surcoat is very similar in construction to the men's short cotehardie. Follow the instructions for the short cotehardie for the basic construction, but as an overgarment, the surcoat must be large enough to fit over the cotehardie. Some men's surcoats were pulled on over the head, while others buttoned up the front. The surcoat in the main illustration is pulled over the head. If yours is going to follow this design, it must be even looser-fitting than one that is buttoned. Note that the large, loose sleeves in the main illustration are part of the cotehardie, not the surcoat.

Make the pattern in four sections, as you did with the cotehardie, but if the surcoat is going to be pulled over the head, pin the front sections together as well as the sides and back. Put the pattern on the wearer, and adjust the seams for a comfortable fit, keeping in mind the amount of clothing that will be worn underneath. Be sure the surcoat can be taken off without removing any of the pins. This should be no problem if it has a button front, but if it's a pullover, it needs to fit fairly loosely.

When the coat has been assembled, fit it on the wearer and find the proper hem length. The main illustration shows the surcoat at mid-thigh, which is the length in the pattern. You may decide to decorate the hem with dags, such as those shown in the picture. Alternative dag styles are shown later in this chapter. If you decide to add dags to the bottom, or even if you don't, you may want to consider the interesting shoulder dags shown in the illustration. A pattern for these is provided here. It is best if the individual dags are made separately. Each dag should be lined with a matching or contrasting material. Sew the dag and lining together, turn inside out to hide the seamed edge, and attach to the body of the surcoat. The two longest dags should go on either side of the shoulder seam, with the shorter ones progressing down the front and back of the arm opening. They should come down no farther than those shown in the main illustration.

You can make your surcoat entirely from leather for a huntsman or woodsman look. Another option is the addition of a collar, but the collar on the surcoat should not come as high as that of the cotehardie. To add interest, consider painting the surcoat with your coat of arms. As with other garments, the surcoat should be fully lined, unless it is the work garment of a woodsman, but this is up to you.

Monk's Robe

The monk's robe was a very traditional garment similar to those previously worn in secular society by both sexes. By the fourteenth century, these long tunics were pretty much limited to members of the clergy. Ecclesiastical tunics were universally made of heavy, coarsely woven cloth in gray, black, white, or brown, depending on the specific order of the monk; select your fabric accordingly. The waist of the tunic was cinched with a belt, usually made of hemp rope. The rope was wrapped twice around the body and knotted in the front. The ends of the belt were allowed to hang to mid-calf length. One end of the belt rope had three knots tied in it three or four inches apart; the knots symbolized the Holy Trinity of Father, Son, and Holy Spirit. A large rosary was usually tucked into the belt. All monks wore cowls, or hoods. Some were attached to the tunic, but most were a separate piece of clothing. The monks' cowls, like the robes, were much looser-fitting than the more fashionable secular models. Directions for making a cowl are in the section on headgear (see page 180).

Far from form-fitting, monk's habits were loose and baggy, so with slight adjustments to the hem and sleeve length, one size should fit nearly anyone. The body of the gown can be cut from a single length of cloth folded over at the shoulder line. To be sure you have enough length to adjust for the height of the wearer, begin with a piece of cloth ten feet in length, folded over on itself to make a double-thick piece five feet long. Lay out the basic lines of the habit as shown in the illustration. Make sure the neck opening falls slightly lower in the front than in the back. Sew the sides of the gown from the front edge of the sleeves to the point where the side gores will be inserted, as illustrated. Next, cut two gores and sew them into the openings at the sides of the gown. Turn the gown inside out so the seams are hidden on the inside.

Have the wearer try on the gown, and mark the hem line so it falls to the ankle. Turn the hem to the inside of the gown and sew. To allow the gown to flow properly, allow a wide, double-turned hem. You may also hem around the neck.

Next, cut four of the sleeve sections shown in the illustration. Depending upon the length of the wearer's arms, you may have to make the sleeve sections slightly longer or shorter. The ends of the sleeves should come to the ends of the fingertips when the wearer's arms are extended. Sew the front and back sections of the sleeves together, and sew them into the body of the gown. The

MONK'S ROBE

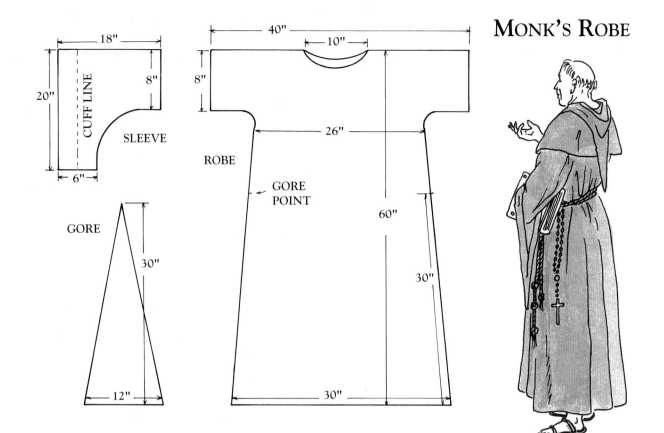

18"

CUFF LINE

20"

8"

6"

SLEEVE

40"

10"

8"

26"

ROBE

GORE POINT

60"

30"

GORE

30"

12"

30"

SHOES

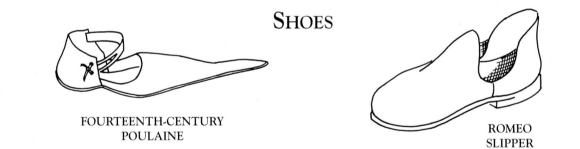

FOURTEENTH-CENTURY
POULAINE

ROMEO
SLIPPER

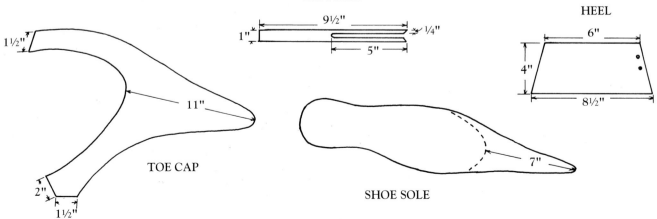

1½"

11"

2"

1½"

TOE CAP

TIE STRAP

9½"

1"

¼"

5"

SHOE SOLE

7"

HEEL

6"

4"

8½"

gown needn't be turned inside out to do this; simply turn under the edges of the arm openings on the gown and slide the ends of the sleeves inside the opening, pinning them in place before stitching. To adjust the length of the sleeves, have the wearer put on the gown and turn back the cuffs approximately at the position of the dotted line in the illustration. The cuffs should be three to four inches in depth and ideally should be turned back twice to add fullness and weight to the sleeves.

Shoes

Available in a variety of styles, the most fashionable fourteenth-century shoes were long, pointed affairs known as poulaines. Sometimes the toes reached more than a foot in length and were pulled upward on the end by a chain attached to a garter below the knee (we don't advise you try walking in these). All fourteenth-century shoes had soft soles, making them little more than slippers. When people went outside, they frequently wore pattens, sandals with wooden soles two or three inches thick, over their shoes. Since there is no way to turn out a pair of medieval shoes quickly, unless you are good at leatherwork, we suggest wearing a pair of hard-soled slippers, such as Romeo slippers, shown in the illustration. Romeos have a semicircular elastic inset on the sides, which can be cut out if you want the shoe to look more authentic. For either the monastic or common-man look we suggest wearing sandals. For those of you who are both fashionable and daring, we have included a pattern for a poulaine.

The Poulaine

The poulaine was not only the most fashionable shoe of the fourteenth century, it was also the simplest to construct. Begin by making a pattern for the sole by standing on a piece of light cardboard and tracing around your foot. Allow an extra three-eighths inch all around the edge so you can sew the shoe together without losing any footroom. Now extend the toe forward six or seven inches; this will give you enough toe to look impressive, but it will be short enough that you can still walk in the shoes.

When the pattern has been cut, trace a left and right sole onto a piece of leather about three-sixteenths inch thick, or onto two layers of thinner leather. If you use a single piece of thick leather, the smooth side of the leather should be the bottom surface of the sole. If you use two thinner pieces, cut them so they can be placed with the rough sides together, giving you smooth surfaces on both the bottom and inside surfaces of the sole. Glue these together with leather glue before sewing the shoe together.

Next, cut two heel sections, two tie straps, and two toe pieces from leather slightly less than one-eighth-inch thick. To ensure that the toe pieces fit properly over your foot, first make a pattern from a piece of heavy cloth. Stand on the sole of the shoe, and lay the toe pattern over your foot. It should drape comfortably over the foot and hang down far enough on the sides to allow the toe to be sewn onto the sole without making the shoe too tight.

Sew the toe piece onto the sole, keeping the seam about three-sixteenths inch from the outside edge of the sole and making the stitches about a quarter inch in length. The best way to sew these multiple layers of leather together is with the help of a sewing awl. When the front of the shoe is sewn together, sew the heel piece onto the sole, making sure it overlaps the back edges of the toe piece by at least a quarter inch. With both pieces sewn to the sole, sew up the side seams to join the heel and toe pieces.

Finally, position the narrow tie strap on the inner face of the heel, so that when the ties are brought across the shoe, they will be facing the outside of your foot. Sew the tie strap in place. Punch two small holes in the side of the shoe so the ends of the tie strap can be drawn through and tied in a knot or bow, as shown in the picture of the completed poulaine.

Monks wore sandals, no matter what the weather. Modern sandals will be fine as long as they are made from leather and are simple in design.

Hats and Headgear

No member of proper medieval society would ever go out in public without some form of headgear. Men's and women's hats came in a wide variety of styles, but the most universally popular among the working classes was the hood. Men's hoods tended to be more elaborate than women's, having a long tail known as a liripipe. These might be no more than a foot in length or might drag on the floor; the longer the liripipe, the greater the

fashion statement. Next to the hood, women of all stations wore a wimple and veil, an arrangement still seen on members of conservative orders of nuns.

Hood with Liripipe

The hood can either be cut from a single piece of cloth and folded along the top seam or made from two halves sewn together. For the outer edge of the hood, known as the mantle, to fall properly over the shoulders, insert a quarter-circle-shaped wedge of cloth into the mantle at the gore point indicated in the diagram. The mantle can be made as long or as short as desired. It can hang from just below the edge of the shoulder to just above the elbow. The bottom edge of the mantle can be ornamented with shaped dags, shown in the dag illustration later in this chapter.

The entire hood, with the exception of the liripipe, should be lined with a matching, coordinating, or contrasting color. The more well-off would have been likely to have the lining in a contrasting color.

The liripipe is made from a separate piece of cloth sewn into the hood at the back of the head. The liripipe should be made from a single piece of cloth seven inches wide and as long as you want it to be. After it has been attached to the hood, lightly stuff the liripipe with cotton batting or small scraps of soft fabric, to help it retain its round shape. Do not overstuff the liripipe, or it will not drape properly.

Women's hoods should not have a liripipe and were often worn open and turned back as shown in the illustration.

Monk's Cowl

Monks' hoods, properly known as cowls, were fuller than the hoods worn in secular society. Like the hood, the cowl can be made from a single piece of cloth folded along the top seam or from two separate pieces sewn together. Cut the cowl into a forty-inch-radius semicircle or two quarter circles. Mark and cut out the shaded, wedge-shaped area. Sew around the edges of the wedge-shaped cut. Next, sew together the lower twenty-two inches of the front of the cowl, leaving an eighteen-inch opening for the face. The bottom edge of the cowl may be seamed or left ragged, but it should not be cut in decorative dags. The cowl may be lined, but if the cloth is sufficiently heavy, it is not necessary.

Robin Hood Cap

There are several versions of this wonderfully pointy men's hat, which we are calling the Robin Hood cap, but

HOODS AND HATS

HOOD WITH
LIRIPIPE

12"

EXTEND
AS DESIRED

3½"

END HERE FOR
WOMAN'S
HOOD

14"

GORE

2½"

GORE HERE

12"

10"

10"

LIRIPIPE WRAPPED
AROUND HEAD

WOMAN WITH
HOOD OPEN

MONK'S
COWL

28"   40"

14" 20"

18"

12"

ROBIN HOOD
HAT

9"

CONE

7"

FOLD BRIM HERE

5"   2½"

18"
DIAMETER

22"
DIAMETER

17"

5"

APPET

3"

12"

6"

LADY IN A WIMPLE
(SEE TEXT)

CONE HAT
WITH APPET

4"

CLOAK
(WOMEN AND MEN)

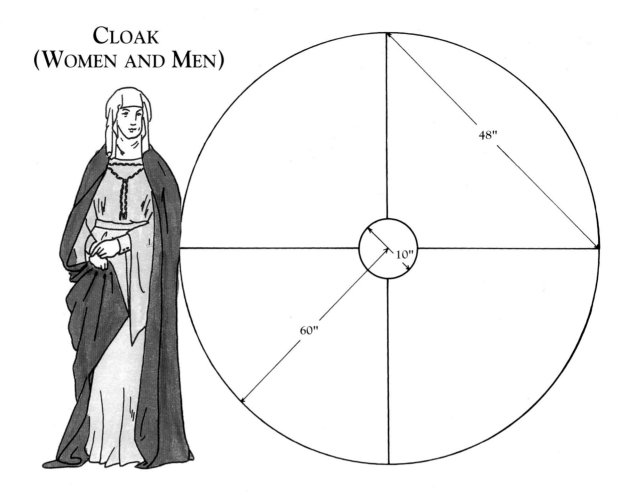

48"

10"

60"

DAG DESIGNS

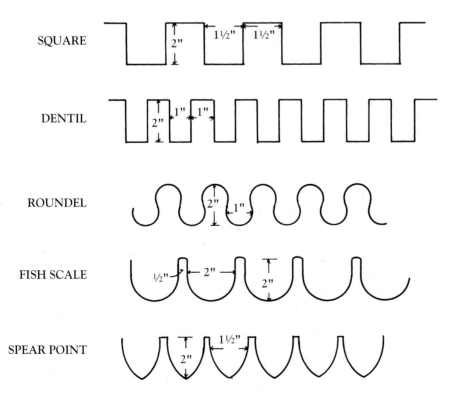

SQUARE

2"   1½"   1½"

DENTIL

2"   1" 1"

ROUNDEL

2"   1"

FISH SCALE

½"   2"   2"

SPEAR POINT

2"   1½"

this is the simplest to make. To provide sufficient body for the snout of the cap to stand out in front of the face without sagging, consider making the cap from medium-weight leather. The cap can be made from two pieces of material sewn together along the two top seams or from a single piece folded along one of the seams and sewn along the other. When you are sewing the rear seam, bear in mind that the long portion of the seam should be sewn on the inside of the hat, and the short, two-and-a-half-inch vertical seam should be sewn so it is exposed on the outside of the hat. This will allow you to turn up the brim of the hat without having any visible seams.

The entire hat should be lined in a coordinating or contrasting color of fabric. When the hat is finished, turn up the brim along the dotted lines shown in the diagram. You may want to tack the edge of the brim to the hat with a few stitches to hold it in place.

Women's Cone Hat with Appet

Make the body of the hat from heavy construction paper or lightweight tag board. Shape a cylinder with an opening circumference of about twenty-three inches. This cylinder should sit on the head so it comes to the hairline in the front and falls to the base of the skull in the rear. The top of the cylinder, the end at the rear of the head, should have a circumference of approximately eighteen inches.

When the cylinder fits the head comfortably, glue, tape, or staple it together. Trim the front edge of the cylinder so it fits comfortably around the ears. Next, cut a circle of the same material that will fit onto the top opening—the small end—of the cylinder. Tape it securely in place. Cover the entire cylinder with inexpensive velvet or felt, wrapping the material around the front edge of the hat so the edge of the construction paper does not show. You may want to sew a few tiny loops of string or cloth ribbon inside the hat so it can be attached to the hair with hairpins.

Next, cut the appet, the horseshoe-shaped piece shown in the diagram, from the same material you used for the body of the hat. Trim the inner edge of the appet so it lays flat along the front edge of the hat. Cover the appet with a contrasting color material, either linen or satin. Now sew the inner edge of the appet to the front edge of the hat from a position just above one ear, around the forehead, and down to just above the opposite ear. Gently shape the bottom ends of the appet so they flare out slightly to lie on a plane with the front of the face.

Wimple and Veil

The wimple is so simple to construct that there is no need to provide pattern diagrams. Simply cut two squares of lightweight fabric thirty inches square. The first piece, the wimple, is fitted under the chin and tied, or pinned, at the top of the head. The second piece, the veil, is positioned on top of the head so one edge falls about three-fourths inch above the eyebrows. Smooth the edge of the veil against the forehead, tucking or pinning the natural pleats that form at the temples behind the edges of the wimple.

Cloak

The cloak was the only outer coat of the Middle Ages. Cloak material could range from lightweight for spring, summer, and early fall to very heavy wool for winter use. Many women had a hood sewn onto the cloak, while men usually depended on a separate hood or hat for head protection. Whether or not the cloak was lined and the expense of the material used in its construction were determined by the social status and wealth of the owner. Most reenactment cloaks are cut from heavy wool blankets, such as old army blankets. They are as warm as you are likely to need, and the weave is coarse enough to pass for medieval wool. You will need to find several blankets with identical coloring to ensure that the segments of the cloak match.

Like the mantle, the full-length cloak is no more than a large circle of cloth with a hole for the head and an opening in the front so it can be thrown over the shoulders. Because of the amount of material required to make a full-circle cloak, it is necessary to cut it in four sections and sew them together. The cloak in the illustration is five feet in length. This should work for a wearer between the heights of five foot seven and five foot ten. For those who fall outside this range, the length of the cloak will have to be adjusted accordingly. If you prefer a knee-length cloak, it can probably be made from two army blankets, rather than four, with each blanket forming a half circle.

When the cloak sections are cut, sew them together, leaving one seam open so the cloak can be thrown around the shoulders. Hem the edges, and line the cloak if you choose. You may want to consider attaching a hood. The cloak may be held together at the neck with string ties sewn to the cloak or with a large, decorative pin.

Belts

Both men and women wore belts during the fourteenth century. Most full-length cotehardies were belted at the waist for both men and women. If a man was wearing a fitted, crotch-length cotehardie, he would more than likely wear his belt around his hips—probably to show that he was still slim enough to do so. The only time a woman would wear her belt at the hips would be if she was wearing a surcoat with huge arm openings on top of the cotehardie or a very form-fitting kirtle. Again, this is a style mostly reserved for those who are comfortable showing off as much of their figure as possible. Belts in the fourteenth century were about two inches in width and frequently covered with metal plates that nearly obscured the belt itself.

Jewelry

Women might wear a cross or jewel on a delicate neck chain, and men of noble rank might wear a collar of maintenance, a large, heavily ornamented chain worn like a necklace, shown on the illustration on page 173 of the man in a full-length cotehardie. Rings, inset with family crests and precious and semiprecious stones, were always popular. Otherwise, jewelry was kept at a minimum.

Knives and Swords

Military men routinely carried broadswords on their left sides at all times. All men above the rank of peasant carried daggers on their right sides. When attending a great feast, an eating knife would be worn by all persons, regardless of social rank or sex. Thus, a military man attending a feast would wear three blades: a sword and eating knife on the left side (with the eating knife located behind the sword in case of an emergency) and a dagger on the right.

CHAPTER 18

Organizing Your Medieval Celebration

If your medieval event is going to run as smoothly as you and your guests expect, it is essential for you to decide well in advance which activity is going to happen when. Organizing the sequence of your events long before the day of your medieval celebration helps you maintain order and allows both your assistants and guests to prepare for the day's activities with as little stress and last-minute confusion as possible.

We suggest that once you have decided which activities you are going to offer, that you compile a list of these activities, listed according to the time they are scheduled to begin, and organize this list in the form of a spreadsheet. At least two weeks prior to your event give copies of this sheet to everyone directly involved in the activities, such as the head of your kitchen staff, your gamesmaster or mistress, anyone in charge of activities that require a supervisor (such as archery), your herald (who will be responsible for announcing when each activity is about to begin), the person in charge of presenting a play, and any hired people such as musicians or dancers. If your medieval event is going to offer a large number of activities you also might want to include an itinerary sheet with the information package you will be sending out to the guests.

No matter how many, or how few, activities you are going to be offering at your medieval celebration, be sure to allow ample time for the activity to take place and for people to move from one activity to the next without

feeling like they are being rushed or herded like cattle. Everyone, including you, is there to have fun; only schedule enough activities to provide people with something to keep them busy, not so much that they feel exhausted trying to keep up. If you can't get everything you want to do into the schedule without crowding, save a few things for your next medieval event. Remember, this is supposed to be a leisurely, fun day, so don't crowd your schedule—leave plenty of time for each event and plenty of time between events.

Keeping In Touch

No matter how many people know the schedule ahead of time, you should post several copies of the complete itinerary list in and around your feast hall so guests can reference it whenever they want and prepare for those events in which they wish to participate.

But don't rely on everyone checking the schedule and keeping track of when each event is going to take place—they are here to have fun, not to read the directions. Reminding the guests of what is happening, and when, will be the responsibility of your herald. A strong, young set of lungs is essential for this job, particularly if you are including outdoor activities where the herald's voice has to carry over long distances. Even when the day's events are limited to an indoor space, the

Large medieval celebrations require careful, long-term planning if they are going to run smoothly. CARA McCANDLESS

herald's voice has to be strong enough to rise above the constant din and buzz of the guests' conversation and any music that might be playing in the background.

The herald will have to wear a watch so he can keep a constant eye on the time and compare it to the list of activities and the times they are scheduled to begin. Because there may be several activities taking place simultaneously, the herald will have to announce each upcoming event fifteen minutes before it is scheduled to begin and again about five minutes prior to the start of the activity.

Medieval heralds usually called attention to themselves and the fact that they were about to make an announcement by walking to the center of a room and calling out as loudly as they could "Oyez, Oyez!" Oyez

(pronounced "O-Yea") was the medieval equivalent of the eighteenth-century town crier's call of "Hear Ye, Hear Ye!" Sometimes, if the guests are concentrating on whatever they are doing, the herald may have to call for their attention a second time before the general buzz dies down. When the herald has the crowd's attention, he should begin his announcement with "My lords and ladies . . ." before giving the specific details of the activity or other important piece of information he has to announce. Some guests will grumble about being interrupted by the herald, but when he calls out events they are interested in, or announces dinner, they will appreciate all of his hard work.

While your personal medieval celebration will have its own distinct set of activities that make it unique to you and to the occasion being observed, we have put together a few general outlines that should help you organize your event so that it will run in an orderly fashion.

For these general outlines we are going to assume that your medieval event will begin in the middle of the afternoon, that your feast is planned for early evening, and that there will be additional activities after the feast is over. Your own medieval celebration may be different from the general schedule of events offered below, but these should give you a broad outline that you can change and modify to suit your specific needs.

Summer Celebrations

Medieval events held during the warm months are far more likely to offer outdoor activities that those held in the winter. Bear in mind that while all of your guests will be looking forward to playing in the sunshine, the weather may have ideas of its own. Consequently, you need to plan indoor activities in case of rain. Planning for indoor activities will also offer alternative forms of amusement for those who do not choose to participate in outdoor sports.

If you are going to offer outdoor activities that require full daylight but do not demand that your guests get dirty and sweaty (such as field archery or boules), these can be held simultaneously, while the guests are still arriving. These activities provide great visual impact for the arriving guests, offer a diversion suitable for both men and ladies, and make a good "icebreaker" that encourages people to get acquainted. Allow people to move from one activity to another as they wish. If your event is a May Day celebration the afternoon's activities should include the maypole dance.

SAMPLE SUMMER CELEBRATION SCHEDULE

Start Time	Indoors	Outdoors	Activity	Finish Time
2:30 P.M.		X	Archery	5:00 P.M.
2:30 P.M.		X	Boules	5:00 P.M.
2:30 P.M.	X		Board games	5:00 P.M.
6:00 P.M.	X		Feast (with activities between courses)	8:00 P.M.
8:30 P.M.		X	Palio race	9:00 P.M.
9:00 P.M.	X		Dancing	11:30 P.M.
9:00 P.M.		X	Tug-of-war	9:45 P.M.

Even while these early events are taking place, you should also offer simultaneous indoor activities. Not only does this provide pastimes for those guests who are not inclined to outdoor sports, but if it rains the schedule of events (and your entire event) will not be brought to a halt. If your summer celebration begins between 2 and 3 P.M., you should have plenty of time for all the contests, games, and other leisurely sports you want to hold before your banquet begins at, say, 6:00 or 6:30 P.M.

Guests who have participated in the outdoor games will probably want to wash up before the banquet, so the herald's first announcement of the feast should come at least half an hour before everyone is expected to make their way to the table.

As we discussed in chapter 10, "Planning A Medieval Feast," there were often activities (pass the parcel, communal song singing, and making toasts) or performances (such as a play, a juggler, or a dance exhibition)

Outdoor events are a great way to take advantage of fine weather during the spring, summer, and autumn seasons. DICK CLARK

Small, intimate feasts require far less planning than large events, especially if everyone is willing to help. EUGENE SIREN

offered between courses. If you plan to hold any of these activities, it will give your servers and kitchen staff more time to get each course prepared, provide guests with an opportunity to excuse themselves for a minute, and give everyone time for their food to settle before the next course. Offering games, songs, or short performances between courses also inevitably lengthens the amount of time you will need to allot to the banquet. Each course, and each entertainment, should be allotted at least thirty minutes to complete. This may sound longer than necessary, but with serving time taken into account and the fact that people will spend more time than usual talking about the food, you will be glad you provided for a little extra time. Take this additional time into account when planning your schedule.

Depending upon your particular guest list and the weather, you may want to devote the after-dinner time to refined, indoor activities such as a play, a court of love, or dancing. Alternatively, if you have a fairly young crowd and the weather is fine, you may want to continue with outdoor activities. Since this is the end of the day, you can now engage people in more physical sports like tug-of-war, a palio race, or chasing a greased pig; it will not matter in the least if everyone goes home a little dirty and sweaty.

Winter Celebrations

Unlike medieval events held during fair weather, a winter celebration means that your guests will be confined inside throughout the course of the day's activities, so you will need to have a variety of diversions planned for both before and after your banquet to ensure that no one gets bored.

Since everyone will be confined to indoor pursuits, this is a good time to hold game tournaments. Chess, merrills, and a number of other games covered in chapter 13 make good elimination games in which the winner from each pair, or group, of players can go on to compete against the winner of another group. It is always good to have a small prize to offer the "champion," and their victory should be announced to the assembly by the herald.

Dreary winter afternoons also offer a fine time to liven things up with a court of love. While only some of the guests will be active participants, the entire assembled company will unquestionably have a good time and a few laughs will help move the day along.

The course of the banquet itself will undoubtedly follow a pattern similar to that of a feast held at any

SAMPLE WINTER CELEBRATION SCHEDULE

Start Time	Activity	Finish Time
2:30 P.M.	Chess tournament	5:00 P.M.
2:30 P.M.	Merrills tournament	5:00 P.M.
3:30 P.M.	Court of love	4:30 P.M.
4:30 P.M.	Sword-fighting exhibition	5:15 P.M.
5:30 P.M.	Feast (with activities between courses)	7:30 P.M.
7:30 P.M.	Musical performance	8:00 P.M.
8:00 P.M.	Dancing	10:30 P.M.
10:30 P.M.	Carol singing	11:15 P.M.

other time of the year; please refer to the description of banquet activities in the above section.

When the feast is over and the tables are being cleared away and the hall readied for the evening's activities, if you are lucky enough to have medieval musicians, they might put on a short concert following the banquet, while guests are refreshing themselves before the evening's activities.

A dance is a fine after-feast activity to warm a cold winter evening, and your medieval dance might take any one of a number of forms, or a combination of these. You might hire a group of skilled dancers from a local medieval reenactment group to put on an after-dinner performance. Some of these same people would make ideal instructors to lead any willing guests in a few medieval dances. Not everyone is going to join in the fun, but once the first few start, they will entice more to join in and everyone on the sidelines will enjoy watching the show.

Christmas celebrations are a particularly good time to put on a play or hold a communal sing-along. These are particularly wonderful activities for the very end of your event and add tremendously to the medieval feel of the day. If the caroling is accompanied by professional or semi-professional musicians with medieval-style instruments it encourages everyone to take part.

Live entertainers are tremendous fun for everyone and they can often be hired through local medieval recreationist groups or renaissance fairs. SCARBOROUGH RENAISSANCE FESTIVAL, WAXA-HACHIE, TX

EUGENE SIREN

Weddings

Weddings seem to have an established dynamic all their own. Because the actual wedding ceremony is the centerpiece around which the rest of the day revolves, it will almost certainly take place prior to any other activity. For the structure of an actual medieval wedding ceremony, see chapter 7.

Once the wedding ceremony is complete and the guests are in the process of adjourning to the reception hall there will be some inevitable confusion and reorganizing as guests hurry to congratulate the newlywed couple, so be sure to allow plenty of time for people to get reorganized and settle down.

Because everyone's attention will be divided between the newlyweds and whatever else is going on, the opening phase of the reception would be a good time to

SAMPLE WEDDING SCHEDULE

Start Time	Indoor	Outdoors	Activity	Finish Time
1:00 P.M.	X		Wedding ceremony	2:00 P.M.
2:15 P.M.		X	Move to reception hall	2:45 P.M.
2:30 P.M.		X	Maypole dance	3:30 P.M.
3:00 P.M.	X		Jugglers, swordfighting, etc.	5:00 P.M.
5:30 P.M.	X		Feast (with gift opening between courses)	7:00 P.M.
7:30 P.M.	X		Court of love	8:15 P.M.
8:30 P.M.	X		Dancing	11:30 P.M.

hold some type of performance piece such as a short play; a performance by medieval musicians, dancers, swordfighters, or jugglers; or a maypole dance, which would look great during any warm month.

As with any feast, the wedding banquet will generally follow the same progression we laid out in the above section. Pauses between courses might be a good time for the happy couple to open their gifts and these could be brought to them by a member of the serving staff, the herald, or the master or mistress of revels.

As with all wedding receptions, the after dinner-schedule will probably include time for dancing. As stated in our discussion of winter celebrations, this could include an exhibition by a dance troupe after which members of the troupe might lead guests in several medieval dances. If time allows, a court of love, timed to take place immediately after dinner and before the dancing begins, is certainly appropriate to the idea of a wedding, and who better to serve as judges than the new bride and her bridesmaids, or the bride and her mother?

CHAPTER 19

A Medieval Celebration Checklist

Allowing plenty of time to prepare for each step in the planning of your medieval celebration will help ensure that if problems crop up—which they undoubtedly will—you will have a good chance of correcting the problem or making alternative arrangements. In this chapter we provide a step-by-step checklist that should help guide you through each of the major steps of advance planning. If you are hosting a medieval wedding rather than some other type of event, we suggest that you double the allotted time frame for each of the planning phases listed below. Booking your wedding and reception venue, scheduling a minister or priest, having special announcements printed, and the dozens of other elements unique to a wedding make it imperative that you allow additional planning time. But no matter what type of medieval event you are hosting, the more time you allow for the planning and execution of each step the better chance you have of eliminating all of the bugs long before they have a chance to crop up.

Four Months (or More) Ahead of Time

These first, preliminary steps in planning your medieval celebration should be done pretty much in the order listed below. The larger your event is going to be, the farther in advance you should begin your preparations.

1. **When.** Select the time of year (and if possible the date) you want to hold your medieval event. This will allow you to determine whether any of it can take place outdoors, what sort of games to plan for, and the kinds of food that will be most appropriate. If you are planning to have your feast during the holiday season, it is often wise to hold it over Twelfth Night (January 5) rather than just prior to Christmas, when many people have family and work commitments. If you plan to hold a medieval New Year's Eve party, remember that you have the option of either December 31 or March 24. If you are planning to hold a summer event, June or September may be best; a lot of people go on vacation during July and August, and these months are often too hot for guests to dress in medieval clothes.

2. **How Many.** Decide on the number of people you want at your medieval celebration. If you are planning the event for a church or civic organization, or as a wedding, you may be looking at a sizable number of guests. Once you have determined the approximate number of people, you can start looking for an appropriate space in which to hold your feast. You can also make rough estimates for the amount of food you will need to buy.

3. **Who Else.** Before you go too far with the planning, be sure you start lining up all the help you could possibly need to assist you with both the day's activities and the preparation of your feast. In addition to kitchen help and servers, you may well need advance help with publicity and information, and on the big day you will need someone to act as gamesmaster or mistress, individuals to oversee outdoor activities like archery or other competitions, and a herald to announce each activity prior to the time it begins. You will also probably need help making the decorations and building any special equipment necessary for outdoor games. Once you have determined the approximate number of guests you will be having, and whether it is to be held indoors or out, or both, you can begin to figure out how many people it will take to help run the feast, the kitchen, and any games you have planned.

Although you won't need kitchen help until the week before the feast, and people to help with the activities only a few days before the event, you should start lining up competent people now. If you are going to need help making a sizeable number of costumes yourself, or with making or painting banners or wall hangings, you will need these people as far in advance as possible to ensure that even if one or more people fail to perform you still have plenty of time to recruit new assistants. Always get more help than you need; some will fade away just when you need them most, and the amount of work is always going to be greater than you think.

4. **Where.** Locate a space in which to hold your feast. If it is to be in your home, determine whether it is going to be in the dining room, basement, garage, or elsewhere. If the feast is to be held in a church, club, or community center, the size of this space will probably help determine how many people you can have at the event. If you plan on hiring a hall for the occasion, keep in mind what it is you are trying to recreate when you look at halls. An old barn can be made to look more appropriately medieval than a starkly modern banquet center with a nine-foot-high ceiling. Assembly halls in Victorian gothic churches or Victorian clubs such as Masonic lodges are about the best type of space you could ever hope to find; most cities of any size probably have at least one or two nineteenth-century churches that would be glad to rent out their hall. If you are holding a summer event with lots of outdoor activities, you might do well to check into hiring a pavilion or shelter at a local park or, if you have a big lawn or similar space available, consider renting a large marquee tent for your banquet and other tents for ancillary activities. Whether your event is indoors or outdoors, you will need to consider accommodations for each type of activity you plan to include in your event. If you are going to have outdoor activities, is there an appropriate exterior space attached to the hall, or at least one in very close proximity, that you can use? Is there a place where people can change into their medieval clothes? Some people will insist on changing at the party, and if there are outdoor games, some will want to change clothes or clean up afterward. Above all, be sure there is a kitchen adequate to your needs.

5. **Extras.** If you are planning to hire any professional or semi-professional help—musicians, caterers, people to lead outdoor activities, or any other extra help—now is the time to line them up. If you are planning your event for June or December you may need to book the caterers five, six, or more months in advance to avoid being shut out by other people's weddings and Christmas parties. If you are having the food catered, look for caterers who are willing to make medieval food from the recipes that you provide. Some caterers only serve from their own list of foods; others will insist they can do a medieval feast and you will discover too late that they have included mashed potatoes and chocolate cake on the menu.

Finding good medieval entertainers, such as musicians, singers, jugglers, and fire-eaters, can be difficult in some areas, but it is not impossible. A good place to start is local colleges and universities. Most of them have student medieval groups, some of whom can be hired for a nominal fee to help in the kitchen, and who will be glad to give advice. Many more have choral societies that perform medieval music; most of them also have a medieval dance group that can be hired to coach your guests. If there are superior church choirs in your area, they may be able to put together a small group of singers to perform medieval choral music. Through your search for singers and other forms of help, you are likely to run across musicians who can play medieval instruments, jugglers, dancers, and other entertainers.

Once you have settled on a space and determined about how many guests you want to accommodate, arrange to rent any necessary tables, tablecloths, and seats. You may want to make special arrangements for plates, serving platters, and drinking vessels. Nothing looks less medieval than a table full of lovely white china and pressed-glass wine goblets.

Three Months (or More) Ahead of Time

6. **Who.** If your feast is going to be a public affair, such as a fundraiser held by a church or community group, you should get publicity out as soon as you have located the room in which the feast will be held. The more lead time you give people, the better your response will be. Put on as aggressive a promotional campaign as possible, with posters, information on your website and the websites of affiliated groups, and Facebook posts. Try to get radio interviews and put up flyers at any sympathetic businesses, churches, and libraries. Don't forget to use good old word of mouth. If you are planning a private party, see number 9, below.

7. **Food Choices.** When the approximate number of guests has been determined, you need to prepare the final menu, begin making your shopping list and another list of any large pots, pans, and roasting dishes you may need. Also locate plates, serving platters, and drinking vessels that will look appropriately medieval (see our suggestions in the resources section on page 199). It may seem early, but a month or six weeks from now, you will be very glad you have this nasty little job out of the way. If you are working with a caterer, you need to give them as much advance notice as possible so they can make any special arrangements necessary to accommodate your medieval menu.

8. **Looking Pretty.** Depending on the size of the hall you are using for your feast, you will probably need an absolute minimum of two months to prepare all the decorations and carry out any special construction necessary for the games. If you are dealing with a space that is not your own, you probably will not be able to begin hanging banners and arranging furniture until a few

Even medieval hosts knew the importance of making lists of important names, dates, and places. DICK CLARK

days before the event, but you want to have everything ready to put in place when the time comes. This is the time to begin calling in all those people who said they would be happy to help you sew and paint banners, sew costumes, and do all the other things that you won't have time to do yourself.

9. **Please Come.** If this is a private party, send out the invitations at least two months in advance. Prepare informational packets containing material on costumes, the menu, the day's activities (particularly if there are games or outdoor sporting activities), table manners, and anything else

that seems important. If your event is going to include more than a feast you may also want to include a schedule of the day's activities. You, your assistants, and your guests should all know exactly what to expect and when. These information packets will help people get into the spirit of the event. Send these out as soon as you begin getting confirmations on attendance. If people haven't answered by one month prior to the event, call them; you need to know if they are coming, and they need to know what to expect.

If your event is going to be a wedding, Christmas, or Twelfth Night affair, three months' advance notice of the details is not out of line. Not only do you need to be relatively sure that people have not made other plans before they hear about your event, but they will need time to pull together a costume and get excited about what you are doing.

10. **Getting Dressed.** Prepare your own costumes now. The larger the number of people for whom you are responsible, the bigger this job is, so get this done in advance. If you are not experienced with a needle and thread or have more than two or three costumes to prepare, you may want to delegate this. If you can't find anyone who can make, or help you make, the banners and costumes, you can always hire someone. Don't wait till the last minute to do that, either. If you are going to rent your costume and you expect a significant number of people at your feast, remember that the really good medieval costumes will go fast. If you are ordering costumes from an online source, order them long enough in advance that if there is a problem you have time to exchange them in plenty of time for your event.

One Month Ahead

11. **Checking the List.** Take a day or two to confirm every item on your checklist. Be certain there is no problem with the hall, rental tables, seating, musicians, table service, borrowed or rented pots and pans, and performers. Make sure your kitchen staff is lined up and you know who is going to pick up all the groceries. Check that your decorating committee and the people who are in charge of the games all know what they are doing and when.

12. **Distribute Schedules.** Give a complete copy of the day's itinerary, along with the time each activity is scheduled to take place, to your herald and activities master or mistress. Keep at least two copies for yourself. If you are using a rented tent be sure it is scheduled to be set up at least one day early so you are not going crazy trying to decorate it on the morning of your event.

13. **The First Foods.** If you plan on making any dishes well ahead of time and freezing them, now is the time to do so. Allow as many days for this as you and your kitchen help will need.

One Week Before the Event

14. **Pulling It Together.** As soon as you can get into the space where you are holding the feast, begin decorating and arranging the furniture. You should allow at least an entire day for you and your helpers to do this, even if it is just in your own dining room. The reshuffling, moving, and hanging will take more time and energy than you imagine. When the hall is decorated, put all of the games and entertainments in one secure place where they cannot be disturbed, and ensure that the gamesmaster or mistress knows where they are and the order in which they are to take place.

15. **Copying It Out.** A trip to the local copy shop four of five days before the feast is a good idea. Copy song sheets, dance sheets, and game rules for each guest, or at the very minimum, make one copy for every two guests. If you are using an activities master or mistress give the copies to him or her to distribute to people at the appropriate time.

16. **Shopping and Cooking Ahead.** Reconfirm your kitchen help. Three or four days before your feast, you should do all the shopping, and some help there would be a great thing. As soon as possible after everything has been bought and moved to the kitchen, you need people to start cooking anything that will keep for a few days.

Three Days Before the Event

17. **Last-Minute Details.** Check over your entire list to be sure you haven't forgotten anything. With three days still ahead of you, you should have plenty of time to take care of any last-minute problems without going into a tailspin. Be sure all of your assistants know what time they are expected on the site, know how to get there, and are ready for the big day. Don't let anyone get overexcited; be very calm and reassuring, and convince them that everything is going like clockwork. Make sure to tell them that you really appreciate their help—that's what you have to tell them, even if you are ready to pull your hair out. Whatever you do, don't let panic set in! It really will come together on the big day.

The Day Before the Event

18. **Getting Set.** Along with a few of your helpers, set up as many finishing touches as possible. Put table service on the tables, set up archery targets, make sure candles are in place and that the kitchen staff have absolutely everything they need, and so on.

The Big Day

19. **Last Time Around.** Early in the day, check to see that everything and everyone is in place in the hall and that the kitchen is up and running according to schedule. Everything and everyone should be in place at least two hours before your guests begin to arrive. With the exception of the kitchen and serving staff, your activities master or mistress and your herald are the two people you will be most reliant on to keep things running in a timely manner. If everything happens on schedule, it will be a near miracle, but what really matters is that your guests and help all have the best time of their lives, and that even you manage to find time to enjoy yourself.

Medieval Sources and Resources

❧

I t's not always easy to find all the things you are going to need when you start organizing your medieval celebration and banquet. While many of your needs can be met locally, finding some specialty items and services will require you to reach out into the world beyond, usually through the Internet, in order to find everything you need. In the following pages we have tried to give you information that will help make your search easier, less time-consuming, more cost-effective, and more fruitful. The sources and resources list here is broken into two main sections: those listings primarily for those of you who are in the U.S. and another for readers in the U.K. Under each of these main headings we have listed appropriate Internet searches, self-help guides, and specific businesses that cater to the medieval market under a variety of topical headings. Many of the online searches listed below have been noted in individual chapters earlier in this book but are given again, here, for your convenience and ease of reference. Bear in mind that many suppliers are more than happy to ship internationally if you are willing to pay the extra freight charges. For any item that you special order,

make sure to allow at least twice as much time for delivery as you think you are going to need; should something go wrong you will need plenty of time to make alternate arrangements. While we have attempted to locate the best, most reliable suppliers of medieval goods, the authors and publisher are not responsible for the quality or service provided by any of the suppliers listed below.

General/United States

Medieval Arms and Armor
There are hundreds of professional and semi-professional armorers offering reproduction armor of varying quality for sale. Some of these items are purely decorative and some are amazingly accurate reproductions of actual battle-quality armor. The prices for armor can range from $50 for a shield suitable for use as a wall decoration in your recreated medieval feast hall to more than $10,000 for an astoundingly accurate reproduction of a full suit of Gothic battle armor. Most of the sites

offering armor also offer swords, battle-axes, and pole weapons. eBay offers many good-quality reproduction items at reasonable prices. Even if none of the items within your budget will stand up to the rigors of a medieval battle they will look great as costumes or decorative pieces for your great hall.

The easiest way to obtain a suit of armor is to rent it from a local costume company. If there is not a costume company near you that has a decent-looking suit of armor, there are companies that will rent armor and will ship it to you. There are hundreds of such listed online; we recommend looking at OnlineCostumeStore .com (www.onlinecostumestore.com/default.asp), Medieval Fantasies Company (www.medievalfantasiesco .com), Broadway Costumes (www.broadwaycostumes .com), and Valentine Armouries (www.varmouries.com).

Most of the companies listed above also offer a wide selection of medieval-style weapons that range from swords to battle-axes and pole arms.

If you plan on hitting each other, even if you are wearing armor, *do not* use metal weapons. Instead, use foam or latex weapons of the type used by live-action role players. There are any number of sites that offer safe, nonmetallic weapons that look appropriately medieval. Among the many to check out are: Calimacil (www .calimacil.com/larp.html), Strongblade (www.strong blade.com), Medieval Collectibles (www.medieval collectibles.com), and Museum Replicas (www.museum replicas.com), all of which also sell real weapons of various degrees of authenticity. If you don't know how to tell good reproduction medieval weapons from "fantasy" weapons, a good rule of thumb is that the simpler the design is, the more likely they are to be in a real medieval style.

Medieval Clothing

There are many online retailers offering medieval clothing patterns. Some will provide better-quality patterns than others, but no matter what style of clothing or time period you are looking for, there would seem to be a pattern to suit the most demanding and specific taste. One of the oldest and most reliable pattern companies in the U.S. is Simplicity, whose medieval patterns are available through a variety of retailers. You can find a Simplicity pattern retailer by visiting the Simplicity pattern website at www.simplicity.com.

If you are renting your medieval clothing the best place to start is your local costume shop. Most costume companies have a limited supply of medieval-type clothing available; make sure that their selection meets your standards. If you live in a large city where there are costume companies that rent to theatrical or movie companies, they will probably have a far better selection and offer better quality than companies that normally supply Halloween costumes. You may decide that the only way to get what you actually want is to purchase your medieval clothing from an online company. An amazing variety of companies supply medieval clothing—both off-the-rack and custom-tailored—and you can also find a selection of medieval clothing on eBay. The quality, authenticity, and cost of this clothing varies nearly as much as the companies that supply them, so research the company and ask about their guarantees and return policy before handing over large amounts of your hard-earned cash. You may find that some of the companies that sell ready-made medieval clothing are also willing to rent it out—especially if you are renting multiple costumes.

Medieval Cookbooks

There are dozens of collections of recipes from the Middle Ages and Renaissance. The cookbooks listed below are among the best we have found. Many of these books are currently in print and even those that have gone out of print can usually be found as used titles on Amazon .com or through Alibris (www.alibris.com), which specializes in out-of-print and hard-to-find books.

Food and Feast in Medieval England by P. W. Hammond (ISBN 0-7509-0992-7)

Food and Feast in Tudor England by Alison Sim (ISBN 0-7509-1476-9)

Pleyn Delit: Medieval Cookery for Modern Cooks by Constance B. Hieatt (ISBN 0-8020-7632-7)

Take A Thousand Eggs or More: A Collection of 15th-Century Recipes (Volumes I and II) by Cindy Renfrow (ISBN 0-9628598-0-X)

To The King's Taste: Richard II's Book of Feasts and Recipes by Lorna J. Sass (ISBN 0-87009-113-7)

The Art of Cookery in the Middle Ages by Terence Scully (ISBN 0-85115-430-1)

The Medieval Cookbook by Maggie Black (ISBN 0-7141-0583-X)

Fabulous Feasts: Medieval Cookery and Ceremony by Madeleine Pelner Crosman (ISBN 0-8076-0832-7)

Medieval Furniture

We have written two books that explain how to build medieval furniture yourself. If either of these books is not in stock at your local bookstore they can be ordered by providing your bookseller with the title, publisher, and ISBN number, or they can be ordered online through Amazon.com or other Internet booksellers.

Constructing Medieval Furniture: Plans and Instructions with Historical Notes by Daniel Diehl (ISBN 978-0-8117-2795-2)

Medieval Furniture: Plans and Instructions for Historical Reproductions by Daniel Diehl and Mark Donnelly (ISBN 978-0-8117-2854-4)

If you want to purchase ready-made medieval furniture, there are dozens of companies now producing reproduction medieval furniture to fit a variety of tastes and pocketbooks. We have found numerous websites that offer ready-made and custom-built furniture in the medieval style.

Medieval Music

There are now two ways to obtain prerecorded medieval music: buying CDs, or downloading it as MP3 or MIDI files from sites such as iTunes. For those who want their medieval music on CD, reliable online booksellers and resale sites like eBay have a wide selection of both new and used medieval CDs that can be found by searching their music section.

Metal and Pewter Plates and Goblets

Inexpensive mugs, goblets, and tankards made from modern pewter regularly appear at flea markets, yard sales, and Goodwill, St. Vincent DePaul, or Salvation Army thrift stores. Also look for plates and tankards made of aluminum; they look like pewter but are far less expensive. Be very careful when buying reproduction medieval pewter; a lot of companies specialize in fantasy-type pewterware depicting fairies, dragons, wizards, and other characters and claim they are in the medieval style. These have absolutely no place on the medieval table and should be avoided like the plague.

Wooden Plates, Goblets and Bowls

For reasons unknown, the best, cheapest place to find a fairly reliable supply of wooden bowls of all sizes (and sometimes plates) at rock-bottom prices is your local thrift store (see previous section). There are also a number of online retailers who supply medieval tableware. One online company that sells both wooden and metal table service at competitive prices is Medieval Fantasies Company (medievalfantasiesco.com).

Without question the best, most authentic, medieval-style wooden tableware available anywhere in the world is produced by English craftsman Robin Wood. You can visit his website at www.robin-wood.co.uk. Don't let Robin's fame and the fact that he is in England put you off; his bowls, plates, and spoons are quite affordable even with the cost of shipping and are so astoundingly beautiful that you will want to use them all year long. Do bear in mind that Robin, like a lot of individual specialty suppliers, may have a list of customers waiting for his goods—so be sure to allow sufficient time for him to get to your order.

Painted Wall Hangings and Tapestries

Many images of original tapestries now in museums can be found on the Internet, giving you an endless supply of ideas for creating your own painted wall hanging as described in chapter 8. Hundreds of sites offer real woven tapestries of varying sizes and quality, ranging in price from under $25 to thousands of dollars. We suggest Tapestry Standard (www.european-wall-tapestries .com) and Charlotte Home Furnishings (www.saveon tapestries.com/tapestries/Medieval-tapestries.htm), just two of the hundreds of companies offering a wide selection of medieval-themed, woven tapestries to fit every budget.

Medieval Banners and Flags

Dozens of websites can supply you with flags, banners, and armorial devices in more styles and sizes than you can imagine. Many of these custom-made banners are very reasonably priced, beginning at less than $25 a piece. Sizes, styles, price, and quality differ greatly from supplier to supplier, so check out prospective retailers carefully before you buy.

Medieval Wedding Planners

There are numerous planners and suppliers who can play some role in helping you plan your medieval wedding. The best way to find a wedding planner in your area who specializes in medieval weddings is to execute a search by state or by a major metropolitan area near you. Such searches are bound to provide you with a variety of companies that can provide you with the amenities and services you are looking for. Be sure to compare prices and ask for references from previous medieval weddings before making your final selection.

United Kingdom

Medieval Armour

The prices for armor can range from £30 for a shield suitable for use as a wall decoration in your recreated medieval feast hall to more than £7,000 for a suit of astoundingly fine reproduction armour that would stand up in a battle against the French. Using the British spelling "armour," we turned up exactly the same eBay results as when we used the American spelling "armor."

There are dozens listed online and we recommend looking at: EntsWeb Directory of Entertainment, Music & Leisure (www.entsweb.co.uk/suppliers/costume), The Knight Shop International (www.theknight shop.co.uk), and The Costumer's Manifesto (www. costumes.org/history/100pages/militaryuniforms.htm). Hightower Crafts (www.hightowercrafts.com) offers stage-prop quality swords and weapons made from latex, for sale and hire. eBay also has a category specifically for medieval swords.

Medieval Clothing

Petty Chapman (www.pettychapman.co.uk), a medieval clothing pattern company in the UK, supplies medieval-quality fabrics and trims and is known to offer good products.

If you are renting ready-made medieval clothing the best place to start is your local fancy dress hire shop. Most fancy dress companies have a limited supply of medieval-type clothing available; make sure their selection meets your standards. If you live in London, Birmingham, or another large city where there are companies that rent to theatrical or movie companies, they will probably have a far better selection and offer better quality than companies that normally supply fancy dress for Halloween and Christmas parties

Medieval Cookbooks

Refer to the listings on page 200.

Medieval Furniture (build-it-yourself guides)

Refer to the listings on page 201.

Medieval Music

Refer to the listings on page 201.

Metal and Pewter Plates and Goblets

Inexpensive mugs, goblets, and tankards made from modern pewter regularly appear at car boot sales as well as at charity and thrift shops. England still manufactures the finest pewter in the world but the good stuff is more than just a bit pricey; if your budget is limited you are far better off going for the aluminum replicas.

Wooden Plates, Goblets, and Bowls

The best, least expensive place to find a fairly reliable supply of wooden bowls of all sizes (and sometimes plates) at rock-bottom prices is your local car boot; people seem determined to sell wonderful wooden bowls for a few pence.

There are also a number of online retailers who supply medieval tableware. If you are buying in quantity for your feast you should be able to buy wholesale even if you are not a business. Without question the best, most authentic, medieval-style wooden tableware available anywhere in the world is that produced by Robin Wood. You can visit his website at www.robin-wood.co.uk.

Painted Wall Hangings and Tapestries

Hundreds of sites offer real woven tapestries in varying sizes ranging in price from under £100 to thousands of pounds. We have found that Tapestries Direct (www. tapestriesdirect.co.uk) offers a selection of tapestries at reasonable prices; many American companies offer a wide selection of medieval-themed, woven tapestries at prices low enough that even with the cost of international shipping they can be cheaper than many suppliers in the UK.

Medieval Banners & Flags

At least one company, Classique Promotions (www. classiquepromotions.co.uk), specializes in hiring out medieval flags and banners.

Medieval Wedding Planners

There are a number of professional wedding planners in the UK who can take over the planning and execution of your medieval-themed wedding. One of the more reliable and experienced medieval wedding planners is Fantaysia Limited (www.fantaysia.co.uk).

Filmography

The following list of films should help give you a feeling for the era as a whole: how people looked, dressed, and decorated their homes. Not all the films included on this list are set in the mid-1300s, the period of our recreated feast, but even those films that take place in other time periods are informative, if only by comparison, and all of them are a lot of fun. The period of each film is indicated in the brief synopsis that follows the title.

There are certainly a lot more films about the Middle Ages than those listed below, but these are the best. We have omitted some films because they are in black and white, which gives you no sense of the colors used; others have been left out because they are simply so inaccurate, or so bad, that they will not provide useful reference or, in many cases, do not even bear watching.

Listings are by the date of the film and do not indicate any particular ranking in historical accuracy. An asterisk (*) indicates the inclusion of a wedding scene, but none of them are carried out according to medieval tradition.

Alexander Nevsky (Mosfilm, 1938). In Russian with subtitles. Set 150 years before our feast. Although it is in black and white, it is still a startlingly realistic and spectacularly executed medieval epic.

Becket (Paramount, 1964). Starring Richard Burton, Peter O'Toole, and John Gielgud. Although the setting is fairly early in the Middle Ages, the film is an Oscar-winning piece that is well worth watching, if only for its gritty realism.

The War Lord* (Universal, 1965). Starring Charlton Heston. Although it is set 250 years before our feast, this film includes a well-done medieval wedding scene. It is also a very exciting movie and well worth watching.

The Lion in Winter (Arco/Embassy, 1968). Starring Katherine Hepburn and Peter O'Toole. Set 150 years before our feast, this is probably the most realistic-looking medieval film ever produced. It takes place at Christmastime, helpful for those planning a Christmas celebration. Hepburn and O'Toole are at their best.

Romeo and Juliet (BHE Films, 1968). Lush, lavish, beautifully set and costumed, this Oscar-winning film by Franco Zeffirelli is a marvelous production of one of Shakespeare's most beloved love stories.

Robin and Marian (Columbia, 1976). Starring Sean Connery and Audrey Hepburn. One of the best and most realistic costume set pieces. The time period is the early 1300s, the early end of our time period. Good costumes, great fun.

Ladyhawke (Warner, 1985). Starring Rutger Hauer, Michelle Pfeiffer, and Matthew Broderick. Set two hundred years earlier than our feast and pure fantasy, but great fun.

The Name of the Rose (TCF, 1986). Starring Sean Connery and Christian Slater. Set during the early years of our time period, this is one of the great medieval movies. Unfortunately, virtually everyone in the film is a cleric, so they are all wearing monastic habits, but for those coming to the feast as priests or monks, it is great reference.

The Navigator: A Medieval Odyssey (Recorded Releases/Arena, 1988). No big-name stars. Although this is a fantasy, it is set in the time period of our feast; unfortunately, everyone in the film is a dirt-poor peasant and everything looks pretty grim. But it's an interesting film.

Henry V* (Curzon, 1989). Starring Kenneth Branagh and Brian Blessed. Set at the end of our time period, this absolutely spectacular film provides some of the best visual reference for your party. It also contains some of the finest recreated medieval interiors ever on screen. Notice how simple and spare the sets are, but how realistic they look and feel.

Robin Hood (TCI/Working Title, 1991). Starring Patrick Bergin. By far the best of the three early-1990s Robin Hood movies. The sets and costumes are very well done and authentic to period, and since this is the same period as our recreated feast, it offers the best visual reference. The story is also quite true to many of the Robin Hood legends. This should have done far better at the box office than it did; it simply didn't have Kevin Costner's name attached to it.

*Robin Hood: Prince of Thieves** (Warner, 1991). Starring Kevin Costner. Set at the right period for our recreated feast; the costumes are good and the interior sets are fine. The problem is the story itself. You've probably seen it and heard all the jokes, but this film presents good visual reference for your feast. Just watch it with the sound turned off and you'll be fine.

*Robin Hood: Men in Tights** (TCI/Brooksfilm, 1993). Starring Cary Elwes. Again, the Robin Hood story is the right time period, and even though this is a bit of Mel Brooks fluff, it is probably better costumed than the Kevin Costner version. The wedding at the end is also fairly accurate and provides good visual reference.

Anchoress (BFI/Corsan, 1993). No big-name stars. Set in the right time period for our feast, this rather grim account of medieval life is well set and costumed and provides good visual reference.

*Braveheart** (TCF, 1995). Starring Mel Gibson. Set fifty years before our feast. Although the Scots' costumes are inaccurate (they would have been wearing kilts that came almost to their ankles), the English costumes are quite good, particularly the court clothes. There are also two versions of medieval weddings—one between William Wallace and his Scottish girlfriend, and another between the crown prince of England and a French princess—that are very good wedding reference and an accurate portrayal of how wedding ceremonies differed at various levels of society.

*Snow White: A Tale of Terror** (Polygram, 1996). Starring Sam Neill and Sigourney Weaver. Although it is set 100 to 125 years later than our feast, this unsettling version of the familiar fairy tale is spectacularly costumed and set. The characters are all fairly convincing, and despite its failure at the box office, this is an excellent medieval fantasy.

Knight's Tale (Black & Blu/Columbia 2001). A bit of medieval fluff starring the late Heath Ledger, the rock soundtrack is a little bit distracting but there is nothing serious about this film except its sense of fun. The jousting scenes are well done and give one of the screen's best portrayals of a medieval tournament.

Tristan & Isolde (Twentieth Century Fox, 2006). This classic, early-medieval love story is lavish, tragic, and well worth watching for anyone who likes a real tearjerker. The period is too early to provide much information relevant to a medieval event but it is a fine film.

Black Death (Egoli Tossell Films, 2010). Set in the 1340s, this grim look at life during the Black Plague is extremely well acted, well set, and costumed, if a bit tragic.

Ironclad (Mythic, 2011). Set during the reign of England's King John (1199–1216), this is a bit earlier than the setting of our medieval event, but it has fine costumes and sets and some great battle scenes.

In addition to these few examples, a simple internet search with the keywords "Medieval Film" or "Medieval filmography" or "Middle Ages Film" should reveal many many others that may serve as useful reference—or at least as entertaining diversions.

Bibliography

Books

Arbeau, Thoinot. *Orchésographie*. Translated by Mary Stewart Evans. New York: Dover, 1967.

Bayard, Tania, trans. and ed. *A Medieval Home Companion*. New York: HarperCollins, 1991.

Betty Crocker's Cookbook. New York: Golden Press, 1981.

Black, Maggie. *Food and Cooking in Medieval Britain*. English Heritage, 1985.

———. *The Medieval Cookbook*. London: British Museum Press, 1966.

Boase, Roger. *Dictionary of the Middle Ages*, Vol. 3, s.v. "Courtly Love." Oxford: Oxford University Press, 1986.

Braun, and Schneider. *Historic Costume in Pictures*. New York: Dover, 1975.

Cantor, Norman. *The Civilization of the Middle Ages*. New York: HarperCollins, 1993.

Capellanus, Andreas. *The Art of Courtly Love*. New York: Columbia University Press, 1964.

Catholic Encyclopedia. 1913.

Cosman, Madeleine. *Fabulous Feasts: Medieval Cookery and Ceremony*. New York: George Braziller, 1976.

Coulson, John, ed. *The Saints*. Bristol, England: Nicholas Adams, 1757.

Cox, Harvey Gallagher. *The Feast of Fools: A Theological Essay*. New York: Harvard University Press, 1969.

Dances for Queen Elizabeth and Her Court. Dolmetsch Historical Dance Society Summer School, 1983.

Davis, William Stearns. *Life on a Medieval Barony*. New York: Harper and Brothers, 1923.

Davidson, Clifford. *Festivals and Plays in Late Medieval Britain*. Farnham, UK: Ashgate Publishing, 2007

Day, Brian. *A Chronicle of Folk Customs*. London: Hamlyn Books, 1998.

Diehl, Daniel. *Constructing Medieval Furniture*. Mechanicsburg, PA: Stackpole Books, 1997.

Diehl, Daniel, and Mark Donnelly. *Medieval Furniture: Plans and Instructions for Historical Reproductions*. Mechanicsburg, PA: Stackpole Books, 1999.

———. *Siege: Castles at War*. Dallas: Taylor Publishing, 1998

Dixon, Peggy. *Dances from the Courts of Europe*. Vol. 3. Nunsuch Early Dance, 1986.

Duby, Georges, ed. *A History of Private Life*. Cambridge, MA: Belknap/Harvard University, 1988.

Dyer, Christopher. *Standards of Living in the Later Middle Ages*. New York: Cambridge University Press, 1994.

Egan, Geoff, et. al. *Dress Accessories*. London: HMSO, 1992.

Erler, Mary, and Maryanne Kowaleski, eds. *Women and Power in the Middle Ages*. Athens, GA: University of Georgia, 1988.

Gies, Frances, and Joseph Gies. *Life in a Medieval Village*. New York: Harper Perennial, 1990.

———. *Women in the Middle Ages*. New York: Harper Perennial, 1980.

Gies, Joseph, and Frances Gies. *Life in a Medieval City*. New York: Harper Perennial, 1981.

Gomar, Pippa. *Warwickshire Country Recipes*. Horsham, Sussex, UK: Ravette Books, 1988.

Hammond, P. W. *Food and Feast in Medieval England*. Stroud, England: Sutton, 1993.

Hassall, W. O. *How They Lived: 55 B.C.–1486*. Oxford: Blackwell, 1962.

Hieatt, Constance, Brenda Hosington, and Sharon Butler. *Pleyn Delit: Medieval Cookery for Modern Cooks*. Toronto: University of Toronto, 1979.

Holt, Arden. *How to Dance the Revived Ancient Dances*. London, 1907.

Holt, Richard, and Gervasa Rosser, eds. *The Medieval Town, 1200–1540*. Harlow, UK: Longman, 1990.

Houston, Mary. *Medieval Costume in England and France: The 13th, 14th, and 15th Centuries*. New York: Dover, 1996.

Laver, James. *Costume and Fashion: A Concise History*. London: Thames and Hudson, 1992.

Lewis, K., Noel Menuge, and K. Phillips, eds. *Young Medieval Women*. Sutton, Gloucester, UK: St. Martin's Press, 1999.

McLean, Teresa. *The English at Play in the Middle Ages*. Windsor Forest, Berkshire, UK: Kensal Press, 1994.

Moore, John C. "'Courtly Love': A Problem in Terminology." *Journal of the History of Ideas* 40 (Oct. 1979).

Piponnier, Francois, and Perrine Mane. *Dress in the Middle Ages*. New Haven, CT: Yale University Press, 1997.

Reeves, Compton. *Pleasures and Pastimes in Medieval England*. Gloucestershire, UK: Allan Sutton Publishers, 1995.

Renfrow, Cindy. *A Sip Through Time: A Collection of Old Brewing Recipes*. Self-published, 1995.

———. *Take a Thousand Eggs or More*. Vols. 1 and 2. Self-published, 1993.

Rowling, Marjorie. *Life in Medieval Times*. New York: Perigree, 1973

Sass, Lorna. *To the King's Taste*. New York: Metropolitan Museum of Art, 1975.

Scully, Terence. *The Art of Cookery in the Middle Ages*. Woodbridge, Suffolk, UK: Boydell Press, 1995.

Sim, Alison. *Food and Feast in Tudor England*. Stroud, UK: Sutton, 1998.

Singman, Jeffrey, and Will McLean. *Daily Life in Chaucer's England*. Westport, CT: Greenwood Press, 1995.

Tabourot, Jean. *Orchésographie*. Paris, 1588

Tarrant, Naomi. *The Development of Costume*. New York: Rutledge, 1994.

Thomas, Bernard, and Jane Gingell. *The Renaissance Dance Book*. London: Pro Musica, 1988.

Tuchman, Barbara. *A Distant Mirror: The Calamitous Fourteenth Century*. New York: Knopf, 1978.

Virgoe, Roger, ed. *Illustrated Letters of the Paston Family*. London: Guild Publishing, 1989.

Woolgar, C. M. *The Great Household in Late Medieval England*. New Haven, CT: Yale University Press, 1997.

Yarwood, Doreen. *Outline of English Costume*. London: Batsford, 1972.

Websites

www.backgammonclassic.com/backgammon-history

www.backgammonclassic.com/news-details/687-medieval-backgammon-pieces-exhibited-in-louisville-museum.html

www.cs.cmu.edu/afs/andrew.cmu.edu/org/Medieval/www/src/contributed/grm/games/piquet.html

www.dartfordarchive.org.uk/medieval/leisure.shtml

www.essortment.com/all/backgammonhisto_rquv.htm

www.expertfootball.com/history/soccer_history.php)

home.comcast.net/~sylvanarrow/archery.htm

www.medieval.net/bloodsports.htm

www.medieval-spell.com/Medieval-Entertainment.html

www.oxfordcroquet.com/history/origins1.asp

tennis.about.com/od/history/a/earlyhistory_2.htm

www.tradgames.org.uk/games/baccarat.htm

www.tradgames.org.uk/games/Billiard-Family.htm

www.tradgames.org.uk/games/Bowls.htm#TableBowls

www.tradgames.org.uk/games/Chess.htm

www.tradgames.org.uk/games/Cribbage.htm

www.tradgames.org.uk/games/Poker.htm

www.tradgames.org.uk/games/ShovelBoard.htm

www.tradgames.org.uk/games/Tafl.htm

Metric Conversions

INCHES TO MILLIMETERS

in.	mm	in.	mm
1	25.4	51	1295.4
2	50.8	52	1320.8
3	76.2	53	1346.2
4	101.6	54	1371.6
5	127.0	55	1397.0
6	152.4	56	1422.4
7	177.8	57	1447.8
8	203.2	58	1473.2
9	228.6	59	1498.6
10	254.0	60	1524.0
11	279.4	61	1549.4
12	304.8	62	1574.8
13	330.2	63	1600.2
14	355.6	64	1625.6
15	381.0	65	1651.0
16	406.4	66	1676.4
17	431.8	67	1701.8
18	457.2	68	1727.2
19	482.6	69	1752.6
20	508.0	70	1778.0
21	533.4	71	1803.4
22	558.8	72	1828.8
23	584.2	73	1854.2
24	609.6	74	1879.6
25	635.0	75	1905.0
26	660.4	76	1930.4
27	685.8	77	1955.8
28	711.2	78	1981.2
29	736.6	79	2006.6
30	762.0	80	2032.0
31	787.4	81	2057.4
32	812.8	82	2082.8
33	838.2	83	2108.2
34	863.6	84	2133.6
35	889.0	85	2159.0
36	914.4	86	2184.4
37	939.8	87	2209.8
38	965.2	88	2235.2
39	990.6	89	2260.6
40	1016.0	90	2286.0
41	1041.4	91	2311.4
42	1066.8	92	2336.8
43	1092.2	93	2362.2
44	1117.6	94	2387.6
45	1143.0	95	2413.0
46	1168.4	96	2438.4
47	1193.8	97	2463.8
48	1219.2	98	2489.2
49	1244.6	99	2514.6
50	1270.0	100	2540.0

The above table is exact on the basis: 1 in. = 25.4 mm

U.S. TO METRIC

1 inch = 2.540 centimeters
1 foot = .305 meter
1 yard = .914 meter
1 mile = 1.609 kilometers

METRIC TO U.S.

1 millimeter = .039 inch
1 centimeter = .394 inch
1 meter = 3.281 feet or 1.094 yards
1 kilometer = .621 mile

INCH-METRIC EQUIVALENTS

Fraction	Customary (in.)	Metric (mm)	Fraction	Customary (in.)	Metric (mm)
1/64	.015	0.3969	33/64	.515	13.0969
1/32	.031	0.7938	17/32	.531	13.4938
3/64	.046	1.1906	35/64	.546	13.8906
1/16	.062	1.5875	9/16	.562	14.2875
5/64	.078	1.9844	37/64	.578	14.6844
3/32	.093	2.3813	19/32	.593	15.0813
7/64	.109	2.7781	39/64	.609	15.4781
1/8	.125	3.1750	5/8	.625	15.8750
9/64	.140	3.5719	41/64	.640	16.2719
5/32	.156	3.9688	21/32	.656	16.6688
11/64	.171	4.3656	43/64	.671	17.0656
3/16	.187	4.7625	11/16	.687	17.4625
13/64	.203	5.1594	45/64	.703	17.8594
7/32	.218	5.5563	23/32	.718	18.2563
15/64	.234	5.9531	47/64	.734	18.6531
1/4	.250	6.3500	3/4	.750	19.0500
17/64	.265	6.7469	49/64	.765	19.4469
9/32	.281	7.1438	25/32	.781	19.8438
19/64	.296	7.5406	51/64	.796	20.2406
5/16	.312	7.9375	13/16	.812	20.6375
21/64	.328	8.3384	53/64	.828	21.0344
11/32	.343	8.7313	27/32	.843	21.4313
23/64	.359	9.1281	55/64	.859	21.8281
3/8	.375	9.5250	7/8	.875	22.2250
25/64	.390	9.9219	57/64	.890	22.6219
13/32	.406	10.3188	29/32	.906	23.0188
27/64	.421	10.7156	59/64	.921	23.4156
7/16	.437	11.1125	15/16	.937	23.8125
29/64	.453	11.5094	61/64	.953	24.2094
15/32	.468	11.9063	31/32	.968	24.6063
31/64	.484	12.3031	63/64	.984	25.0031
1/2	.500	12.7000	1	1.000	25.4000